Ohio Confederate Connection

Facts You May Not Know about the Civil War

Curtis A. Early
and Gloria J. Early

iUniverse, Inc.
New York Bloomington

Ohio Confederate Connection
Facts You May Not Know about the Civil War

Picture on front cover is Camp Chase in Columbus, Ohio

iUniverse books may be ordered through booksellers or by contacting:

iUniverse
1663 Liberty Drive
Bloomington, IN 47403
www.iuniverse.com
1-800-Authors (1-800-288-4677)

ISBN: 978-1-4502-7372-5 (sc)
ISBN: 978-1-4502-7373-2 (ebk)

Library of Congress Control Number: 2010916853

Printed in the United States of America

iUniverse rev. date: 3/16/2011

DEDICATED

To our children
and
Grandchildren
Laurie-Bob
Wendi-Jay
Sheri- D.J.
Dustin, Ashley, Patrick, Sabrina
Amy, Noah, Emma and
Future grandchildren

INTRODUCTION

This book will give you an idea of what was going on before, during and after the War for Southern Independence and how the State of Ohio was connected. The South was tired of being told what to do from the North. Slavery wasn't the cause of the war. After the South started to secede from the voluntary union. Lincoln supported the Corwin Amendment which would have made forever slavery in states that had slavery and it could never be repealed. Only the states that had slavery could end it. The South said "NO" because slavery wasn't the reason for leaving the union. It was taxes. Soon as Lincoln became president he supported the Morrill Tariff Act which would have taken the import tax from 20% to 47%. This is why the South withdrew from the union. Lincoln threatened war if the South didn't pay the taxes. Slavery was on its way out. Just like the North had slavery for over 200 years and the North ended slavery in 1832. This book will show you that whites were slaves too and blacks also owned slaves. African black leaders sold their people to the Jewish slave traders. The New England states controlled the slave trade. There were hundreds of rum factories that made rum to trade to the black African leaders in trade for the slaves. The New Englanders sold the slaves to the North and South. Everyone is to blame for slavery during that time period, but not in today's world.

Contents

Chapter I

Ohio Born, Foreign or Northern Born and resided in Ohio Before the War Between the States

10 Years ago my wife and I started looking for Confederate graves in Ohio and we thought we would find a few but we found many. We started in Lake County; this is the smallest county in Ohio. There are 88 counties and we have checked hundreds of cemeteries in many of these counties. The two things that we didn't expect was most of the Confederate soldiers were born or resided in Ohio and another thing we didn't expect was their families were from the New England States or Foreign born. My estimate of Ohioans who went South and joined the Confederate Army and came back home will be approximately 1000+. When we find Confederate graves I check the soldier's records, history record and the 1860 and 1870 census. This chapter will show who the soldiers were, their age, trade unit they fought for and other information. The records are not 100% accurate do to who filled out the record and due to the age are hard to read. We will never know how many Ohioans joined the Confederate Army; many never made it back and are buried in the South.

Robert E. Lee

April 20, 1861 – **Resignation of Lee**, Robert E. Lee, son of a Revolutionary War hero, and a 25 year distinguished veteran of the United States Army and former Superintendent of West Point, resigns his commission in the United States Army. "I cannot raise my hand against my birthplace, my home, my children" Lee had been offered command of the Union Army on April 18. He travels to Richmond, Virginia, and is offered and accepts command of the military and naval forces of Virginia.

Name: **Anthony F. Card**
Birth date: **1835**
Birth place: **Alabama**
Occupation: **Carpenter**
Service record: **11th Michigan Infantry Company G, USA Pvt.**
1st Alabama Infantry Company H. CSA. Junior 2nd Lieutenant
Death place: **Painesville, Ohio**
Cemetery: **Evergreen Cemetery, Painesville, Lake County, Ohio**

There are also two unknown Confederate Veterans in Evergreen Cemetery, Painesville, Ohio who have no stones. No information on these two soldiers, but they are listed in the Evergreen cemetery records.

Aaron H. Conrow
Born: June 19, 1824 near Cincinnati, Ohio
Died: August 25,, 1865 in Mexico
Buried: Shotwell Cemetery, Richmond, Missouri
Colonel Missouri State Guards
Confederate States of America

Aaron H. Conrow was born June 19, 1824, near Cincinnati, Ohio. He spent part of his boyhood days at, or near Pekin, Illinois, and from that place, with his parents, moved to Missouri, and settled in Ray County. Here, by dint of his own energy, he obtained a pretty thorough education, teaching school part of the time in order to get means to complete the same. In this he was very successful. He then chose the law as a profession, and by rigid economy and sedulous application, succeeded in making an eminent lawyer. On the 17th of May, 1848, he was married to Miss Mary Ann Quesenberry, daughter of David H. and Lucinda Quesenberry, of Richmond, Missouri. From this union resulted the following children: David, Benjamin, William S., and Mamie. He was appointed by the governor, judge of the first probate court established in Ray County. From January, 1857, to January, 1861, he was circuit attorney of the fifth judicial circuit of Missouri; an office that had previously been filled by such eminent lawyers as Hamilton R. Gamble, Abiel Leonard, Charles French, Robert W. Wells, Amos Rees, Thomas C. Burch, Peter H. Burnett, George W. Dunn, and others, but by none of them more zealously and efficiently than by the subject of this sketch. He was a brilliant and successful advocate, a fine judge of law, and never descended to even the slightest artifice to gain the advantage of an opposing brother lawyer. He was above all littleness, open, candid, ingenuous. He was the preceptor of three young men who afterward became able and prominent lawyers; one of them is now a circuit judge, and the biography of another, who lives in Richmond, appears in this volume. Aaron H. Conrow was ever the fast friend of education, and no man contributed more liberally than he, in proportion to his means, to the support of institutions of learning. He was ever a safe counselor in matters of moment relative to the town and community in which he lived. In 1860 he was elected to the state general assembly- a democrat worthy to be trusted. He was in the general assembly at the beginning of the war, and sided with the south. He was instrumental in recruiting and equipping the first company organized in Ray for the defense of what he believed to be right. He ranked as colonel in the Missouri state guards, a military organization he had helped to create by his vote in the general assembly. He was by a majority of his comrades elected to represent his district in the confederate congress, and in that capacity, as in all others, served with singular zeal and promptness. He was present at the first meeting and at the final adjournment of that body. At the close of the war the amnesty agreed upon did not extend to members of the confederate congress, and fearing that if he fell into the hands of the successful party his life would be taken, he went to Mexico, and soon after arriving in that country, he was brutally murdered by a band of Mexican soldiers on or about the 25th of August. 1865.

Confederate Soldier
Name: **Peter Alexander**
Spouse: **Prudence Virginia Dunnica**
Birth date: **April 27,1838**
Birth place: **Ohio**
Occupation: **Farmer**
Enlistment place: **Missouri**
State served: **Missouri**
Service record: **Pvt. Missouri State Guard/Pvt. 42nd Reg. EMM**
Death date: **Jan. 10, 1900**
Death place: **Kentucky**
Cemetery: **Centertown Cemetery – Kentucky**

He came to Cole County with his family as a young boy. Peter and his Brother John were well to do farmers in Cole County and both joined the Missouri State Guard. Peter fought at Wilson's Creek, Pilot Knob and Carthage. After being captured, he was forced to join the Union Army Or have his Cole County property taken away from him.

Name: **Adam Beamer**
Spouse: **Mary**
Birth date: **1835**
Birth place: **Ohio**
Father's name and Birth place: **Henry – Ohio**
Mother's name and Birth place: **Sarah – Ohio**
Occupation: **Farmer**
Side served: **Confederate**
Death date: **1929 or 1932**
Death place: **Carroll County, Ohio**

Name: **John Beamer**
Birth date: **1833**
Birth place: **Ohio**
Occupation: **Farmer**
Enlistment date: **Nov. 1, 1862**
Enlistment place: **Opequon, Virginia**
Side served: **Confederate**
Service record: **Pvt. Co. F 2nd Regiment Virginia Infantry**
Death date: **March 6, 1865**
Death place: **Elmira, New York P.O.W. Camp**
Cemetery: **Elmire, New York**

The Beamer family of Convoy, Ohio has a strong and unique perspective of the US Civil War. The family's involvement in the war is a sensitive subject, as the conflict tore apart four brothers, eventually leading two to fight for the Union, and two to fight for the Confederacy. This occurred after the outbreak of the war, when John and Adam returned to their ancestral border state of Maryland. There, with their Beamer cousins, they joined the CSA under abbreviated names. The two youngest brothers, Phillip and Henry remained in Ohio, where they joined the Ohio Volunteer Infantry on September 7th 1861. Half a year later, their father Henry joined Company C. of the Ohio 87th regiment for Volunteer Infantry.

By Robby Beamer
US Civil War

Name: **James W. Blakely**
Spouse: **Jemima**
Birth date: **1836**
Birth place: **Gallia County, Ohio**
Father's name and Birth: **James Blakely 1799 New York**
Mother's name and Birth: **Lucinda Wells 1800 Canada**
Occupation: **Carpenter**
Enlistment date: **July 12, 1861**
Enlistment place: **Pitman's Ferry Arkansas**
Side served: **Arkansas CSA**
Service record: **2nd Sergeant Co. E. 6th Arkansas Cavalry Battalion**
Description: **Blue Eyes Light Hair Height 6'**

Discharged for disability at Bell's Tavern, Kentucky January 28, 1862. Injured his left leg after being thrown from his horse while charging the enemy near Williams in Green County, Kentucky, October 23, 1861

"Thy do not know what they say. If it came to a conflict of arms, the war will last at least four years. Northern politicians will not appreciate the determination and pluck of the 'South, and Southern politicians do not appreciate the numbers, resources, and patient perseverance of the North. Both sides forget that we are all Americans. I foresee that our country will pass through a terrible ordeal, a necessary expiation, perhaps, for our national sins. "

"With all my devotion to the Union and the feeling of loyalty and duty of an American citizen, I have not been able to make up my mind to raise my hand against my relatives, my children, my home. I have therefore resigned my commission in the Army, and save in defense of my native State, with the sincere hope that my poor services may never be needed. I hope I may never be called on to draw my sword."

Quotes: From General Robert E. Lee of the Confederate States of America

Jonathan Bressler, Confederate soldier -Alabama

Jonathan was born in 1832 in Pennsylvania. His parents were John and Elizabeth. His family moved to Ohio. Jonathan learned the carpenter trade and then moved to Mobile, Alabama. Then the War Between the States started. He enlisted in the Confederate army in 1861 at Mobile, Alabama with the Alabama State Artillery Company A. He earned the rank of 2nd Lieutenant and served until the end of the war. Jonathan then married Margaret, a Alabama girl. Somewhere before 1880 Jonathan's wife Margaret passed away and he then lived in Breckenridge, Summit, Colorado. Then he moved back to Ohio.

Jonathan became postmaster and was very respected in the community. He died December 17, 1909 in the city of Reily County of Butler. He is buried at Bunker Hill Universalist Cemetery.

(Alabama) State Artillery Battery

The Alabama State Artillery Battery (also known as Ketchum's-Garrity's Artillery Battery) was organized at Mobile on 4th May 1861, and the officers and men were from that county. It went to Pensacola and remained there until briefly. It lost 7 killed and wounded, and several horses at Shiloh. Attached to General Daniel Ruggles' Brigade, it was engaged at Farmington without loss. Moving into Kentucky as part of General James Chalmers' Brigade, its loss was light at Mumfordville. At Perryville and Wildcat Gap, the battery fought with few casualties. At Murfreeboro, the battery lost 27 men killed and wounded, and 30 horses. The battery was more fortunate at Chickamauga, but it lost several men and two guns at Missionary Ridge. The battery was in Union General William T. Sherman's way both by day and night as he moved on to Atlanta, and it suffered considerably. It fought at Franklin and Nashville, with small losses, and it endured the siege of Spanish Fort with two men k. The battery, numbering about 80, surrendered at Meridian.

Picture above Jonathan Bressler is standing in doorway with white beard. Lower picture is of Jonathan Bressler house in Bunker Hill, Ohio.

Mound Cemetery Washington County, Marietta, Ohio

Name: **Charles F. Buck**
Birth date: **1832**
Birth place: **Ohio**
Father's name: **Frederick**
Mother's name: **Mary**
Enlistment date: **May, 1861**
Enlistment place: **Near New Orleans, Louisiana**
Side served: **Louisiana CSA**
Service record: **1st Special Battalion Louisiana Inf. "Wheats" Pvt. Co. C Louisiana Tigers.**
Death date: **1863**
Death place: **Marietta, Ohio**
Cemetery: **Mound Cemetery, Marietta, Ohio**

James Parks Caldwell

Confederate Soldier
Mississippi

James Parks Caldwell, born in Monroe, Ohio, was just 14 years old when he helped launch Sigma Chi. By the time he was 13, his progress through courses, including Latin and advanced math, caused the principal of the local academy to remark that the boy had covered everything that could be offered there, and he entered Miami University apparently with advanced credits.

Caldwell is best remembered for his spirit of youth and for bringing an element of creative genius. According to Runkle, "Jimmie Caldwell was born with a wonderful brain and a strangely sensitive and delicate organization.. He was from his childhood one of the most lovable of God's creations. Strong men who have become hardened to tender feeling and sympathetic sentiment, remember and love him. Somehow, he seemed closely akin to all of us. I roomed and cared for him for more than a year. Our holidays were spent in the fields and along the streams, one of us carrying a gun, or fishing rod, but Caldwell his copy of Poe or his Shakespeare. His contributions, essays, poems, plays, and stories read in the literary hall, in the chapter meetings, and on Saturdays before the whole corps of students, were the most remarkable productions that I ever heard. Few of us escaped the pointed witticisms that flowed from his pen, or ever lost the nicknames that he gave us in his dramas. He never seemed to study as other boys. What he knew appeared to be his intuitively. He wrote Latin and Greek poetry, and he was more widely versed in literature, and more accurate in his knowledge, than any other student in the college. He left the university with the respect and the whole hearted affection of every soul from president to janitor."

He graduated Miami University soon after his sixteenth birthday. Following college he practiced law in Ohio, and began a career as an educator in Mississippi. He enlisted in the Confederate army as a 1st Sergeant in Company C of Mississippi Hudson Light Artillery Battery, and during the Civil War, he was captured and taken prisoner. He rejected an offer of freedom on condition that he renounce allegiance to the Confederacy, even though it came from a northern soldier who loved him as a brother.

Following the war, he returned to Mississippi and was admitted to the Bar. Being a bachelor, he traveled frequently, writing as a journalist and practicing law. His death came in 1912, at Biloxi, where in his room were found the latest issues of The Sigma Chi Quarterly. He is buried in Biloxi Cemetery.

Soldiers' and Sailors' Monument

Completed 1894 on Public Square in Cleveland, Ohio. Union Soldiers and Sailors from Cuyahoga County that were in the War Between the States. The monument room is open daily, Monday through Saturday 9 A.M. to 4:00 P.M. except on Thanksgiving, Christmas and New Year's Day. Admission is free. A 125' column topped with a statue of the goddess of freedom.

"The education of a man is never completed until he dies."

Quote by: General Robert E. Lee

Name: **Edward Asa Ferris**
Spouse: (1) **Elsia Abbey from Ohio**
Spouse: (2) **Matilda Robinson from Yorkshire, England**
Birth date: **May 3, 1823**
Birth place: **New York**
Father's name: **John**
Mother's name: **Hannah H. Black**
Occupation: **Farmer**
Side served: **Texas**
Service record: **1st Texas Heavy Artillery Co. D. Ordinance Sergeant**
Death date: **October 20, 1872**
Death place: **Newbury, Ohio**
Cemetery: **Newbury Center Cemetery on St. Rt. 87 & Auburn Rd. Newbury, Ohio**

"The gentleman does not needlessly and unnecessarily remind an offender of a wrong he may have committed against him. He can not only forgive; he can forget; and he strives for that nobleness of self and mildness of character which imparts sufficient strength to let the past be put the past."

Quote: General Robert E. Lee

Name: **E. W. Fuller**
Birth date: **1815**
Birth place: **Ohio**
Enlistment place: **Louisiana**
Side served: **Confederate**
Service record: **Captain Co. D. Louisiana 16th Cons Infantry Reg.**
Death date: **July 25, 1863**
Death place: **Johnson Island P.O.W.**
Cemetery: **Fuller Family Cemetery- Lawrence County, Ohio**

His wife had his body exhumed and moved to family cemetery next to his brother that fought for the Union army and died in battle of Proctorville, Oh.

E.W. is now in the Fuller Family cemetery in Lawrence County, Oh.

Name: **George J. Grossman**
Spouse: **Elizabeth - Switzerland**
Birth date: **1837**
Birth place: **Wurttemberg-Wurttemberg, Germany**
Immigrated: **To Wooster, Wayne County, Ohio**
Ancestry birth place: **Germany**
Occupation: **Cabinet maker**
Enlistment place: **Tennessee**
Side served: **Confederate**
Service record: **Corporal-Sergeant 1st Regiment Tenn. Infantry (Field's) Co. E.**
Death date: **1917**
Death place: **Wooster, Wayne County, Ohio**
Cemetery: **Wooster Cemetery at 983 Madison Ave. Wooster, Ohio**

George Grossman immigrated to Ohio, U.S.A. in 1854. In the 1860 census George was in Nashville, Tennessee working at a horse farm making carriages. When the War Between the States started George joined the Confederate army. After the war George returned to Wooster, Wayne County, Ohio until his death.

Dr. Henry Ebenezer Handerson

Born: Mar. 21, 1837 Cuyahoga Co. Ohio
Died: Apr. 23, 1918 Cleve. Ohio

Confederate Soldier
Louisiana

Owing to Dr. Handerson's modesty, even we who were for years associated with him in medical college, in organization, and professional work, knew but little of him. He would much rather discuss some fact or theory of medical science or some ancient worthy of the profession than his own life. Seeing this tall venerable gentleman, sedate in manner and philosophical in mind, presiding over the Cuyahoga County Medical Society or the Cleveland Medical Library Association, few of the members ever pictured him as a fiery, youthful Confederate officer, leading a charge at a run up-hill over fallen logs and brush, sounding the "Rebel yell," leaping a hedge and alighting in a ten-foot ditch among Federal troopers who surrendered to him and his comrades. Yet this is history. We could perhaps more easily have recognized him even though in a military prison-pen, on finding him dispelling the tedium by teaching his fellow prisoners Latin and Greek, or perusing a precious volume of Herodotus.

Henry Ebenezer Handerson was born on March 21, 1837, here in Cuyahoga County, in the township of Orange, near the point now known as "Handerson's Cross-Roads." On the Chagrin river. His mother's maiden name was Catharine Potts. His father was Thomas Handerson, son of Ira Handerson. The family immigrated to Ohio from Columbia county, New York, in 1834. Thomas Handerson died as the result of an accident in 1839, leaving the widow with five children, the eldest thirteen years of age, to support. Henry and a sister were adopted by an uncle, Lewis Handerson, a druggist, of Cleveland. In spite of a sickly childhood the boy went to school a part of the time and at the age of fourteen was sent to a boarding school, Sanger Hall, at New-Hartford, Oneida County, New York. Henry's poor health compelled him to withdraw from school. No one at that time would have predicted that the delicate youth would live to be the sage of four score years and one. With his foster father and family he moved to Beersheba Springs, Grundy County, Tennessee.

In 1854, in good health, the boy returned to Cleveland, prepared for college, and entered Hobart College, Geneva, New York, where he graduated as A.B. in 1858. Returning to Tennessee, he occupied himself for about a year with surveying land and in other work and then became private tutor in the family of Mr. Washington Compton on a cotton plantation near Alexandria, Louisiana. There he remained a year or more, then in the autumn of 1860 matriculated in the Medical Department of the University of Louisiana (now Tulane University), where he studied through the winter, and also heard much of the political oratory of that exciting period.

The bombardment of Fort Sumter, April 12, 1861, followed by the call of President Lincoln for 75,000 troops to suppress the rebellion, found young Handerson again employed as tutor, this time in the family of General G. Mason Graham, a veteran of the Mexican War.

With his friends and acquaintances, Handerson joined a company of "home guards" consisting mostly of planters and their sons, formed for the purpose of maintaining "order among the negroes and other suspicious characters of the vicinity."

Many years afterward Dr. Handerson wrote, in a narrative for his family, concerning this period of his life: "Without any disposition to violent partisanship, I had favored the party of which the standard-bearers were Bell and Everett and the battle cry "The Constitution and the Union." And I had grieved sincerely over the defeat by the Radicals of the North, aided by the 'fire-eaters' of the South."

And again: "Born and educated in the North, I did not share in any degree the fears of the Southerners over the election to the Presidency of Mr. Lincoln. I could not but think the action of the seceding States unwise and dangerous to their future prosperity. On the other hand, this action had already been taken, and without any prospect of its revocation. Indeed, in the present frame of mind of the North, any steps toward recession seemed likely to precipitate the very evils which the secession of the state had been designed to anticipate. I believed slavery a disadvantage to the South, but no sin, and, in any event, an institution for which the Southerners of the present day were not responsible. An inheritance from their fore-fathers, properly administered, it was by no means an unmitigated evil, and it was one, moreover, in which the North but a few years before had shared. All my interests, present and future, apparently lay in the South and with Southerners, and if the seceding States, in one of which I resided, chose deliberately to try the experiment of self-government, I felt quite willing to give them such aid as lay in my feeble power. When I add to this that I was 24 years of age, and naturally affected largely by the ideas, the enthusiasm and the excitement of my surroundings, it is easy to understand to what conclusions I was led."

So on June 17, 1861, he volunteered in the Stafford Guards under Capt. (afterward Brigadier General) L.A. Stafford. The Guards became company B of the 9th Regiment Of Louisiana Volunteers, Confederate States of America, Colonel (later Brigadier General) "Dick" Taylor (son of "Old Zach." The President of the U.S.), in command. During the year that followed until the close of the war, Handerson experienced the adventures and trials of a soldier's life. He knew picket, scouting, and skirmishing duty, the bivouac, the attack and defense in battle formation, the charge, the retreat, hunger and thirst, the wearisome march in heat and dust, in cold, in rain, through swamps and stony wildernesses. He was shot through the hat and clothing and once through the muscles of the shoulder and neck within half inch of the carotid artery, lay in a hospital, and had secondary hemorrhage. At another time he survived weeks of typhoid fever.

He was a successively private soldier and accountant for his company, quarter-master, 2nd Lieutenant of the line, Captain of the line, and finally Adjutant General of the 2nd Louisiana Brigade, A.N. Virginia, under Lee and Jackson, with rank of Major. On May 4, 1864, Adjutant General Handerson was taken prisoner, and from May 17th until August 20th he was imprisoned at Fort Delaware in the Delaware River. He was then confined in a stockade enclosure on the beach between Forts Wagner and Gregg on Morris Island, until about the end of October, when he was transferred to Fort Pulaski at the mouth of the Savannah river, and in March, 1865, back to Fort Delaware. In April, after Lee's surrender, many of the prisoners were liberated on taking the oath of allegiance to the Federal Government. But Handerson did not consider his allegiance to the Southern Confederacy ended until after the capture of President Davis, and it was not until June 17, 1865, that he signed the oath of allegiance and was liberated in Philadelphia.

Since that time, with that spirit of tolerance and openness to truth which characterized the man, he was said, "in the triumph of the Union, the war ended as it should have ended."

Mr. Handerson then resumed his medical studies, this time in the College of Physicians and Surgeons of New York, Medical Department of Columbia University, taking the degree of M.D. in 1867. Hobart College conferred the A.M. in 1868. On October 16, 1872, he married Juliet Alice Root, who died leaving him a daughter.

February 25, 1878, Dr. Handerson read before the Medical Society of the County of New York an article entitled, "The School of Salernum, an Historical Sketch of Mediaeval Medicine." This essay attracted wide attention to his scholarly attainments and love of laborious research. For example, Professor Edward Schaer of the chair of Pharmacology, and Pharmaceutical Chemistry, of Neumunster-Zurich, pronounces this pamphlet "a valuable gift...a remarkable addition to other historical materials...in connection with the history of pharmacy and of pharmaceutical drugs'; that he found in it "a great deal of information which will be sought for in vain in many even renowned literary works."

Dr. Handerson practiced medicine in New York City, from 1867 to 1885, removing to Cleveland in 1885.

On June 12, 1888, he married Clara Corlett of Cleveland.

Then in 1889 appeared the American edition of the "History of Medicine and the Medical Profession, by John Hermann Bass, M.D.," which was translated, revised and enlarged by Dr. Handerson, to whom, in the words of Dr. Bass, "we are indebted for considerable amplification, particularly in the section on English and American medicine, with which he was, of course, better acquainted than the author, and for numerous corrections." ...As a matter of fact, the learning and judgment, and the conscientious industry of the translator and American editor of this work are evident throughout the book.

Concerning Dr. Handerson's writings, Dr. Fielding H. Garrison writes (Medical Pickwick, March, 1915, P. 118): "The earliest of Dr. Handerson's papers recorded in the Index Medicus is 'An unusual case of intussusception' (1880). Most of his other medical papers, few in number, have dealt with the sanitation, vital statistics, diseases and medical history of Cleveland, and have the accuracy which characterizes slow and careful work. This is especially true of his historical essays of which that on "The School of Salernum" (1883) is a solid piece of original investigation, worthy to be placed beside such things as Holmes on homoeopathy, Weir Mitchell on instrumental precision, or Kelly on American gynecology.

"To the cognoscenti, Dr. Handerson's translation of 'Baas' History of Medicine' (1889) is known as 'Handerson's Book.' He modestly describes himself as its 'editor,' but he is more than that. As the witty and effective translator of a witty and effective work, he has added sections in brackets on English and American history which are based on original investigation and of permanent value to all future historians. Handerson's Baas is thus more complete and valuable than the Rhinelander's original text."

Confederate Soldier
Name: **Edgar A. Manley**
Spouse: **Gracey**
Birth date: **November 8, 1845**
Birth place: **Ohio**
Father's birth place: **Massachusetts**
Mother's birth place: **Massachusetts**
Occupation: **Farmer**
Service record: **Private co. D 10th cavalry Tenn.**
Death date: **April 19, 1902**
Death place: **Leroy, Ohio**
Cemetery: **Brakeman Cemetery Leroy, Ohio on St. Rt. 86**

Do your duty in all things. You cannot do more, you should never wish to do less.

Quote from: Robert E. Lee

10th Regiment, Tennessee Cavalry (DeMoss')

10th Cavalry Regiment was organized in February, 1863, by consolidating Cox's and Napier's Tennessee Cavalry Battalions. Its companies were raised in the counties of Perry, Humphreys, Decatur, Hickman, Davidson, Montgomery, and Henry. The unit served in Forest's Humes', J.B. Bifle's, and Dibrell's Brigade. It fought at Brentwood, Denmark, and Chickamauga, then saw action in the Atlanta Campaign and Hood's operations in Tennessee, During February, 1865, it was consolidated with the 11th Tennessee Cavalry Regiment and in May contained 30 officers and 280 men. The unit ended the war in Alabama and surrendered with the Department of Alabama, Mississippi, and East Louisiana. Its field officers were Colonels Nicholas N. Cox and William E. DeMoss, Lieutenant Colonel Edward B. Trezevant, and Major John Minor.

Name: **John E. Moser**
Birth date: **1841**
Birth place: **Alsace-Lorraine**
Occupation: **Farmer**
Enlistment date: **N.A.**
Enlistment place: **Kentucky**
Side served: **C.S.A.**
Service record: **2nd Kentucky Cavalry Co. D. Pvt.**
Death date: **January 25, 1925**
Death place: **Lucas County, Ohio**
Cemetery: **Willow Cemetery Oregon, Ohio**

2nd Regiment, Kentucky Cavalry (Woodward's)

2nd (Woodward's) Cavalry Regiment was organized in December, 1862, using Woodward's Kentucky Cavalry Battalion as its nucleus. The unit served in F. C. Armstrong's, J. W. Grigsby's, and J. S. Williams' and J. H. Lewis' Brigade, Army of Tennessee. It was involved in many conflicts in Tennessee, Alabama, and Kentucky, then took an active part in the **Atlanta** Campaign. The regiment want on to aid in the defense of Savannah and the campaign of the Carolinas. On April 26, 1865, it surrendered. Its commanders were Colonel Thomas G. Woodward and Major Thomas W. Lewis.

Name: **William Pritchard**
Spouse: **Mary**
Birth date: **1832**
Birth place: **Ohio**
Father's Birth place: **Tennessee**
Mother's Birth place: **Tennessee**
Occupation: **Carpenter—Farmer**
Side served: **Arkansas CSA**
Service record: **Pvt. Co. 3rd. Cavalry Reg. Arkansas**

"July 3, 1863...We built fires all over the battle field and the dead of the blue and gray were being buried all night, and the wounded carried to the hospital. We made no distinction between our own and the confederate wounded but treated them both alike, and although we had been engaged in fierce and deadly combat all day and weary and all begrimed with smoke and powder and dust, many of us went around among the wounded and gave cooling water or hot coffee to drink. The confederates were surprised and so expressed themselves that they received such kind treatment at our hands, and some of the slightly wounded were glad they were wounded and our prisoners.

But in front of our breastworks, where the confederates were massed in large numbers, the sight was truly awful and appalling. The shells from our batteries had told with fearful and terrible effect upon them and the dead in some places were piled upon each other, and the groans and moans of the wounded were truly saddening to hear. Some were just alive and gasping, but unconscious. Others were mortally wounded and were conscious of the fact that they could not live long; and there were others wounded, how bad they could not tell, whether mortal or otherwise, and so it was they would linger on some longer and some for a shorter time—without the sight or consolation of wife, mother, sister or friend. I saw a letter sticking out of the breast pocket of one of the confederate dead, a young man apparently about twenty-four. Curiosity prompted me to read it. It was from his young wife away down in the state of Louisiana. She was hoping and longing that this cruel war would end and he could come home, and she says, "Our little boy gets into my lap and says, "Now, Mama, I will give you a kiss for Papa." But oh how I wish you could come home and kiss me for yourself." But this is only one in a thousand. But such is war and we are getting used to it and can look on scenes of war, carnage and suffering with but very little feeling and without a shuddr."

Quote by : Corporal Horatio D. Chapman, USA
Co. C 20th Connecticut Volunteers

Captain William Clarke Quantrill

Missouri Confederate
Cavalry Commander

Captain Quantrill, the oldest of 8 children, was born at Canal Dover (now just Dover), Ohio, on July 31, 1837. His father was Thomas Quantrill, formerly of Hagerstown, Maryland. His mother, Caroline Cornelia Clark, was a native of Chambersburg, Pennsylvania. They were married on October 11, 1836, and moved to Canal Dover the following December. Thomas Quantrill died December 7, 1854, apparently of tuberculosis.

Little is known of Quantrill's life in Dover, though it appears that he was raised by his mother in a Unionist family. However, he always had a loathing for its Free-Soil beliefs. After several years working as a teacher, Quantrill traveled to Utah Territory with the Federal Army as a teamster in 1858 as part of the Utah War, but left the army there to try his hand at professional gambling. In 1859, he moved to Lawrence, Kansas, and again taught school.

During the war, Quantrill met fourteen-year-old Sarah Katherine King at her parents' farm in Blue Springs, Missouri. They married and she lived in camp with Quantrill and his men. At the time of his death, she was seventeen.

William Clarke Quantrill (July 31, 1837—June 6, 1865). Was a Confederate guerrilla leader during the American Civil War. After leading a Confederate bushwhacker unit along the Missouri-Kansas border in the early 1860s, which included the infamous raid and sacking of Lawrence, Kansas in 1863, Quantrill eventually ended up in Kentucky where he was killed in a Union ambush in 1865, aged 27.

Top picture: Quantrill's grave marker in Dover, Oh. Quantrill's skull, and other bones are buried in Dover, Oh. and his body is buried in Kentucky. Bottom picture: 1912 Quantrill reunion

Colonel James Reily

Confederate Soldier
Texas

JAMES REILY(1811-1863)-Lawyer, diplomat, legislator, Confederate Army Officer. Born in Hamilton, Ohio on July 3, 1811, the second of five children of John and Nancy (Hunter) Reily. He had an excellent secondary education and received a bachelor's degree in 1829 from Miami University, where his father was a trustee. He began the study of law at Transylvania University, Lexington, Kentucky. According to the customs of the times, Reily boarded in the home of his mentor, Judge Robert Todd. Reily became a great favorite of Todd's daughter Mary, who he "petted and spoiled excessively". Mary grew up to marry Abraham Lincoln of Kentucky.

James Reily married Ellen Hart Ross, a grandniece of Henry Clay, in Lexington on March 4, 1834, at about the same time he was converted from the Episcopal faith. He was also a Mason. After his admission to the bar, he established a practice in Vicksburg, Mississippi, during the summer of 1835, and there his son John was born.

Sometime after March 2, 1836, he moved to Texas, where he received a headright of 1,280 acres. He settled his family in Nacogdoches and served as a major in the Army of the Republic of Texas and aide-de-camp to T.J. Rusk. Reily is listed in the Nacogdoches Mounted Guards, 2nd Regiment, 3rd Brigade Texas Militia, Col. Wm. Sparks in command. By January 1838 Reily had become Rusk's law partner and when Rusk was elected chief justice of the state Supreme Court, they moved their offices to Houston, the capital of the republic. This partnership continued until the summer of 1839, when Reily went into partnership with James Love. About this time Reily served as captain of a volunteer company, the *Milam Guards.*

Reily was one of the founders of Christ Church in Houston in March of 1839, and served several terms as vestyman. He was elected a member of the board of trustees. That year he was appointed by Prisident Mirabeau B. Lamar to sell $1 million in Texas government bonds in New Orleans but was unsuccessful. In 1840 Reily was nominated by Lamar for district attorney for the Fifth Judicial District, but opposition from the Senate led to a withdrawal of the nomination. When the Supreme Court commenced it's first session on January 13,1840, Reily was on the roll of attorneys certified to practice before that high tribunal. He was nominated for the post of District Attorney of the Fifth Judicial District on February 1, 1840, but the Senate failed to confirm him by a vote of nine to one. On October 15 the same year he was initiated into Holland Lodge No. 1.A.F.&A.M. The census of 1840 shows that he owned one town lot in Houston, one slave, two gold watches and one pleasure carriage. He went to Kentucky and returned home to engage in private practice and to make plans to visit Great Britain in April or May 1845. With the beginning of his second administration, in December 1841.Sam Houston named Anson Jones his secretary of State and James Reily replaced Barnard Bee as minister to the United States. On January 26, 1842, Jones gave Reily his instructions. Reily reported to his government that John Tyler, who became president on the death of William Henry Harrison, in April 1841, was in favor of annexation, which was becoming increasingly popular with the Congress. To Reily, Tyler explained that he wished to conclude the matters at once but that he must have the consent of the Senate and that as matters stood it seemed best to mediate with Mexico in an attempt to bring about peace between that country and Texas. Instead of peace in 1842 there came Mexican invasions in March and again in September. On July 20, 1842 upon Reily's resignation, Sam Houston nominated Issac Van Zandt as charge the affairs to the United States. Van Zandt wrote on December 23, 1842, that Tyler and a majority of his cabinet were in favor of annexation but they feared that they; could not secure the necessary two-thirds vote in the senate to ratify a treaty. Reily represented Harris County in the House of Representatives of the 5th Congress of the Republic of Texas, 1840-41, and was appointed by Sam Houston as charge d' affaires for the republic in Washington, D.C., where he arrived on March 8, 1842. He negotiated with Daniel Webster a treaty of amity, commerce and navigation, which the United States failed to ratify. Although Houston reappointed him to the same post, Reil's confirmation failed because of his outspoken opposition to annexation. During the Mexican War Reily commanded a Texas Regiment. On May 6, 1852, he served as chairman of the state Whig party convention but soon thereafter broke with the party because the presidential nominee, Winfield Scott, opposed slavery. Reily was elected to the House of the Fifth Texas Legislature, 1853-54, as a Democrat and later, under the administration of James Buchanan, was an ardent secessionist.

On August 20, 1861, he accepted a commission as colonel of the 4th Texas Mounted Volunteers. This regiment served in *Gen. Sibley's Brigade,* with *Lt. Col. William Read (dirty shirt) Scurry* as second in command. The first unit to join Sibley was William Polk Hardeman's Company A, 4th Regiment Texas Mounted Volunteers, which was mustered into Confederate service for the "war" on August 27. By September 20, Colonel James Reily's 4th Regiment, which was mustered in the Alamo Plaza, had reached its full complement of ten companies and training was begun at Camp Sibley, which was on the west bank of Salado Creek about six mile east of San Antonio on the Austin road. After the briefest of training, Sibley was ready to march his command to Fort Bliss. On Oct. 22, Colonel Reily assembled his 4th Regiment at Camp Sibley and delivered an eloquent speech followed by his reading of a stirring prayer written by Alexander Gregg, Episcopal Bishop of Texas. Reily's 4th Regiment reached Fort Bliss on December 17, but was sent to encamp at Willow Bar in Confederate Arizona. On Christmas Day Colonel Reily bade farewell to his troops. Reily's first assignment was a diplomatic mission to Chihuahua and Sonora from January through April 1862, and thus he missed his regiments involvement in the battles of Valverde and Glorieta. His son, John however served in those conflicts as first Lieutenant and commander of the artillery of his father's regiment. Reily was killed April 14, 1863 at the Battle of Bayou Tech near Franklin, La. Reily knew his wound was mortal and told his men they could not afford to take the time to carry him off. He asked them to leave him to die on the battlefield. When his men returned they found that he had propped himself up against a tree. With his hands crossed over his chest and cloth placed over his face, he had prepared himself for death. Another noble leader is gone but not forgotten. Col. James Reily is buried at Lexington Cemetery, Lexington, Kentucky.

McPherson Home Museum Clyde, Ohio
300 East McPherson Highway - Maple Street

Sandusky County, Ohio built in 1833 and is the childhood home of General James B. McPherson, who was the highest ranking Union officer, killed during the War Between the States. Phone for Appointment: Brenda 419-639-3017 or 419-618-3321 or Bob @ 419-547-0870

Name: **Wesley Russell**
Birth date: **1808**
Birth place: **New Hampshire**
Home in 1860: **Mayfield, Ohio**
Father's name: **C.B. Russell**
Mother's name: **Caroline**
Enlistment date: **November 7, 1862**
Enlistment place: **North Carolina**
Side served: **North Carolina CSA**
Service record: **Co. D. 51st. Infantry Reg. North Carolina**
Death place: **Willoughby Hills, Ohio**
Cemetery: **S.O.M. Rd. Cemetery Willoughby Hills, Ohio on St. Rt. 91**
Old name (Willoughby Center Cemetery also (Willoughby Ridge Cemetery
51st Regiment, North Carolina Infantry

51st Infantry Regiment was organized at Wilmington, North Carolina, in April, 1862, with men recruited in the counties of Cumberland, Sampson, Duplin, Columbus, Robeson, and New Hanover. It was assigned to General Clingman's Brigade and Served under him for the duration of the war. After fighting at Goldsboro, it moved to the Charleston area and was prominent in the defense of Battery Wagner. The 51st was then ordered to Virginia, participated in the battles of Drewry's Bluff and Cold Harbor, and endured the hardships of the Petersburg siege south and north of the James River. Returning to North Carolina, it saw action at Bentonville. On July 18, 1863, this regiment lost 16 killed and 52 wounded at Battery Wagner and in August contained

374 effectives. In May, 1864 it contained 1,100 men, and in October there were 145 present. During that time the 51st lost in killed and wounded 160 at Drewry's Bluff, 194 at Cold Harbor, and 104 at Fort Harrison. Very few surrendered with the Army of Tennessee. The field officers were Colonels John L. Cantwell and Hector McKethan, Lieutenant Colonels William A. Allen and Caleb B. Hobson, and Major James R. McDonald.

Name: **Hiram Saxton**
Spouse: **Rebecia**
Birth date: **1830**
Birth place: **Ohio**
Father' Birth place: **Ohio**
Mother's Birth place: **Ohio**
Occupation: **Farmer**
Enlistment date: **Nov. 10, 1863**
Side served: **Arkansas**
Service record: **Wrights Reg. 12th Arkansas Cavalry Co. F. & 23rd. Ark. Co. G. Private.**
Death date: **Sept. 6, 1922**
Death place: **Mississippi, Arkansas**

"Believing as we did that the war was a war of subjugation, and that it meant, if successful, the destruction of our liberties, the issue in our minds was clearly drawn as I have stated it,- The Union without Liberty without the Union. And if we are reminded that the success of the Federal armies did not involve, in fact, the destruction of liberty, I answer by traversing that statement, and pointing out that during all the long and bitter period of "Reconstruction," the liberties of the Southern States were completely suppressed. Representative government existed only in name. In the end, by the blessing of God, the spirit of the martyred Lincoln prevailed over the spirit of despotism as incarnated in Thaddeus Stevens and Charles Summer, and after long eclipse the sun of liberty and self-government again shone south of Mason and Dixon's line."

Quote by : Lt. Randolph Harrison McKim, CSA
1st. . Lt. Army of Northern Virginia, CSA

My chief concern is to try to be a humble, earnest Christian.

Quote by: Robert E. Lee

Name: **James Sewell Smith**
Spouse: **Mary**
Birth date: **1837**
Birth place: **Ohio**
Father's Birth place: **New York**
Mother's Birth place: **New York**
Occupation: **Policy Dealer**
Side served: **CSA**
Service record: **Confederate Spy**
Death date: **September 29, 1926**
Death place: **Cincinnati, Ohio**
Cemetery: **Spring Grove Cemetery in Cincinnati, Ohio**

Smith was at the Ford Theater the evening Lincoln was shot. He was wounded at the battle at Gettysburg, left on the field thought to be dead.

Get correct views of life, and learn to see the world in its true light. It will enable you to live pleasantly, to do good, and, when summoned away, to leave without regret.

Quote by: **Robert E. Lee**

Name: **John M. Snyder**
Spouse: **Libbie**
Birth date: **December 30, 1838**
Birth place: **Ohio**
Father's Birth place: **Virginia**
Mother's Birth place: **Virginia**
Occupation: **Farmer**
Enlistment place: **Missouri**
Side served: **Confederate Missouri CSA**
Service record: **6th Regiment Missouri Infantry Co. H. Private**
Death date: **April 24, 1902**
Death place: **Shelby, Ohio**
Cemetery: **St. Peter's London at Lutheran Church Cemetery. Shelby, Ohio**

Name: **Hiram K. Squires**
Spouse: **Caroline**
Birth Date: **Nov. 1816**
Birth place: **New Hampshire**
Father's Birth place: **England**
Mother's Birth place: **Connecticut**
Side served: **North Carolina CSA.**
Service record: **Co. F 7th. Battalion Cavalry Reg. & Co. A 6th Cavalry**
Regiment Private
Death date: **1902**
Death place: **Lake County, Ohio**
Cemetery: **West Kirtland Cemetery on St. Rt. 6 Kirtland, Ohio**

Name: **Edward Tanner**
Birth date: **1837**
Birth place: **Canfield, Mahoning, Ohio**
Ancestry birth place: **Connecticut**
Father's name and Birth place: **E.P. Tanner – Connecticut**
Mother's name and Birth place: **Fanny – Connecticut**
Occupation: **Laborer**
Enlistment place: **Arkansas**
State served: **Arkansas**
Service record: **Pvt. 24th Regiment Arkansas Infantry Co. E**
Death date: **Sept. 8, 1862**
Death place: **Arkansas**
Cemetery: **Camp White Sulphur Spring, Arkansas**

24th Regiment, Arkansas Infantry was organized during the spring of 1862, and after being involved in the fight of Arkansas Post, moved east of the Mississippi River. The regiment was assigned to Deshler's, Liddell's, and Govan's Brigade, and in September, 1863, consolidated with the 19th (Dawson's) Regiment and in December with the 2nd and 15th (Cleburne's-Polk's-Josey's) Regiments. It served with the Army of Tennessee from **Chickamauga** to **Atlanta,** fought with Hood in Tennessee, and ended the war in North Carolina. The 19/24th lost thirty-eight percent of the 226 engaged at **Chickamauga**, and the 2nd/15th/24th totaled 295 men and 202 arms in Dec. 1863. During the spring of 1864 part of the 24th served in Dawson's Regiment in the Trans-Mississippi Department. At the Battle of Atlanta only the 2nd and 24th were united, and this command sustained 130 casualties. Very few surrendered in April, 1865. The field officers were Colonel E.E. Portlock, Jr: Lieutenant Colonels W.R. Hardy, E. Warfield, and T.M. Whittington; and Major F. H. Wood.

"The battle is over, and although we did not succeed in pushing the enemy out of their strong position, I am sure they have not any thing to boast about. They have lost at least as many in killed and wounded as we have. We have taken more prisoners from them then they have from us. If that is not the case, why did they lay still all to-day and see our army going in the rear? An army that has gained a great victory follows it up while the enemy is badly crippled, but Meade, their commander, knows he has had as much as he gave, at least, if not more. As yet I have not heard a word from my brother Morris since the first day's fight."

Quote: Private Louis Leon, CSA
Pvt. Co. B 53rd Regiment, NC.
After the battle of Gettysburg

Name: **Memphis F. Thompson**
Spouse: **Emily**
Birth date: **May 19, 1847**
Birth place: **Leroy, Lake County, Ohio**
Ancestry birthplace: **Connecticut**
Father's name and Birth place: **Gordon Thompson – Connecticut**
Mother's name and Birth place: **Martha – Connecticut**
Occupation: **Farmer**
Enlistment place: **Virginia CSA**
Side served: **Confederate**
Service record: **Pvt. Richardson's Co. Va. Artillery "James City Artillery"**
Death date: **April 6, 1886**
Death place: **Leroy, Lake County, Ohio**

Confederate Soldier
Name: **William Henry Wheeler**
Spouse: **Minerva**
Birth date: **1842**
Birth place: **Lake County, Ohio**
Father's name and birth place: **James Harvey Wheeler – New York**
Mother's name and birth place: **Adaline - Ohio**
Occupation: **Farmer**
State served: **Virginia**
Service record: **Private 2nd. Regiment Virginia cavalry co. K**
Death date: **March 29, 1873**
Death place: **Lake County, Ohio**
Cemetery: **Northeast Cemetery – Leroy, Ohio on Ford & Trask Rd.**

Name: **John Wilson**
Spouse: **Ella 1845**
Birth date: **1836**
Birth place: **Ohio**
Father's name and Birth: **Pennsylvania**
Mother's name and Birth: **N.A.**
Occupation: **Farmer**
Enlistment date: **N.A.**
Enlistment place: **N.A.**
Side Served: **Virginia CSA**
Service record: **23rd Regiment Virginia Infantry Co. F. Corporal**
Death date: **October 17, 1917**
Death place: **Licking County, Ohio**
Cemetery: **North Lawn Cemetery Utica, Ohio**

23rd Regiment, Virginia Infantry

23rd Infantry Regiment completed its organization in May, 1861. Its members were recruited at Richmond and in the counties of Louisa, Amelia, Halifax, Goochland, Prince Edward, and Charlotte. This regiment participated in Lee's **Cheat Mountain** Campaign, saw action at **Greenbrier River,** and took part in Jackson's Valley operations. Later it was assigned to Taliaferro's, Colston's, Stuart's, and W. Terry's Brigade, Army of Northern Virginia. The Unit was involved in the campaigns of the army from the Seven Days' Battles to **Cold Harbor**, then moved with Early to the Shenandoah Valley and ended the war at **Appomattox**. It reported 28 casualties at Carrick's Ford, 4 at **Laurel Hill,** 49 at **First Kernstown**, and 41 at **McDowell.** During May, 1862, it contained 600 effectives, lost 5 killed and 27 wounded at **Cedar Mountain**, had 1killed and 13 wounded at **Second Manassas**, and reported 10 killed, 70 wounded and 2 missing at **Chancellorsville**. Of the 251 engaged at **Gettysbur**g, seven percent were disabled. It surrendered with 8 officers and 49 men. The field officers were Colonels Alexander G. Taliaferro and William B. Taliaferro; Lieutenant Colonels Clayton G. Coleman, Jr., James H. Crenshaw, George W. Curtis, John P. Fitzgerald, and Simeon T. Walton; and Majors. J.D Camden, Joseph H. Pendleton, Andrew J. Richardson, and Andrew V Scott.

Confederate Soldier
Name: **George W. Wood**
Birth date: **1845**
Birth place: **Lake County, Ohio**
Father's name and Birth Place: **Elisha - New York**
Mother's name and Birth Place: **Polly - New York**
Occupation: **Farmer**
State served: **Virginia**
Service record: **Private 2nd. Regiment Virginia cavalry co. K**
Death date: **July 25, 1919**
Death place: **Lake County, Ohio**
Cemetery: **Fairview Memorial Park-Madison, Ohio on St. Rt. 528**

"So the case stands, and under all the passion of the parties and the cries of battle lie the two chief moving causes of the struggle. Union means to many millions a year lost to the South; secession means the loss of the same millions to the North. The love of money is the root of this, as of many other evils. The quarrel between the North and South is, as it stands, solely a fiscal quarrel.

Charles Dickens Dec. 28, 1861

Stone of Thomas's wife and his ashes are believed to be buried there also.

Name: **Thomas Worrall**
Spouse: **Mary**
Birth date: **1807**
Birth place: **Ohio**
Side served: **C.S.A.**
Service record: **3rd Virginia Artillery Company**
Death place: **Earl LaSalle, Illinois**
Cemetery: **West Kirtland Cemetery Kirtland, Ohio on St. Rt. 6**

3rd Artillery Company was organized at Richmond, Virginia, in January, 1862. Ordered to Knoxville, the unit served in Tennessee and Kentucky**,** then was assigned to A. W. Reynold's Brigade, Department of Mississippi and East Louisiana. During the spring of 1863 a detachment served on board the Confederate gunboat Queen of the West and suffered many casualties. The remaining part of the battery was captured at **Vicksburg.** After being exchanged, the officers and men were consolidated with the Stephens Georgia Light Artillery. It was commanded by Captains Henry B. Latrobe and William L. Ritter.

Name: **Christopher C. Shaw**
Spouse: **Martha L.**
Birth date: **1844**
Birth place: **Newark, Licking County, Ohio**
Ancestry birth place: **North Carolina**
Enlistment place: **Virginia**
Side served: **Confederate**
Service record: **Mosby's Regiment Virginia Cavalry Co. A-C Private**
Description: **Partisan Rangers**
Death place: **Newark, Licking County, Ohio**
Cemetery: **Cedar Hill Cemetery, Newark, Licking County, Ohio**

Name: **Shedrick Truman**
Spouse: **Ruth**
Birth date: **1853**
Birth place: **Ohio**
Occupation: **Farmer**
Side served: **Confederate Virginia CSA**
Service record: **19th Virginia Cavalry Co. H Private**

Shedrick Truman was the youngest soldier in the 19th Virginia Cavalry

Name: **John J. Wilson**
Spouse: **1st Katherine Magill – 2nd Laura Crawford**
Birth date: **January 19, 1845**
Birth place: **Licking County, Ohio**
Father's name and Birth place: **Louis – Ohio**
Mother's name and Birth place: **Mary Margaret McLaughlin – Ohio**
Occupation: **Farmer – Carpenter**
Enlistment date: **May 14, 1861**
Enlistment place: **Richmond, Virginia**
Side served: **Confederate**
Service record: **23rd Virginia Infantry Regiment Co. H. Promoted to full 2nd Lt. on Feb. 15, 1863**
Description: **5'8" Dark complexion, Dark eyes, Dark hair**
Death date: **October 17, 1917**
Death place: **Eden, Licking County, Ohio**

Name: **Hugh William Hickok**
Birth date: **1820**
Birth place: **Ohio**
Service record: **11th Battalion Texas Volunteer, Cavalry, Artillery & Infantry Company B Corporal**
Death date: **1863 Battle at Fordoche Bayou, Louisiana**
Death place: **Louisiana**

Name: **James A. Kelley**
Birth date: **1842**
Birth place: **Ohio**
Father's Birth place: **Virginia**
Mother's Birth place: **Virginia**
Home in 1880: **Cabell, West Virginia**
Occupation: **Farmer**
Side served: **Confederate Virginia**
Service record: **63rd Regiment Virginia Infantry – McMahon's Co. K**

Name: **James M. Kelley**
Birth date: **1840**
Birth place: **Ohio**
Home in 1910: **St. Clair, Missouri**
Father's Birth place: **Pennsylvania**
Mother's Birth place: **Pennsylvania**
Side served: **Alabama CSA**
Service record: **10th Regiment Alabama Infantry Co. B Pvt.**

Name: **Sarden Lott**
Birth date: **1839**
Birth place: **Ohio**
Father's name and Birth place: **J.D. – Pennsylvania**
Mother's name and Birth place: **Margaret – Tennessee**
Occupation: **Farmer**
Side served: **Arkansas CSA**
Service record: **6th Battalion Arkansas Cavalry Co. C Pvt.**
Description: **With the Crittenden Rangers**

What a cruel thing is war: to separate and destroy families and friends, and mar the purest joys and happiness God has granted us in this world; to fill our hearts with hatred instead of love for our neighbors, and to devastate the fair face of this beautiful world.

Quote by: **General Robert E. Lee of Confederate States of America**

Name: **Dennis O'Brian**
Spouse: **Dora Steels**
Birth date: **1846**
Birth place: **Ireland**
Lived in: **Ohio**
Side served: **Maryland – Confederate**
Service record: **2nd Battalion Maryland Cavalry Co. B Pvt.**
Death date: **1930**
Cemetery: **Claysville Mt. Zion Cemetery Guernsey County, Ohio**

Name: **George Riddle**
Birth date: **1828**
Birth place: **Ireland**
Home in 1860: **Ohio**
Occupation: **Farmer**
Enlistment date: **November 10, 1863**
Enlistment place: **Arkansas**
Side served: **Arkansas CSA**
Service record: **Arkansas 12th Cavalry Regiment Co. F Pvt.**

Name: **Richard Brindley Ryan**
Spouse: **Margaret –Born in Ohio**
Birth date: **1801**
Birth place: **Ireland**
Home in 1860: **St. Clairsville, Belmont, Ohio**
Occupation: **Merchant**
Enlistment date: **May 1, 1861**
Enlistment place: **Norfolk County, Virginia**
Side served: **Confederate Virginia CSA**
Service record: **6th Infantry Regiment Virginia Co B**
Discharged: **September 1, 1861**
Death place: **Belmont County, Ohio**
Cemetery: **Methodist Cemetery St .Clairsville, Belmont County, Ohio**

Three members of the 15th Tennessee Infantry CSA Came from Ohio

Name: **William L. Baldwin**
Birth Date: **1845**
Birth Place: **Ohio**
Occupation: **Carpenter and Farmer**
Enlistment Date: **June 5, 1861**
Enlistment Place: **Union City, Tennessee**
Side Served: **Confederate States of America**
Service record: **15th Tennessee Infantry Company G. Pvt.**
Death Date: **October 27, 1934**
Discharged: **March 1864**

Name: **W. J. Davis**
Birth Date: **1841**
Birth Place: **Ohio**
Occupation: **Farmer**
Enlistment date: **June 5, 1861**
Enlistment place: **Union City, Tennessee**
Side served: **Confederate States of America**
Service record: **15th Tennessee Infantry Company G. Pvt.**
Death date: **April 6, 1862**
Death place: **Shiloh, Tennessee**

Name: **J. G. Patterson**
Birth date: **1839**
Birth place: **Ohio**
Occupation: **Carpenter**
Enlistment date: **June 5, 1861**
Enlistment place: **Union City, Tennessee**
Side served: **Confederate States of America**
Service record: **15th Tennessee Infantry Company G. Pvt.**

They went from the North to fight for the South:

Pro-southern Paducah, Illinois citizens brought food, clothing and other gifts to the 21 members who were leaving to join the Confederate Army. One of the citizens of Paducah, Illinois presented the Southern Illinois captain with a beautiful Confederate flag. These men by the time they got to Tennessee was 99 strong an joined the 15th Tennessee Infantry Company G.

Major General Bushrod Rust Johnson was born in Ohio.
15th Regiment, Tennessee Infantry:

15th Infantry Regiment was organized at Jackson, Tennessee, in June 1861 and in July totaled 744 men. Its members were from Memphis and the counties of Weakley, Lake, Madison, and Shelby. Company G contained men from Kentucky and Southern Illinois. After fighting at **Belmont**, **Shiloh,** and **Perryville**, the unit was assigned to Bate's ,Tyler's, and Palmer's Brigade, Army of Tennessee. During June, 1863, it was consolidated with the 37th Regiment. It was active at Hoover's Gap, then participated in the campaigns of the army from Chickamauga to Atlanta, returned to Tennessee with Hood, and saw action in North Carolina. This regiment reported 200 casualties at Shiloh and had 34 disabled at Perryville. The 15th/37th lost fifty-eight percent of the 202 engaged at Chickamauga and in December, 1863, totaled 234 men and 148 arms. Only a handful surrendered on April 26, 1865. the field officers were Colonels Charles M. Carroll and Robert C. Tyler; Lieutenant Colonels Thorndike Brooks and James H.R. Taylor: and Majors John W. Hambleton, John F. Hearn, and John M. Wall.

Chapter II

Confederate Soldiers that Settled in Ohio

Confederate Soldiers Buried in Ohio

There were Confederate soldiers that moved to Ohio after The War Between the States. After the war the South was virtually destroyed. I know people that had families in the Shenandoah Valley. It was passed down through the family that they had to walk 80 miles to get food. A big part of the Shenandoah Valley was virtually burnt to the ground; the Virginia Military Institute was burnt down by Union General Hunter. Towns throughout the South were destroyed. After the war the Union League went south and committed atrocities on Southern people and Carpet Baggers went south and robbed the people both black and white, towns, counties and states. On page 258 you will see the debt of some southern states. White Southerners weren't allowed to vote in any election for 7 years. Reconstruction lasted 12 years. The worst cases of atrocities ever committed on American citizens by the U.S. Government were committed on Southern people.

Name: **Squire Adkins**
Spouse: **Nancy**
Birth date: **1837**
Birth place: **Virginia**
Father's name: **Mathew Adkins**
Mother's name: **Elizabeth**
Occupation: **Carpenter**
Enlistment date: **November 10, 1862**
Enlistment place: **Giles County, Virginia**
Side served: **Confederate States of America**
Service record: **Co. A 30th Battalion Sharpshooters Regiment Virginia Pvt.**
Death date: **October 1, 1909**
Death place: **Near Bidwell, Ohio**
Cemetery: **Fairview (Long) Cemetery, Springfield Twp. Gallia County, Ohio**

30th Battalion, Virginia Sharpshooters (Clarke's)

30th Battalion Sharpshooters was organized in August, 1862, with six companies. The unit was assigned to G.C. Wharton's and A. Forsberg's Brigade and fought in various engagements in East Tennessee and the Shenandoah Valley of Virginia. After the Battle of Waynesborough, it disbanded. Lieutenant Colonel J. Lyle Clarke and Major Peter Otey were in command.

"My experience through life has convinced me that, while moderation and temperance in all things are commendable and beneficial, abstinence from spirituous liquors is the best safeguard of morals and health."

"You can have anything you want – if you want it badly enough. You can be anything you want to be, have anything you desire, accomplish anything you set out to accomplish – if you will hold to that desire with singleness of purpose."

Quotes by: **General Robert E. Lee, Confederate States of America**

Name: **James P. Andrews**
Birth date: **1834**
Birth place: **Virginia**
Home in 1860: **Cumberland, Tennessee**
Mother's name: **Ann**
Occupation: **Farmer**
Service record: **28th Regiment Tenn. Infantry (also known as 2nd Tenn. Mountain Volunteers)**
Death date **June 28, 1862**
Death place: **Clinton County, Ohio**
Cemetery: **Waldschmidt Cemetery at Camp Dennison, Ohio then later moved to Spring Grove Cemetery on July 4, 1869**

Andrews fought with his Regiment at the Battle of *Fishing Creek* also known as *Mill Spring* on January 19, 1862. They were then sent to Corinth, Mississippi and fought at the Battle of Shiloh, where Andrews was wounded and captured by the Union forces. He was sent up the river to Cincinnati, Ohio where he was held as a wounded prisoner of war in a military hospital at Camp Dennison. He died twelve weeks later.

28th regiment, Tennessee Infantry (2nd Tennessee Mountain Volunteers)

28th Infantry Regiment (also called 2nd Mountain Volunteers) was organized during September, 1861, at Camp Zollicoffer, Overton County, Tennessee. The men were recruited in the counties of Cumberland, Overton, Putnam, Wilson, Jackson, Smith, and White. It fought at *Fishing Creek, Shiloh,* and *Port Hudson,* served at Jackson, Mississippi, then was assigned to M.J. Wright's and Maney's Brigade, Army of Tennessee. On March 8, 1863, the 84th Regiment merged into this command. The 28th took an active part in the campaigns of the army from *Murfreesboro* to *Atlanta,* returned to Tennessee with Hood, and saw action in North Carolina. During January, 1862, it contained 748 effectives, had 12 men disabled at *Fishing Creek*, and sustained 76 casualties at *Murfreesboro.* The regiment lost thirty-four percent of the 254 at *Chickamauga* and totaled 254 men and 169 arms in December, 1863. Very few surrendered on April 26, 1865. The field officers were Colonels Uriah T. Brown, David C. Crook, Preston D. Cunningham, and John P. Murray; Lieutenant Colonel Jonathan Eatherly; and Majors John B. Holman, Eli D. Simrell, and James R. Talbet.

American Civil War Museum of Ohio

217 S. Washington St. Tiffin, Ohio 44883 Info@acwmo.org Website www.acwmo.org
419-509-0324
Well stocked gift shop with over 600 book titles "Put it on" – Dress in a reproduction civil war uniform.

Name: **Samuel M. Berry**
Spouse: **N.A.**
Birth date: **N.A.**
Birth place: **N.A.**
Father's name: **N.A.**
Mother's name: **N.A.**
Occupation: **N.A.**
Enlistment date: **N.A.**
Enlistment place: **N.A.**
Side served: **Louisiana CSA**
Service record: **20th Regiment Louisiana Infantry Co I Pvt.**
Death date: **February 20, 1912**
Death place: **Blanchester, Clinton County, Ohio**
Cemetery: **Blanchester I.O.O.F. Cemetery Clinton County, Ohio**

20th Regiment, Louisiana Infantry

20th Infantry Regiment (often times called the Lovell Regiment) was assembled and mustered into Confederate service at Camp Lewis, Louisiana, in February, 1862. Some of the men were recruited in Orleans Parish. The unit participated in the conflicts at *Shiloh* and Farmington, shared in the Kentucky Campaign, then was assigned to D. W. Adams' and Gibson's Brigade, Army of Tennessee. It was consolidated with the 13th Louisiana Regiment from December, 1862, to April, 1864. The unit fought with the army from *Murfreesboro* to *Atlanta,* served with Hood in Tennessee, and ended the war defending Mobile. At Shiloh this regiment took 507 men into action, but only 289 moved to Farmington. The 13th/20th reported 20 killed, 89 wounded, and 78 missing at Murfreesboro, lost forty-three percent of the 289 engaged at *Chickamauga*., and totaled 191 men and 71 arms in December, 1863. The 20th had 59 effectives in November, 1864 and surrendered with the Department of Alabama, Mississippi, and East Louisiana. The field officers were Colonels Augustus Reichard and Leon Von Zinken, and Lieutenant Colonels S.L. Bishop, Samuel Boyd, and Charles Buillet.

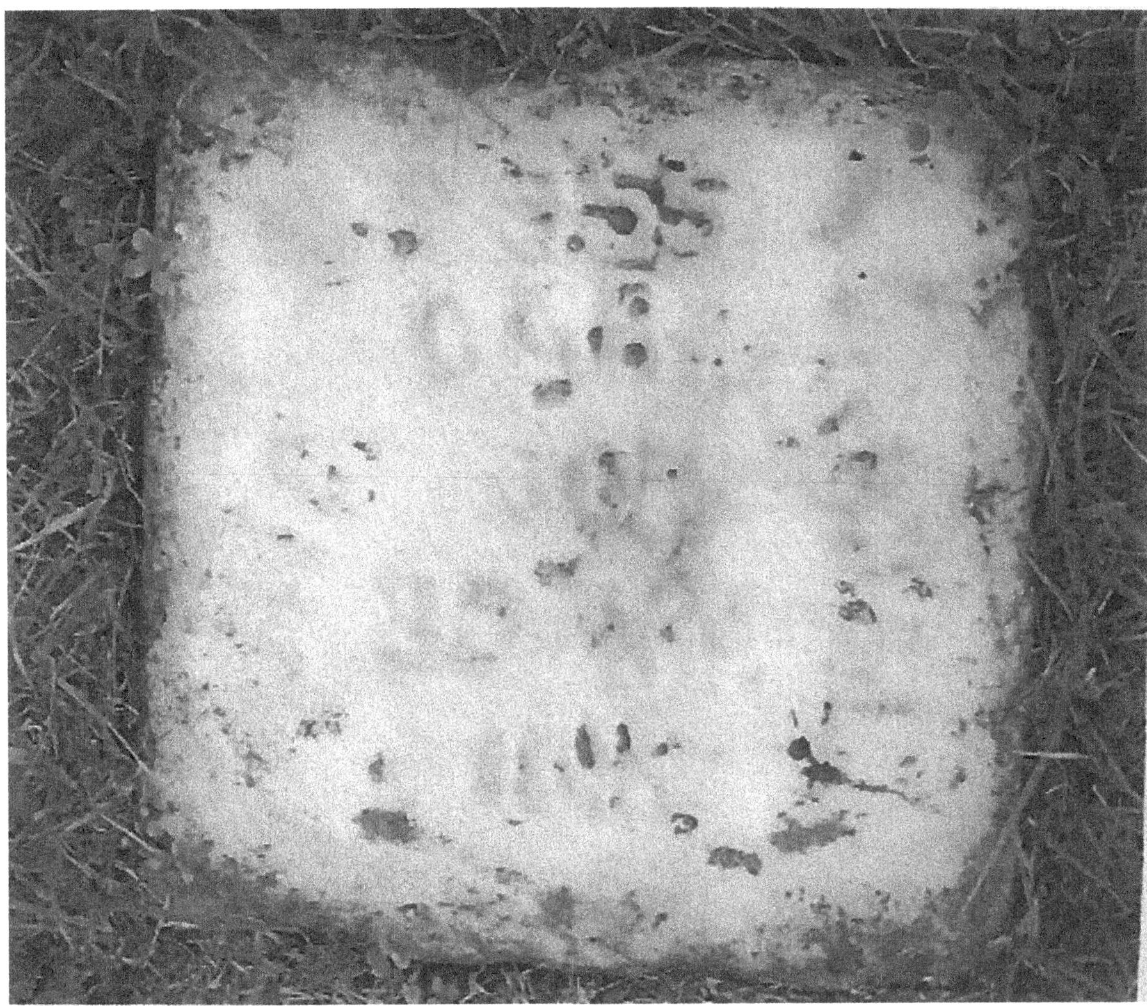

Name: **Stephen Berry**
Birth date: **1835**
Birth place: **New York**
Home in 1860: **Mobile, Alabama**
Occupation: **Clerk**
Service record: **2nd Battalion Alabama Light Artillery**
Death date: **May 10, 1862**
Death place: **Camp Dennison – Hamilton County, Ohio**
Cemetery: **Camp Dennison**

Berry was wounded and captured by Union forces in the battle of Shiloh. He was taken as a prisoner of war and sent to a military hospital at Camp Dennison near Cincinnati. Ohio He died 5 weeks later. Berry's grave was removed from Waldschmide cemetery at Camp Dennison, Ohio and moved to Spring Grove Cemetery July 4, 1869.

2nd Battalion, Alabama Light Artillery

2nd Artillery Battalion was formed at Mobile, Alabama, in January, 1862, with five companies; later reduced to three. It was attached to the Department of the Gulf, and after January, 1864, the Department of Alabama, Mississippi, and East Louisiana. The unit was stationed at or near Mobile throughout the war, and participated in the conflicts at *Forts Gaines and Morgan, Spanish Fort,* and *Fort Blakely. With 64 Officers and men it surrendered on May 4, 1865. Lieutenant Colonel James H. Hallonquist was in.*

Civil War Soldiers Monument, Willoughby, Ohio

On Public Square and Dedicated July 4, 1885 14'tall 3'6" wide. Made of Richmond granite. Union army private on top of statue
http://wepl.lib.oh.us/willoughby_historical_society.htm
There are thousands of statues & monuments in the North & South dedicated to the Civil War Soldiers.

Name: **Joseph Bolton**
Spouse: **Mary**
Birth date: **1836**
Birth place: **Kentucky**
Home in 1860: **Bullitt, Kentucky**
Side served: **Kentucky CSA**
Service record: **5th Reg. Kentucky Inf. Co. F –9th Kentucky mounted Inf.**
Death date: **May 9, 1862**
Death place: **Camp Dennison**
Cemetery: **Waldschmidt Cemetery at Camp Dennison & moved to Spring Grove Cemetery July 4, 1869.**

At Shiloh, Bolton was wounded and captured by the Union forces at Pittsburg Landing. He was taken as a prisoner of war and sent to a military hospital at Camp Dennison near Cincinnati, Ohio. Bolton died 5 weeks later.

5th Regiment, Kentucky Mounted Infantry

5th Infantry Regiment, assembled during the late summer of 1861, included Freeman's Kentucky Infantry Battalion Its members were raised in the counties of Pendleton, Breathitt, Morgan Magoffin, Bath, Owen, Grant, Jessamine, Henderson, Harrison, Shelby, and Franklin. Being a twelve-month unit, when it became time to reenlist some of its members refused and were transferred to the 9th Kentucky Regiment. Later men of the 5th did reenlist for the duration of the war. It became part of the Orphan Brigade or Louisville Legion. The regiment reported 134 casualties in the Battle *Shiloh,* then was active at *Baton Rouge* before being assigned to Kelly's and J. H. Lewis' Brigade, Army of Tennessee. It was prominent at *Chickamauga* and later took an active part in the *Atlanta* Campaign. In the fall of 1864 it was mounted, aided in the defense at Savannah, and fought in the Carolinas. The unit had 91 men disabled at Chickamauga, totaled 201 men and 165 arms in December, 1863, and surrendered on April 26, 1865. Its field officers were Colonels Hiram Hawkins, Andrew J. May, and John S. Williams; Lieutenant Colonels John W. Caldwell and George W. Conner' and Majors Richard Hawes and William Mynheir.

9th Regiment, Kentucky Mounted Infantry

9th Infantry Regiment [also called 5th (Hunt's) Regiment] was organized at Russellville, Kentucky, during the fall of 1861. The men were recruited in the counties of Logan, Jefferson, Nelson, Harrison, Ohio, and Scott. It became part of the Orphan Brigade or Louisville Legion. The 9th served under General Hanson, Helm, and J.H. Lewis. It fought at *Murfreesboro,* was active in and around *Jackson,* saw action at *Chickamauga,* then participated in the *Atlanta* Campaign. During the fall of 1864 it was mounted and took part in the defense of Savannah and the campaign of the Carolinas. The regiment lost 1 killed and 28 wounded at Murfreesboro and forty-four percent of the 230 engaged at Chickamauga. In December, 1863, it totaled 235 men and 157 arms, but only a remnant surrendered with the Army of Tennessee. The field officers were Colonels John W. Caldwell and Thomas H. Hunt; Lieutenant Colonels Alexander Casseday, Robert A Johnston, and J.C. Wickliffe; and Major Ben Desha.

Name: **Samuel H. Bowman**
Spouse: **Mary M**
Birth date: **1833**
Birth place: **Virginia**
Father's name and Birth place: **Henry – Pennsylvania**
Mother's name and Birth place: **Eliza - Pennsylvania**
Occupation: **Farmer**
Enlistment place: **Virginia CSA**
Side served: **Confederate**
Service record: **33rd Regiment Virginia Infantry Co. C. Captain**
10th Regiment Virginia Cavalry 1st Cavalry Reg. (Wise Legion) Co. H. 1st Sergeant
Death place: **Clinton County, Ohio**
Cemetery: **Blanchester Cemetery Clinton County, Ohio**

10th regiment, Virginia Cavalry (1st Cavalry Regiment, Wise Legion)

10th Cavalry Regiment, formerly called 1st Cavalry Regiment, Wise Legion, and 8the Battalion, was organized in May, 1862. Many of the men were from Richmond and Albermarle, Rockingham, and Henrico counties. The unit served in Hampton's W.H.F. Lee's, Chambliss', and Beale's Brigade, Army of Northern Virginia. After fighting in the Seven Days' Battles, it saw action at *Sharpsburg, Fredericksburg, Brandy Station, Upperville, Gettysburg, Bristoe,* and *Mine Run.* The regiment was involved in the *Wilderness* Campaign, the defense of Richmond and *Petersburg,* and the *Appomattox Courthouse* operations. It took 236 effectives to Gettysburg and surrendered with 3 officers and 19 men. Its commanders were Colonels Robert A. Caskie, William B. Clement, and J. Lucius Davis; Lieutenant Colonel Zachariah S. McGruder; and Major J.

Name: **Jacob S. Broughman**
Spouse: **Sarah L. Varney Birth: 1850 Ohio**
Birth date: **October 20, 1841**
Birth place: **Botetourt, Virginia**
Father's name and Birth: **Jacob Broughman 1791 in Virginia**
Mother's name and Birth: **Christene Deel 1801 Virginia**
Occupation: **Farmer**
Enlistment date: **April 10, 1862**
Enlistment place: **Fincastle, Virginia**
Side served: **Virginia CSA**
Service record: **Bedford Light Artillery Reg. Virginia Pvt.**

Surrendered April 9, 1865 at Appomattox Court House, Virginia

The Ross County Heritage Center

Ross County Historical Society- Museum

Visitors may tour exhibits on the Northwest Territory and Ohio statehood. Founding of Ohio first Capital Chillicothe. The prehistoric cultures of the Scioto River Valley, The Civil War Years in Ross County, Camp Sherman and World War I. Heritage center patrons may also visit the society's McKell Library and Museum store. Museum tour hours: Call 740-772-1936 during regular office hours; 9:00 A.M.to 5:00 P.M. Website http://www.rosscountyhistorical.org/museum.html

Confederate Soldier
Kentucky

"Daddy"
Name: **John Benjamin Bryant**
Birth date: **November 4, 1820**
Birth place: **Louisiana**
His parents died from Yellow fever and his uncle raised him until he was 3 years of age then put into the East Baton Rouge Orphanage in Louisiana.
Father's Birth place: **Louisiana**
Mother's Birth place: **Louisiana**
Occupation: **Laborer**
Enlistment place: **Lexington, Kentucky**
Side served: **Kentucky CSA**
Service record: **7th Kentucky Cavalry Co. K Pvt.**
Death date: **January 5, 1913**
Death place: **Turtle Creek Twp. Warren County, Infirmary, Ohio**
Cemetery: **Unmarked grave at Lebanon Cemetery, Warren County, Ohio**

Loved Her in Youth (John Benjamin Bryant), The Western Star, Lebanon, Ohio, Thursday, August 19, 1909. When the Civil War broke out he enlisted in the Confederate army under General Butler as a 'Bushwhacker," and later under Colonel Hines swam the Ohio river in Morgan's celebrated raid. That was a wintry night but no one faltered and "Daddy" was right in the lead. He was not with the section that infested Cincinnati but made on toward Pomeroy where they were repulsed and driven back to Nashville. Our hero was in the battle of *Gettysburg* and was mortally wounded, a large portion of the bone being shot from his left leg. From this he never fully recovered."

A Tale of True Love
Loves Her in Death

Grand Old Gentleman of Southern Type, with a Remarkable History, Spending Last Days at County Hospital in Memories of Bygone Days—Loved But One Girl

You who believe in the beauty of mankind's devotion in a love that endures for a life-time and is true through the trials of life's journey, list to this tale of a lover, hoary, but faithful to the one he loved when the blush of youth flushed his cheeks, now furrowed by the onward marsh of time. Over at the county hospital among other unfortunates from many causes, is a grand old gentleman nearly a century old, but sill bearing the striking characteristics of youth, happy as the day is long and as cheerful as a lark in springtime.

Although he as not been endowed with very much of this world's goods, having met disappointments upon all hands, he has a remarkable history and talks entertainingly of the days that are no more.

Such as **John Benjamin Bryant,** now in his eighty-ninth year. No matter how hot the day nor how inclement the weather, "Daddy," as the force is want to call him, makes his daily journey to the offices of the Western Star. His ever beaming smile always drives away the clouds and after he is gone life somehow seem to be just a little more worth while.

First seeing the light of the day in New Orleans, November 4, 1820, he remained ever true to his native land and fought through the war of the Rebellion under the flag of Lee and was in Morgan's raid when he dashed for the Ohio shore. He well remembers James Monroe as President and the death of John Quincy Adams.

When but a month old "Daddy" was left an orphan, both his father and mother being stricken down by the fearful plague of Yellow Fever. He was cared for by an uncle until three years old and then placed in a orphans asylum where he stayed until he was 10 years of age. It was while in this institution that life's young dream of love had its inception, the boy being attracted by a little playmate orphan girl. Often they played together side by side gathering daisies in the meadow and wathing the frogs and minnows at the babbling brook. In youthful terms he told her of the future he had planned and all was sealed with a kiss of innocent love.

As the years grew on, they renewed their vows and when at maturity finding the flame of affection burning even brighter than ever, they named the day for the chiming of wedding bells. That day never came. Seemingly as a curse upon his young life the Yellow Fever again broke out and his sweetheart was claimed as a victim at the very dawn of their nuptial morning.

Thus for three quarters of century, this true love has trod down life's pathway caring little for the affection of women but with the highest regard for all, never seeing the counterpart of his first love.

Thinking he would forget his troubles he enlisted in the state militia and served two years; but at the end of this time he could not think of returning to his youthful scenes but came northward to a farm in Logan county, Kentucky, where he found work. He made the journey up the Mississippi in a boat and took a stage from Clarksburg to his destination paying a fare of $6.50, while he is now reduced to 75 cents on the railroad.

In 1852 he joined Robinson's circus driving the lion wagon, the longest trip he made being that of overland from New York to New Orleans. His experiences in this line would fill a large volume. When the Civil War broke out he enlisted in the *Confederate army* under General Butler as a "Bushwhacker," and later under Colonel Hines swam the Ohio river in Morgan's celebrated raid. That was a wintry night but no one faltered and "Daddy was right to the lead. He was not with the section that infested Cincinnati but made on toward Pomeroy where they were repulsed and driven back to Nashville.

Our hero was in the battle of Gettysburg and was mortally wounded, a large portion of the bone being shot from his left leg. From this he never fully recovered. This ended his war career and he came to Ohio in 1871 and to Warren County soon after where he engaged at various jobs here and there over the country.

Infirmities of old age and overwork soon bore heavily upon his shoulders and being without kin or friend he was placed upon the mercy of the county.

There he lives enshrouded in the dignity of venerable old age, happy that he still lives, eager and anxious to still live on that he may enjoy the beauty in life God has given him, he still lives in the thoughts and fancies of the past when as a sprightly boy he played with that old sweetheart of his.

7th Regiment, Kentucky Cavalry

7th Cavalry Regiment was organized in September, 1862, using Gano's Texas Cavalry Battalion as its nucleus. The unit skirmished in Tennessee and Kentucky, then fought with J. H. Morgan. Most of its men were captured at *Buffington Island* on July 19, and the rest at New Lisbon on July 26, 1863. The regiment was not reorganized. Colonel Richard M. Gano, Lieutenant Colonel J.M. Huffman, and Major Theophilus Steele were in command.

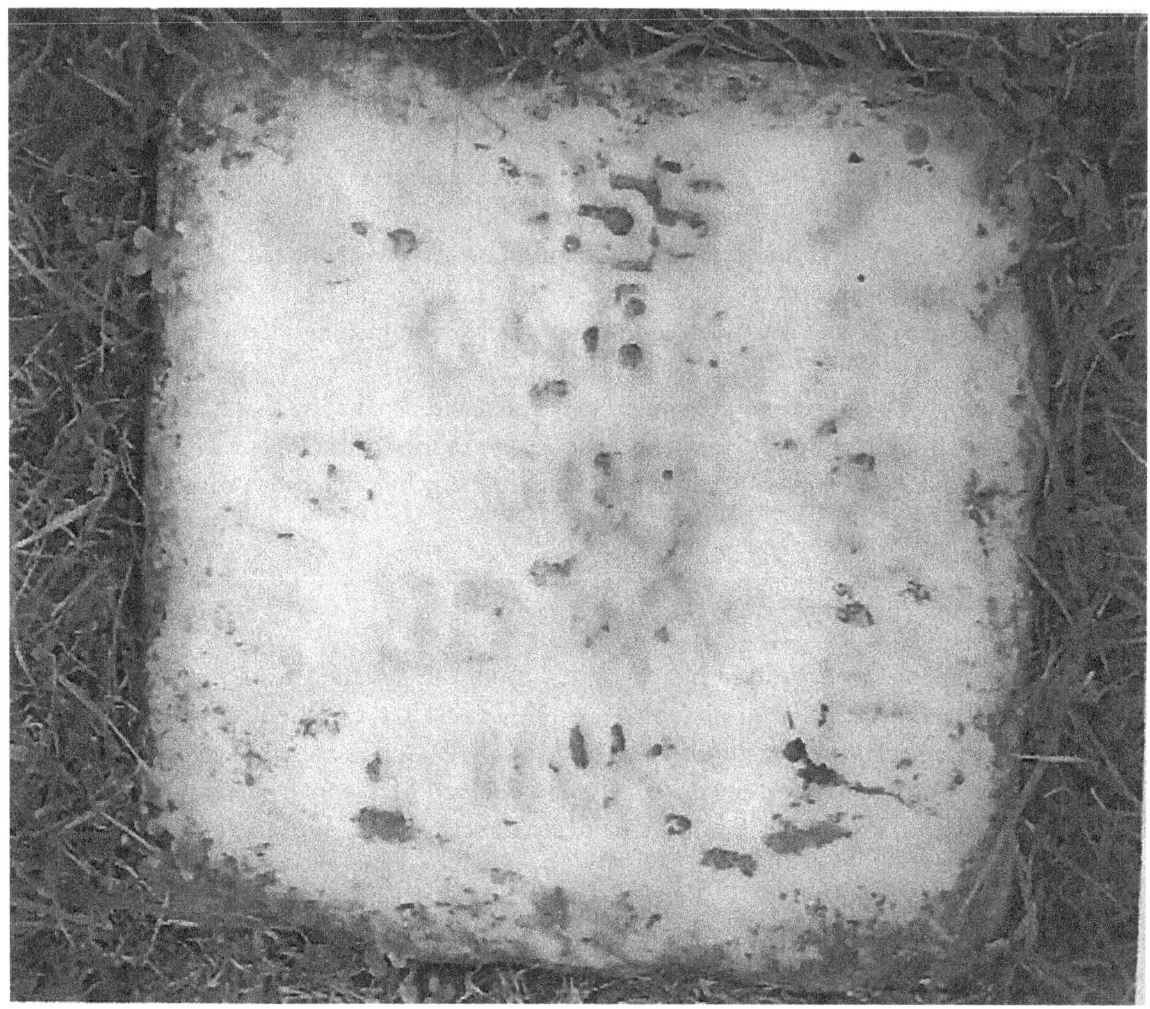

Name: **John Lee Carmichael**
Birth date: **1835**
Birth place: **Kentucky**
Home in 1860: **Jefferson, Kentucky**
Mother's name and Birth place: **Hannah – Kentucky**
Enlistment place: **Camp Boone Montgomery County, Tenn.**
Side served: **Kentucky, CSA**
Service record: **3rd Kentucky Mounted Infantry Co. I Private**
Death date: **April 24, 1863**
Death place: **Camp Dennison- Hamilton County, Ohio**
Cemetery: **Waldschmidt Cemetery-at Camp Dennison**

Carmichael fought with his regiment at the Battle of Shiloh in April of 1867. He was wounded and captured by the Union forces. He was taken as a prisoner of war and sent to a military hospital at Camp Dennison near Cincinnati Ohio. Carmichael died 13 months later. His grave was removed from Waldschmidt cemetery at Camp Dennison, Oh. and sent to Spring Grove Cemetery on July 4, 1869.

3rd regiment, Kentucky Mounted Infantry

3rd Infantry regiment was organized during July 1861, at Camp Boone, Tennessee. Many of the men had previous service in the Kentucky State Guard. The unit took an active part in the Battle of *Shiloh* and reported 174 casualties. Later it was assigned to Rust's and Buford's Brigade, Department of Mississippi and East Louisiana. It lost 26 men at *Baton Rouge*
Then participated in various conflicts around *Vicksburg* and *Jackson*. During the spring of 1864 the regiment was mounted and continued the fight by confronting the Federals in Mississippi, Georgia, and Alabama. It was included in the surrender on May 4, 1865. The field officers were Colonels Gustavus, A.C. Holt, Albert P. Thompson, and Lloyd Tighman; Lieutenant Colonels Benjamin Anderson, T.T. Barnett, and Alfred Johnston; and Majors James H. Bowman, William P. Johnston, and Al McGoodwin.

General George Armstrong Custer-Ohio History Center

General Custer's memorial statue. Born in New Rumley in 1839. Monument is located in New Rumley, Harrison County, Ohio

Name: **William N. Cherryholmes**
Spouse: **Nancy**
Birth date: **1838**
Birth place: **Virginia**
Home in 1860: **Hardy, Virginia**
Home in 1870: **Paxton, Ross County, Ohio**
Father's Birth place: **Virginia**
Mother's Birth place: **Virginia**
Occupation: **Farmer**
Enlistment date: **June 2nd 1861**
Enlistment place: **Petersburg, Virginia**
Side served: **Virginia CSA**
Service record: **18th Cavalry Regiment Virginia Co. E – 25th Infantry Regiment Virginia Co. K Pvt.**
Description: **6'1" Blue eyes Dark hair**
Death place: **Clinton County, Ohio**
Cemetery: **Sabina Cemetery Clinton County, Ohio**

25Th Regiment, Virginia Infantry (Heck's)

25th Infantry Regiment was organized during the early summer of 1861 and included the four companies of the 9th Battalion Virginia Infantry. Its members were raised in Upshur, Augusta, Highland, Bath, Pendleton, and Rockbridge counties. The unit participated in the Lee's *Cheat Mountain* Campaign and Jackson's Valley operations before being assigned to General Early's Jr. R. Jones', and W. Terry's Brigade, Army of Northern Virginia It took an active part in the campaigns of the army from the Seven Days' Battles to *Cold Harbor,* then fought with Early in the Shenandoah Valley and in various conflicts around *Appomattox.* This regiment reported 18 casualties at *Camp Alleghany,* 72 at *McDowell,* and 29 at *Cross Keys* and *Port Republic.* It lost 1 killed and 24 wounded at *Cedar Mountain,* had 3 killed and 20 wounded at *Sharpsburg,* and reported 1 killed and 13 wounded at *Fredericksburg.* Of the 280 engaged at *Gettysburg,* twenty-five percent were disabled. There were no members of the 25th at Appomattox on April 9, 1865. The field officers were Colonels John C. Higginbotham, George A. Porterfield, and George H. Smith; Lieutenant Colonels Patrick B. Duffy, Jonathon M. Heck, Robert D. Lilley, and John A. Robinson; and Majors Wilson Harper, Albert G. Reger, and William T. Thompson.

Name: **Phillip David Crume**
Spouse: **Georgia Hawkins**
Birth date: **October 6, 1840**
Birth place: **Nelson, Kentucky**
Home in 1860: **Collin, Texas**
Father's name and Birth place: **Phillip W.- Kentucky**
Mother's name **Christiann**
Occupation: **A miller and farmer in Kentucky after the war**
Enlistment date: **July 1862**
Enlistment place: **Texas**
Side served: **Texas CSA**
Service record: **8th Texas Cavalry also know as Terry's Texas Rangers Co. H. Pvt.**
Death date: **Sept 17, 1896**
Death place: **Hamilton, Ohio**
Cemetery: **Spring Grove Cemetery Hamilton, Ohio**

8th Regiment, Texas Cavalry(Terry's) (1st Rangers) (8th Rangers)

8th Cavalry Regiment, usually called Terry's Texas Rangers, was organized with 1,170 men at Houston, Texas, in December, 1861. Its members were raised in Houston, Richmond, Columbus, Gonzales, and Wharton, and Bastrop County. The regiment was one of the hardest fighting cavalry units in the war. It was assigned to Wheeler's , Wharton's and T. Harrison's Brigade, and fought at *Shiloh, Murfreesboro,* and *Chickamauga,* Later it was active in the Knoxville and *Atlanta* Campaigns, the Defense of Savannah, and the campaign of the Carolinas. On April 26, 1865, it surrendered with about 30 men. The field officers are Colonels Gustave Cook, Thomas Harrison, Thomas S. Lubbock, Ben. Franklin Terry, and John A. Wharton; Lieutenant Colonels Samuel P Christian, Marcus L. Evans, Stephen C.Ferrell, and John G.Walker; and Majors William R. Jarmon and Leander M. Rayburn.

Civil War Soldiers and Sailors Monument

Veterans Park, Public Square, Painesville, Ohio
Dedicated July 3, 1880 and stands 48' Tall
Http://www.downtownpainesville.org

Name: **John Dedrick**
Spouse: **Anna**
Birth date: **1834**
Birth place: **Germany**
Home in 1860: **Reading, Hamilton County, Ohio**
Side served: **Virginia CSA**
Service record: **7th Virginia Cavalry (Ashby's Cav.) Co. I Pvt.**
Death date: **January 16, 1914**
Death place: **Oak Harbor, Ohio**
Cemetery: **New Berlington, Clinton County, Ohio**

7th Regiment, Virginia Cavalry (Ashby's)

7th Cavalry Regiment was organized during the late spring of 1861. In October authority was given to increase its size, and by the summer of 1862 the regiment contained twenty-nine companies. In June it was reduced to ten companies. Then companies formed the 12th Regiment Virginia Cavalry, seven became the 17th Battalion Virginia Cavalry, one transferred to the 14th Regiment Virginia Cavalry, and one became J. W. Carter's Battery. The unit served in W. E. Jones', Rosser's and J. Dearing's Brigade in the Army of Northern Virginia. It took part in Jackson's Valley Campaign and the conflicts at *Cedar Mountain, Second Manassas, Sharpsburg, Upperville, Fairfield, Bristoe, Mine Run, the Wilderness, Spotsylvania* , and *Cold Harbor.* Later the regiment was involved in Early's Shenandoah Valley operations and disbanded in mid-April, 1865. None of is members were at *Appomattox* on April 9. The field officers were Colonels Turner Ashby, Richard H. Dulany, William E. Jones, and A. W. McDonald; Lieutenant Colonel Thomas Marshall; and Majors O.R. Funsten, Daniel C. Harcher, and Samuel B. Myers.

Name: **Thomas F. Dedrick**
Birth date: **1845**
Birth place: **Virginia**
Father's Birth place: **Virginia**
Mother's Birth place: **Virginia**
Service record: **25th Battalion Virginia Infantry also known as (Richmond Battalion) and (City Battalion) Co. C Pvt.**
Death date: **March 28, 1923**
Death place: **Clinton County, Ohio**
Cemetery: **New Burlington Cemetery Clinton County, Ohio**

Name: **Lawrence F. Patten**
Birth date: **1836**
Birth place: **New Hampshire**
Service record: **47th. Regiment Virginia Infantry Co. N.B. Pvt.**
Cemetery: **Sugar Grove Cemetery Clinton County, Ohio**

47th Regiment, Virginia Infantry

47th Infantry Regiment was formed in June, 1861, with men recruited in Caroline, Middlesex, Essex, and Stafford counties. The unit served under the command of Generals Pettigrew, Field, Heth, H.H. Walker, and Barton. It fought with the Army of Northern Virginia from Seven Pines to *Cold Harbor,* then was active in the trenches of *Petersburg* and around *Appomattox.* This regiment totaled 444 effectives in April, 1862, and sustained 34 casualties of the 156 engaged as Frayser's Farm. It reported 29 casualties at *Second Manassas,*45 at *Fredericksburg,* and disabled. During February, 1865, the 47th and 55th Regiments were consolidated, but only 2 sergeants of the 47th surrendered on April 9. The field officers were Colonels Robert M. Mayo and George W. Richardson; Lieutenant Colonels James D. Bruce, William J. Greene, and John W. Lyell; and Majors Charles J. Green and Edward P. Tayloe.

Name: **Elias Davis**
Spouse: **Elder J**
Birth date: **1840**
Birth place: **Grayson County, Virginia**
Father's name: **David**
Mother's name: **Lucindy**
Occupation: **Farmer**
Enlistment date: **May 15, 1862**
Enlistment place: **Camp Jackson, Virginia**
Side served: **Confederate States of America**
Service record: **Co. G Virginia 63rd Infantry Regiment**
Description: **5' 11" Hazel Eyes Black Hair**
Death date: **May 20, 1909**
Death place: **Clark, Clinton County, Ohio**
Cemetery: **Martinsville Cemetery, Clinton County, Ohio**

63rd Regiment, Virginia Infantry (McMahon's)

63red Infantry Regiment was organized in May, 1862. It served in Western Virginia, then joined the Army of Tennessee. The unit was assigned to Kelly's, Reynolds', Brown's and Reynolds' Consolidated, and Palmer's Brigade. It participated in the campaigns of the army from *Chickamauga* to *Atlanta*, moved with Hood to Tennessee, and was active in North Carolina. The 63rd lost about one-third of its force in the fight at Chickamauga, and in December, 1863, totaled 303 men and 188 arms. It contained 129 effectives in December, 1864, and on April 9, 1865, merged into the 54th Battalion Virginia Infantry. Few surrendered on April26. The field officers were Colonels James M. French and John J. McMahon, and Lieutenant Colonels David C. Dunn and Connally H. Lynch.

Name: **Issac Long Frye**
Spouse: **Elizabeth**
Birth date: **August 2, 1842**
Birth place: **Virginia**
Father's name and Birth place: **Jacob – Virginia**
Mother's name and Birth place: **Catherine Moss – Virginia**
Occupation: **Farmer**
Enlistment date: **August 5, 1862**
Enlistment place: **Frederick County, Virginia**
Side served: **Virginia CSA**
Service record: **17th Virginia Cavalry Co. H – 11th Virginia Cavalry Co H -14th Virginia Militia**
Description: **5'10" Blue eyes, Brown hair**
Death date: **September 23, 1918**
Death place: **Wayne Twp. Warren County, Ohio**
Cemetery: **Miami Cemetery Corwin, Warren County, Ohio**

Miami Cemetery Corwin, Warren County, Ohio

11th Regiment, Virginia Cavalry

11th Cavalry Regiment was organized in February, 1863, by consolidating the 17th Battalion Virginia Cavalry, one company from the 24th Battalion Virginia Cavalry, and two companies of the 5th Regiment Virginia Cavalry. The unit served in W.R. Jones', Lomax's, Rosser's, and J. Dearing's Brigade, Army of Northern Virginia. It was active in the conflicts at *Upperville, Fairfield, Bristoe,* and *Mine Run.* Later the regiment participated in The *Wilderness* Campaign, the defense of Richmond, and Early's Shenandoah Valley operations. It then disbanded as there were no members of the 11th at Appomattox. The field officers were Colonels Oliver R. Lunsten and Lunsford L. Lomax, Lieutenant Colonel Matt D. Ball, and Majors William H. Harness and Edward H. McDonald.

Name: **John L. Hunley**
Spouse: **Martha A.**
Birth date: **March 1835**
Birth place: **Tennessee**
Home in 1900: **Wilmington, Clinton County, Ohio**
Father's Birth place: **Virginia**
Mother's Birth place: **Virginia**
Side served: **Tennessee CSA**
Service record: **11th Regiment Tennessee Infantry Pvt.**
Cemetery: **Sugar Grove Cemetery, Clinton County, Ohio**

11th Regiment, Tennessee Infantry

11th Infantry Regiment was organized at Camp Cheatham, Tennessee, in May, 1861. Its companies were recruited in the following counties: Humphreys, Dickson, Davidson, Cheatham, Robertson, and Hickman. In July the unit contained 880 effectives, moved to Kentucky, then skirmished at Cumberland Gap and Tazewell. Later it joined the Army of Tennessee and served in P. Smith's, Vaughan's, and Palmer's Brigade. The 11th participated in the campaigns of the army from *Murfreesboro* to *Atlanta,* endured Hood's winter operations, and fought in North Carolina. It reported 8 killed, 64 wounded, and 11 missing at Murfreesboro and 8 killed and 44 wounded at *Chickamauga.* In December, 1863, it totaled 340 men and 267 arms. After the Atlanta Campaign the regiment was consolidated with the 29th Regiment and was included in the surrender on April 26, 1865. Its commanders were Colonels George W. Gordon, James A. Long, and James E. Rains; Lieutenant Colonels Thomas P. Gateman, William Thedford, and Howell Webb; and Majors John E. Binns, William Green, Hugh R. Lucas, and Philip Van Horn Weems.

Newton J. Kidwell

Confederate Soldier
Virginia

Newton Kidwell was a former Confederate soldier who lived in central Ohio after the Civil War but never lost his loyalty to the South.

Kidwell was born on July 4, 1846, in Loudoun County, Virginia. On February 14, 1863, at the age of fourteen, he enlisted in the Eighth Virginia Infantry Regiment. He remained in the Confederate army for the duration of the American Civil War. Kidwell participated in the Battle of Gettysburg, where he was captured during Pickett's Charge. He was held as a prisoner of war at Fort Delaware until December 1863, when he was released. Kidwell returned to active duty with the Eighth Virginia and served with this unit until April 7, 1865, when he was captured once again. He took the oath of allegiance to the United States and was released on April 12, 1865. He returned to his family home at Upperville, Virginia.

Loudoun County, Virginia was devastated at the end of the Civil War. Kidwell, like many of his neighbors, left the South and hoped for more opportunity in the North. This trend had begun even before the Civil War as land availability declined in Virginia and other Southern states. It continued throughout the nineteenth and twentieth centuries until well after World War II. Kidwell moved to a farm near Groveport, Ohio, where he became a tenant farmer. He arrived with his new bride, Elinorah Bradfield, whom he had married in 1874. She had also migrated from Virginia after the Civil War. In return for turning over the entire crop to the landowner, Kidwell received one dollar a day in pay and the right to live in a five-room house located on the property. He remained on the farm until old age caused him to move to Columbus, Ohio. There, Kidwell found employment as a landlord and groundskeeper.

Kidwell, like many of the Southerners who migrated to the North after the Civil War, never forgot his Confederate service. Kidwell was the Commander of the Ohio Camp of United Confederate Veterans at the time of his death. In 1919, the Grand Army of the Republic held its fifty-third annual encampment in Columbus. Upset with the large number of Union veterans parading through the street, Kidwell put on his Confederate uniform and marched through the streets, mocking the Union soldiers. Two Northern soldiers "captured" Kidwell and paraded their "prisoner" through the streets as a joke. The veterans then decided to make the former Confederate an honorary member of the Seventy-Sixth Ohio Volunteer infantry.

Newton J. Kidwell died in Columbus on April 19, 1920

Name: **Thomas B. Latta**
Spouse: **N.A.**
Birth date: **1841**
Birth place: **Hickman County, Kentucky**
Father's name and Birth: **John 1812 Tennessee**
Mother's name and Birth: **Mary S. 1812 Tennessee**
Occupation: **Farmer**
Enlistment date: **December 9, 1861**
Enlistment place: **Columbus, Kentucky**
Side served: **Confederate States of America**
Service record: **Co. A Kentucky 7th Mounted Infantry Pvt.**
Death date: **April 22, 1862**
Death place: **Camp Dennison, Ohio**
Cemetery: **Waldschmidt Cemetery at Camp Dennison then removed to Spring Grove Cemetery Hamilton County, Oh on July 4, 1869**

7th Regiment, Kentucky Mounted Infantry

7th Infantry Regiment was assembled in September, 1861, at Camp Burnett, near Clinton, Kentucky, with men from the western section of the state. This regiment reported 14 casualties at Baton Rouge, then was assigned to Rust's and Buford's Brigade, Department of Mississippi and East Louisiana. It was active in various conflicts around *Vicksburg* and *Jackson* and during the spring of 1864 was mounted and attached to General Lyon's Brigade in Forrest's Corps. The unit saw action in the expedition from Memphis into Mississippi, June 1-13, and reported 39 casualties. During July there were 73 disabled at *Harrisburg*. Later it skirmished in Alabama and surrendered on May 4, 1865. The field officers were Colonels Edward Crossland and Charles Wickliffe, Lieutenant Colonels Williams D. Lannom and L. J. Sherrill, and Majors H. S. Hale and W.H.N. Welborn.

Name: **Phillip Noland Luckett**
Birth date: **1824**
Birth place: **Virginia**
Home in 1860: **Corpus Christi, Texas**
Father's name and Birth place: **Otho Holland Williams – Virginia**
Mother's name and Birth place: **Elizabeth C. Graham – Virginia**
Enlistment date: **1861**
Enlistment place: **Texas**
Side served: **CSA**
Service record: **3rd Regiment Texas Infantry Col.**
Death date: **May 21, 1869**
Death place: **Avondale, Hamilton County, Ohio**
Cemetery: **Spring Grove Cemetery Hamilton County, Ohio**

Civil War Confederate Army officer. Born in Virginia, he was educated in medicine when his family moved to Chillicothe, Ohio and he became a physician. He was appointed to the United States Military Academy at West Point in 1847 though he never enrolled, and moved to Texas instead, where during the 1840's he became a surgeon of Captain John S. Ford's Company of Texas Rangers. He represented Nueces and Webb Counties of Texas in the state Secession Convention. He was ordered by the Committee along with Thomas J. Divine, Samuel A. Maverick, and J. H. Rogers on January 28, 1861 to visit Federal General David E. Twiggs in San Antonio to demand and recover United States Military property in the state of Texas. He was then appointed as Quartermaster-General of Texas and served on the staff of Earl Van Dorn, who commanded the Department of Texas. Elected as Colonel of the 3rd Texas Infantry in the fall of 1861, he assumed command of the regiment in June, 1862 until October when the unit was reassigned to Colonel Ford's Western Sub-district of Texas. The regiments were scattered from Fort Brown to Laredo guarding the state's border with Mexico. He was appointed as "acting Brigadier General" by General John B. Magruder in June of 1863. The 3rd Texas Infantry was sent to Galveston, Texas in July of 1863. His regiment was attached to the 3rd Brigade(under Brigadier General

William R .Scurry) in the 1st Division that was commanded by Major General John G. Walker and participated in the Red River Campaign the following year. His regiment is credited with the repulsion of Major General Frederick Steele's forces in the Battle of Jenkins' Ferry, Luckett assumed command of the brigade when General Scurry was killed. He continued to command the brigade until December 21, 1864 when he took ill and was relieved of command. The 3rd Texas disbanded in June of 1865 just before the Trans-Mississippi Department surrendered to the Union Army. He then accompanied William Preston, Hamilton P. Bee, and General Walker to Mexico with about forty men to escape being captured by the Union forces. He returned to Texas in November and was subsequently arrested by federal officials along with fellow commissioner of public safety, Thomas J. Divine. He was imprisoned for several months at Fort Jackson in Louisiana. After he was paroled and released he lived in nearby New Orleans. He eventually returned to Ohio and was living with relatives in Cincinnati when he died in Avondale from a bronchial infection in 1869.

3rd Regiment, Texas Infantry

3rd Infantry Regiment completed its organization during the fall of 1861. Some of its members were recruited in Austin and San Antonio. It served along the Texas coast at various points and in October , 1862, totaled 648 effectives. Because the regiment never saw any action, during the latter part of the war morale deteriorated. It disbanded before the Trans-Mississippi Department surrendered in June, 1865. The field officers were Colonel Philip N. Luckett, Lieutenant Colonels Augustus Buchel and Edward F. Gray, and Major John H. Kampmann.

Name: **James F. Marlow**
Birth date: **1836**
Birth place: **Lee County, Virginia**
Father's name and Birth place: **Mark - North Caroline**
Mother's name: **Polly**
Enlistment date; **September 13, 1862**
Enlistment place: **Virginia**
Side served: **Virginia CSA**
Service record: **6th Cavalry Regiment Virginia Co. A. Pvt.**
Death place: **Clinton County, Ohio**
Cemetery: **Sugar Grove Cemetery, Clinton County, Ohio**

6th Regiment, Virginia Cavalry

6th Cavalry Regiment completed its organization in November, 1861, at Manassas, Virginia. Men of this unit were raised in Loudoun, Rappahannock, Clarke, Rockingham, Pittsylvania, Fairfax, Halifax, Fauquier, and Orange counties. The unit served in Robertson's W. E. Jones', Lomax's, and Payne's Brigade, Army of Northern Virginia. It fought in Jackson's Valley Campaign and in the conflicts at *Second Manassas, Brandy Station, Upperville, Fairfield, Bristoe, Mine Run, The Wilderness, Todd's Tavern, Spotsylvania Haw's Shop,* and *Cold Harbor.* The regiment went on to take part in Early's Shenandoah Valley operations and the *Appomattox* Campaign. Only 3 men surrendered on April 9, 1865, as most of the cavalry cut through the Federal lines and later disbanded. The field officers were Colonels Charles W. Field, Thomas S. Flourney, John S. Green, and Julien Harrison; Lieutenant Colonels J. Grattan Cabell and Daniel T. Richards; and Majors Cabell E. Flournoy and Daniel A. Grimsley.

Name: **John B. Mason**
Birth date: **1835**
Birth place: **Texas**
Service record: **6th Texas Infantry Co. B. Pvt.**
Death date: **1862**
Death place: **Camp Dennison**
Cemetery: **Spring Grove Cemetery Hamilton County, Ohio**

He was mustered into Co. B as a private when the Regiment was organized at Camp McCulloch, near Victoria, Texas. In the summer of 1861, Mason fought with his regiment at the Battle of Shiloh. In April of 1862 he was wounded and captured by Union forces. He was taken as prisoner of war and sent to a military hospital at Camp Dennison. He died 3 weeks later. His grave was removed from Wildschmidt Cemetery at Camp Dennison and moved to Spring Grove Cemetery on July 4, 1869.

Confederate Soldier
Virginia

Name: **Charles Taylor Mason**
Spouse: **Susie J. - Born in Ohio**
Birth date: **1845**
Birth place: **Virginia**
Home from: **1846 to 1860 Meigs Muskingum, Ohio**
Home in 1870: **Chillicothe, Ross County, Ohio**
Father's name and Birth place: **James W. – Virginia**
Mother's name and Birth place: **Mary Ann – Virginia**
Occupation: **Farmer**
Service record: **Mosby's regiment Va. Cavalry (Partisan Rangers) Co B Pvt.**
Death date: **1918**
Death place: **Chillicothe, Ross County, Ohio**
Cemetery: **Grandview Cemetery Ross County, Ohio**

Name: **Sidney Clark Mooney**
Spouse: **Sharolette Matilda**
Birth date: **January 9, 1841**
Birth place: **Hillsville, Carroll County, Virginia**
Father's name and Birth place: **Martin Dickerson – Virginia**
Mother's name and Birth place: **Sarah Amelia – Virginia**
Enlistment date: **March 3, 1862**
Mustered out: **March 15, 1865**
Enlistment place: **Hillsville, Virginia**
Side served: **Virginia CSA**
Service record: **Virginia 24th Infantry Co. C. Pvt.**
Death date: **November 14, 1921**
Death place: **Martinsville, Clinton County, Ohio**
Cemetery: **Martinsville I.O.O.F. Cemetery Clinton County, Ohio**

24th Regiment, Virginia Infantry

24th Infantry Regiment was assembled in June, 1861, with men from Floyd, Franklin, Carroll, Giles, Pulaski, Mercer, and Henry Counties. It served under Early at *First Manassas,* then was assigned to Early's, Kemper's, and W.R. Terry's Brigade, Army of Northern Virginia. The 24th participated in the campaigns of the army from *Williamsburg* to *Gettysburg* except when it was detached to Suffolk with Longstreet. Later it was involved in the engagements at *Plymouth* and *Drewry's Bluff.* And *Petersburg* siege north of the James River, and the Appomattox operations. The regiment contained 740 men in April l, 1862, and reported 189 casualties at *Williamsburg* and 107 at *Seven Pines.* It lost 4 killed, 61 wounded, and 14 missing at Frayser's Farm, had 8 wounded at *Fredericksburg,* and had about forty percent of the 395 engaged at *Gettysburg* disabled. Many were lost at *Sayler's Creek* with no officers and 22 men surrendered on April 9, 1865. The field officers were Colonels Jubal A. Early and William A. Terry; Lieutenant Colonels Peter Hairston, Jr. and Richard L. Maury; and Majors William W. Bentley, Joseph A. Hambrick and J. P. Hammet.

Name: **James H. Moore**
Service record: **4th Regiment Kentucky Mounted Infantry Co. E. Pvt.**
Death date: **1862**
Death place: **Camp Dennison**
Cemetery: **Spring Grove Cemetery Hamilton, Ohio**

After the Civil War began, Moore volunteered to serve in the Confederate Army and enlisted with the 4th Kentucky Mounted Infantry. He was mustered into Company E as a Private when the regiment was organized at Bowling Green, Kentucky in September of 1861. Moore fought with his regiment at the Battle of Shiloh in April of 1862 where he was wounded and captured by the Union forces. He was taken as a prisoner of war and sent to a military hospital at Camp Dennison near Cincinnati, Ohio. Moore died two weeks later. His grave was removed from Waldschmidt Cemetery at Camp Dennison, Ohio to Spring Grove Cemetery on July 4, 1869.

4th Regiment, Kentucky Mounted Infantry

4th Infantry Regiment was organized at Bowling Green, Kentucky, in September, 1861, and became part of the Orphan Brigade or Louisville Legion. Its members were recruited In the counties of Barren, Henderson, Union, Owen, Scott, Green, Jefferson, Taylor, Franklin, Estill, Nicholas, Davies, and Trigg. This unit had 213 men disabled at *Shiloh,* then, was active at *Baton Rouge* and *Jackson.* Later it was assigned to Hanson's, Helm's and J. H. Lewis' Brigade, Army of Tennessee. The 4th took an active part in the Battles of *Murfreesboro* and *Chickamauga* and saw action in the *Atlanta* Campaign. During the fall of 1864 it was mounted, aided in the defense of Savannah, and ended the war in North Carolina. It reported 12 killed, 49 wounded, and 8 missing at Murfreesboro, lost twenty-one percent of the 275 engaged at Chickamauga, and totaled 335 men and 251 arms in December, 1863. Few surrendered on April 26, 1865. The field officers were Colonels Joseph P. Nuckols, Jr. and Robert P. Trabue; Lieutenant Colonels John A. Adair, Andrew R. Hynes, and Thomas W. Thompson; and Majors Joseph H. Millett, Thomas B. Munroe, Jr., and John B. Rogers.

James A. Garfield National Historic Site Mentor, Ohio
Route 20 (8095 Mentor Ave. Mentor, Lake County, Ohio 44060

James A. Garfield National Historic site U.S. National Park Service. Garfield acquired this home in 1876. Garfield was the 20th President of the United States in 1880 and a Union General in the Civil War. Visitor info: 440-255-8722

Name: **Thomas Satterwhitt Noble**
Spouse: **Mary Caroline Hogan**
Birth date: **May 29, 1835**
Birth place: **Near Lexington, Fayette County, Kentucky**
Father's name and Birth place: **Thomas Hart – Kentucky**
Mother's name: **Rosmond Clarke**
Service record: **3rd Regiment Porter's Brigade Missouri Co. A. Pvt. That unit consolidated into the 4th Missouri Cavalry Co. D**
Death date: **April 27, 1907**
Death place: **New York**
Cemetery: **Spring Grove Cemetery, Hamilton, Ohio**

Painter, Born near Lexington, Kentucky, he grew up on a hemp and cotton plantation. Noble attended Transylvania University in Lexington and studied painting with *Samuel Woodson Price* in Louisville in 1852. In 1856 he studied abroad in Paris, France with *Thomas Couture* until he returned to America in 1859. During the Civil War he served in the Confederate Army and enlisted in 1862 while living with his family in St. Louis, Missouri. Noble was mustered into the 3red Regiment of Porter's Brigade as a Private in Company A. His company was eventually consolidated into Company D. of the 4th Missouri Cavalry, also know as Burbridge's Regiment. Noble spent a portion of his service on detached duty at Camden, Arkansas as a bullet molder for the Ordnance Department. After the war he moved to New York City and operated a studio there from 1866 to 1869 where he painted a few of his most famous works including "The Modern Medea" in 1867 and "the Price of Blood" in 1868. He became a prominent painter and Portraitist and was know for painting historical representations. Many of his paintings involved serious issues such as slavery and suicide. He is a noted painter of Black History and was known to have opposed the institution of slavery. In 1869 he accepted a position as the head of the McMicken

School of Design in Cincinnati, Ohio and remained there for 35 years. Noble retired in 1904 and returned to New York City where he died in 1907 at the age of 71.

4th Regiment, Missouri Cavalry

4th Cavalry Regiment was assembled during December, 1861, and included Preston's Missouri Cavalry Battalion. Some of he men were from St. Louis and Barton County, and many had served in the Missouri State Guard. The unit served in the Trans-Mississippi Department and was attached to C. Green's , Shelby's, and J.B. Clarks' Brigade. It participated in Marmaduke's Expedition into Missouri, fought in various conflicts in Arkansas, and shared in Price's Missouri operations. The regiment reported 11 casualties with Marmaduke, 6 at *Poison Spring,* 13 at *Jenkins' Ferry,* and 63 in Price's Expedition. The 4th was included in the surrender in June, 1865. Colonel John Q. Burbridge, Lieutenant Colonel William J. Preston, and Major Dennis Smith were its commanders.

Ulysses S. Grant Birthplace Point Pleasant, Ohio

Grant was a General in the Civil War, and 18th President of the United States. He was born here on April 27th. 1822. The Grant's birthplace was restored and open to the public.

Hours: April thru October only. 9:30 AM to 5:00 PM. Weds. Thur. & Fri, and 12:00 to 5:00 on Sunday. Closed Mon & Tues and each day from noon to 1:00. Located at 1551 Old Route 232 Point Pleasant, Ohio. 1-800-283-8932

Jacob Harvey Plaugher Jr.

Confederate Soldier
Virginia

Name: **Jacob Harvey Plaugher Jr.**
Spouse: **1st. Christina Miller, 2nd. Sarah Francis Judy, 3rd. Mattie Eye**
Birth date: **November 10, 1843**
Birth place: **Rockingham, Virginia**
Home in 1920: **Monroe, Allen, Ohio**
Father's name and Birth place: **Jacob Harvey Plaugher Sr. – Virginia**
Mother's name: **Susan Brown**
Occupation: **Farmer**
Enlistment place: **Virginia**
Side served: **Virginia CSA.**
Prison camp 1863: **Champ Chase, Ohio**
Service record: **Pvt. 7th Virginia Cavalry (Ashby's) Co. I**
Death date: **January 3, 1936**
Death place: **Lima, Ohio**

Jacob Harvey Plaugher Sr. 1794-1881 was with the 146th Virginia Militia Co. C as a private. He is buried at Prospect Cemetery in Brandywine, W.Va. His brother Levi was with the 7th Virginia Co. I. Cavalry Regiment. Brother John was with the 7th Virginia cavalry Co. I. Stepbrother Samuel Henry Plaugher was a Southern Loyalist.

ALLOWANCES MADE TO BLIND OF ALLEN-CO

An allowance of $1,480 was made to beneficiaries under the blind pension law Friday by county commissioners. Eighty-one persons afflicted by blindness will receive allowances Monday for the last quarter of 1928. Two persons included in the allowances made for the prior quarter were dropped and two names added. Gustavus Clements, 81, and Jacob H. Plaugher, 85, were included in the allowances for the last quarter and the names of Timothy Carnell, Spencerville, and Rosalee Jane Smith, Lima, were removed from the list thru death.

Jacob had 29 children

Confederate Army Veteran Dies Near Lima

Jacob Plaugher, 92, possibly Lima district's only veteran of the Confederate army, died at his home near Beaverdam late Friday. Funeral services will be held in the Pleasant View Church of the Brethren at 2 p. m. Monday the Rev. I. C. Paul officiating. Plaugher had been a member of that church 56 years. Services will be in charge of Mortician Harris of Columbus Grove.

Plaugher was born in 1843 in Rockingham, Va. During the war between the states he served four years with the Seventh Virginia cavalry. He came to Allen-co 24 years ago, and had engaged in farming until four years ago when stricken with blindness. He was the father of 29 children, 21 of whom survive with the widow, Mrs. Mattie Plaugher.

Surviving children are Mrs. Maxine Schrider, of Lima; Everett, of Lima; Gilbert, of Beaverdam; Mrs. Harry Wagner, of West Virginia; P. C., J. J. and George of Westminster; S. D., Ortho, Eli, Weldon, Frank and Rollie, of California; John, of South America; Miss Ruth Plaugher, of Philadelphia, and Albelt, Raymond, Woodrow, Charles and Edwin at home. Two sisters, Mrs. Nessie Rexroad, and Miss Susie Plaugher, of Rockingham, Va., also survive. There are 57 grandchildren and 37 great-grandchildren.

Obituary was in the Lima Sunday News on Sunday, Jan. 5th. 1936.

Southern Claims Commission

Claimant	County	State	Commission No.	Office No.	Report No.	Year	Status
Plaster, David H., exr.	Loudoun	VA	16110	—	—	—	B
" " [of Michael]			16122	1628	9	1879	
Plaster, Henry	Loudoun	VA	16121	—	—	—	B
Plato, Telam, est. [Plats]*	Fauquier	VA	16341	—	7	1877	A
Platt, David [Plot, D.]+	Haywood	NC	16313	1062	9	1879	D
Platt, Emily A., admx. of Norman	Hinds	MS	17539	929	9	1879	D
Platt, Joshua A.	Manatee	FL	13695	—	—	—	B
Platt, Obediah H.	Prairie	AR	11896	—	—	—	B
Platts, Benjamin	Beaufort	SC	10088	—	9	1879	A
Platts, Elizabeth	Barnwell	SC	5664	478	6	1876	D
Plauché. See Planché							
Plaugher, Samuel H.	Rockingham	VA	2556	—	1	1871	A
Pleasant Grove Church	Catoosa	GA	15031	222	5	1875	D
Pleasants, Isaac	Henrico	VA	20403	—	4	1874	A
Pledger, Cato	Marlborough	SC	308	—	—	—	B
Pledger, Elizabeth T.	Chattooga	GA	7492	—	7	1877	A
Pledger, Isaac	Franklin	AR	17083	—	—	—	B
Pledger, Pleasant W.	Jefferson	AL	7979	—	6	1876	A
Plischke, Augustine	Shelby	TN	8482	812	2	1872	D
Plonk, Jacob F.	Gaston	NC	262	—	4	1874	A
Plowman, George	Talladega	AL	4036	60	3	1873	D
Plowman, Matilda	Chattooga	GA	7494	—	9	1879	A
Plummer, G. W.	Jefferson	TX	2500	178	1	1871	D
Plummer, Goen W.	Jefferson	TX	14584	—	2	1872	A
Plummer, Zachariah	Cumberland	NC	5439	—	2	1872	A
Plunk, Calvin	McNairy	TN	17796	—	4	1874	A
Plunk, David	McNairy	TN	17797	—	4	1874	A
Poage, Elijah	Roanoke	VA	13907	1062	2	1872	D
Podesta, Joseph	Warren	MS	19433	475	7	1877	D
Poe, Ansel	Hamilton	TN	17575	—	9	1879	A
Poe, Elizabeth E. [Flanagan, William, est.]§	Pulaski	AR	16096	—	—	—	B
Poe, est. of John	James	TN	15436	—	9	1879	A
Poe, Sivility J.	Walker	GA	6882	334	8	1878	D
Poe, Wyatt	Tuscaloosa	AL	6037	—	2	1872	A
Poindexter, John F.	Forsyth	NC	14301	861	3	1873	D

Jacob's stepbrother Samuel was a Southern Loyalist

Name: **John Plauger - Plaugher**
Residence: **Rockingham County, Virginia**
Occupation: **Farm Laborer**
Age at Enlistment: **24**
Enlistment Date: **18 June 1861**
Rank at Enlistment: **Private**
Enlistment Place: **Harrisonburg, VA**
State Served: **Virginia**
Service Record: **Enlisted in Company I, Virginia 7th Cavalry Regiment On 18 June 1861.**
Birth Date: **abt 1837**
Sources: **The Virginia Regimental Histories Series**

Name: **Jacob Plaugher**
Side: **Confederate**
Regiment: **Virginia**
State/Origin:
Regiment Name: **146 Virginia Militia**
Regiment Name: **146th Regiment, Virginia Militia**
Company: **C**
Rank In: **Private**
Rank In Expanded: **Private**
Rank Out: **Private**
Rank Out Expanded: **Private**
Alternate Name: **Jacob/Plauger, Jr. or Sr.**
Film Number: **M382 roll 44**

Name: **Levi J. Plaugher**
Spouse: **Nancy J.**
Birth date: **April 10, 1840**
Birth place: **Rockingham, Virginia**
Home in 1870: **Warren, Washington County, Ohio**
Home in 1880: **Bethel Pendleton, W.Va.**
Home in 1900: **Warren, Washington County, Ohio**
Father's name and Birth place: **Jacob Harvey Sr. – Virginia**
Mother's name: **Susan Brown**
Occupation: **Cooper-Farmer**
Enlistment date: **June 18, 1861**
Enlistment place: **Harrisonburg, Virginia**
Side served: **Virginia CSA**
Service record: **Va. 7th Cavalry Regiment Co. I**
Description: **5'9" dark complexion gray eyes black hair**
Death date: **November 15, 1912**
Death place: **Washington County, Ohio**
Cemetery: **Hopkins Cemetery Nichols Farm Cr. 3 Washington County. Ohio Located in Marietta, Ohio**

This is the Son of Jacob Harvey Sr. and the brother of Jacob Harvey Jr.

7th Regiment, Virginia Cavalry (Ashby's)

7th Cavalry Regiment was organized during the late spring of 1861. In October authority was given to increase its size, and by the summer of 1862 the regiment contained twenty-nine companies. In June it was reduced to ten companies. Ten companies formed the 12th Regiment Virginia Cavalry, seven became the 17 Battalion Virginia Cavalry, one transferred to the 14th Regiment Virginia Cavalry, and one became J.W. Carter's Battery. The unit served in W.E. Jones', Rosser's, and J. Dearing's Brigade in the Army of Northern Virginia. It took part in Jackson's Valley Campaign and the conflicts at **Cedar Mountain**, , **Second Manassas Sharpsburg, Upperville, Fairfield, Bristoe, Mine Run, The Wilderness, Spotsylvania, and Cold Harbor**. Later the regiment was involved in Early's Shenandoah Valley operations and disbanded in mid-April,1865. None of its members were at Appomattox on April 9. The field officers were Colonels Turner Ashby, Richard H. Dulany, William E. Jones, and A.W. McDonald: Lieutenant Colonel Thomas Marshall; and Majors O.R. Funsten, Daniel C. Harcher, and Samuel B. Myers.

Name: **Richard Rickett**
Spouse: **Martha M.**
Birth date: **1845**
Birth place: **Virginia**
Father's Birth place: **Virginia**
Mother's Birth place: **Virginia**
Occupation: **Wagon Maker**
Enlistment date: **April 18, 1861**
Enlistment place: **Lexington, Virginia**
Side served: **Confederate Virginia CSA**
Service record: **5th Infantry Regiment Virginia Co. B and 27th Infantry Regiment Virginia Co. H Pvt.**
Cemetery: **New Burlington Cemetery, Clinton County, Ohio**

27th Regiment, Virginia Infantry

27th Infantry Regiment was organized in May, 1861, and accepted into Confederate service in July. The men were from the counties of Alleghany, Rockbridge, Monroe, Greenbrier, and Ohio. It contained only eight companies and became part of the famous Stonewall Brigade. During the war it served under the command of General T.J. Jackson, R.B. Garnett, Winder, Paxton, J. A. Walker, and W. Terry. The 27th fought at *First Manassas, First Kerns town,* and in Jackson's Valley Campaign. It then participated in the campaign of the Army of Northern Virginia from the Seven Days' Battles to *Cold Harbor,* moved with Early to the Shenandoah Valley, and was active around *Appomattox.* The regiment reported 141 casualties at First Manassas, 57 at First Kerns town, and 4 of the 136 engaged at *First Winchester.* It lost 3 killed at *CedarMountain,*had 4 killed and 23 wounded at *Second Manassas,* and sustained 9 killed and 62 wounded at *Chancellorsville.* Of the 148 in action at *Gettysburg* about thirty percent were disabled. Only 1 officer and 20 men surrendered. The field officers were Colonels John Echols, James K. Edmondson, William A. Gordon, and A.J. Grisby; Lieutenant Colonels Charles L. Haynes and Daniel M. Shriver; and Majors Philip F. Frazer and Elisha F. Paxton.

Dr. Edward Rives
1822-1883
Confederate Physician

Name: **Edward Rives**
Spouse: **1st. Marie T. Thompson – 2nd. Eliza Jane**
Birth date: **August 27, 1833**
Birth place: **Oak Ridge, Nelson County, Virginia**
Father's name and birth place: **Landon Cabell- Virginia**
Mother's name: **Annie Marie**
Service record: **Surgeon with the 28th Virginia Infantry**
Death date: **September 26, 1883**
Death place: **Hillsboro, Ohio**
Cemetery: **Spring Grove Cemetery, Hamilton, Ohio**

Physician, Confederate Civil War Surgeon. Born in Nelson County, Virginia, he was the son of Dr. Landon Cabell Rives and Annie Marie Towles. He studied medicine and practiced as a physician until the start of the Civil War in 1861. Rives was commissioned as an Assistant Surgeon in the Confederate Army with the 28th Virginia Infantry. He later Became a full Surgeon on the General Staff of General George Pickett's Division. After the war he moved to Ohio and practiced as a doctor in Cincinnati. Rives moved to Hillsboro, Ohio after he retired and later died there at his residence in 1883 when he was 50 years old. He was the husband of Marie Thompson Rives. His brother, *Dr. Landon C. Rives Jr.,* also served as a Surgeon during the Civil War. He was the nephew of *William C. Rives,* a Virginia Whig Congressman, and was the brother-in-law of *Rufus King.*

28th Regiment, Virginia Infantry

28th Infantry Regiment completed its organization at Lynchburg, Virginia, in June, 1861. Its members were raised to the counties of Botetourt, Craig, Bedford, Campbell, and Roanoke. After fighting at *First Manassas* the unit was assigned to General Pickett's, Garnett's, and Hunton's Brigade, Army of Northern Virginia. It was active in the campaigns of the army from *Williamsburg* to *Gettysburg* except when it served with Longstreet at *Suffolk.* The 28th moved to North Carolina, then was on detached duty at Richmond. It fought at *Cold Harbor,* endured the battles and hardships of the *Petersburg* trenches, and was engaged in various conflicts around *Appomattox.* The regiment totaled 600 men in April, 1862, and reported 40 casualties at *Williamsburg* and 47 at *Seven Pines.* It lost 12 killed and 52 wounded at *Second Manassas,* had 8 killed and 54 wounded during the Maryland Campaign, and of the 333 engaged at *Gettysburg,* half were disabled. Many were captured at *Sayler's Creek,* and 3 officers and 51 men surrendered on April 9, 1865. The field officers were Colonels Robert C. Allen, Robert T. Preston, and William Watts; Lieutenant Colonels Samuel B. Paul and William L. Wingfield; and Majors Michael P. Spesard and Nathaniel C. Wilson.

The McCook House Civil War Museum

Located in Carrollton, Ohio. The McCook house is a memorial to the Ohio famous fighting McCooks. About 1837 Daniel McCook erected this large brick house on the Southwest corner of the Public Square. Daniel McCook Sr. was a major in the Union army. Operated by Carrollton County Historical Society . Owned by the Ohio Historic Society. Ph. # 330-627-3345 or 1-800-600-7172 Shirley Anderson, Manager

Name: **Charles R. Sheppard**
Spouse: **1st. Mary Jane 2nd. Amelia H. Graves- Ohio**
Home in 1870: **Columbia Florida**
Home in 1880: **Cambridge, Wayne Indiana**
Birth date: **1845**
Birth place: **Georgia**
Father's name: **David**
Mother's name and Birth place: **Temperance – Georgia**
Occupation: **Railroad**
Enlistment date: **April 14, 1861**
Enlistment place: **Georgia**
State served: **Georgia – Confederate**
Service record: **Pvt. 1st. Regiment Georgia Regulars Co. K**
Death date: **1905**
Death place: **Willoughby, Lake County, Ohio**
Cemetery: **Willoughby Sharp Ave Cemetery- Willoughby, Ohio**
POW: **Feb. 4, 1865 Salkehatchie, South Carolina**

Name: **W. O. Smith**
Spouse: **Martha A.**
Birth date: **1831**
Birth place: **Kentucky**
Father's name and Birth: **John N. Smith 1802 Kentucky**
Mother's name and Birth: : **Paulina P. 1813 Virginia**
Occupation: **Physician**
Enlistment date: **1861**
Enlistment place: **Virginia**
Side served: **Virginia CSA**
Service record: **Senior Second Lieutenant 5th Regiment Virginia Cavalry Co. G**
Death date: **1899**
Cemetery: **S.O.M. Rd. Cemetery, Willoughby Hills, Ohio On St. Rt. 91 old names (Willoughby Center Cemetery) and the (Willoughby Ridge Cemetery).**

Name: **John Swaney**
Spouse: **Sarah**
Birth date: **1840**
Birth place: **Maryland**
Occupation: **Carpenter-Farmer-Operated a machine shop a portable sawmill and cider mill**
Enlistment place: **Virginia**
Side served: **Confederate**
Service record: **39th Virginia Cavalry**
Death date: **January 22, 1898**
Death place: **Tiro, Crawford County, Ohio**
Cemetery: **Hanna Cemetery Auburn Twp, St. Rt. 98 & Baker Rd.**

This week's photograph is of the Hanna Cemetery on Baker Road in Tiro. This postcard was postmarked 1911. The Hanna Cemetery is the resting place for Crawford County's only Confederate Soldier, John F. Swaney. Mr. Swaney served with the 39th Virginia Calvary. He moved to Tiro with his wife and family after the end of the Civil War. He lived in rural Tiro and operated a threshing machine, a portable sawmill, and a cider mill. He later lived on Robinson Ave. in Tiro and died on January 22, 1898. On Memorial Day the American Legion decorates his grave with an American Flag along with his former opponents in the Civil War.

Name: **Sanders Taylor**
Spouse: **Scharlotte Simmons**
Birth date: **1824**
Birth place: **Lincoln, Tennessee**
Father's name and Birth place: **Young Taylor – Virginia**
Mother's name: **Sarah C. Poston**
Service record: **44th Tennessee Infantry Co. I Sergeant**
Death date: **April 28, 1862**
Death place: **Hamilton County, Ohio**
Cemetery: **Camp Dennison, Hamilton County, Ohio then moved to Spring Grove Cemetery on July 4, 1869**

Taylor volunteered to serve in the Confederate Army and enlisted with the 44th Infantry. He was mustered into Co. B as a sergeant. Taylor fought with his regiment at the Battle of Shiloh. In April 1862 he was wounded and captured by union forces. He was taken as prisoner of war and sent to a military hospital at Camp Dennison near Cincinnati, Ohio. Taylor died 3 weeks later.

44th Consolidated Regiment, Tennessee Infantry

44th Infantry Regiment, organized at Camp Trousdale, Tennessee, in December, 1861, contained men from Coffee, Grundy, Franklin, Lincoln, and Bedford counties. The unit fought at *Shiloh* and lost seventy-four percent of the 470 engaged. On April 19, 1862, the 55the (McKoin's) regiment, which also suffered heavy losses, merged into the 44th. It now had a force of 489 effectives. After fighting at *Munfordville* and *Perryville* it was assigned to General B.R. Johnson's Brigade, Army of Tennessee. During November, 1863, the unit was consolidated with the 25th Regiment. It participated in the Battle of *Murfreesboro* and *Chickamauga,* was active in the Knoxville Campaign, then joined the Army of Northern Virginia. The regiment went on to fight at *Drewry's Bluff,* was active in the *Petersburg* trenches north of the James River, and ended the war at *Appomattox.* It lost thirty-four percent of the 509 engaged at Murfreesboro and thirty-eight percent of the 294 at Chickamauga. The 25th/44th sustained 95 casualties of the 259 at Drewry's Bluff. This regiment, attached to General McComb's Brigade, surrendered 5 officers and 53 men. The field officers were Colonels John S. Fulton, John H. Kelly, and Coleman A. McDaniel; Lieutenant Colonels John L. McEwen, Jr. and Henry S. Shied; and Majors Gibson M. Craw ford, Henry C. Ewin, and James M. Johnson.

Follett House Museum

The Follett House was built in 1902 and houses artifacts from the Civil War Johnson Island prison camp. The museum has a fine collection of history including the battle of Lake Erie. Learn more about the roll played by local citizens in time of conflict from the war of 1812 to World War II. The Follett House Museum was placed on the National Register of Historic Landmarks on Dec. 31, 1974. Located at 404 Wayne St., Sandusky, Ohio 44870. Ph. # 419-672-9608 website www.sandusky.lob.oh.us/public/folletthousemuseum.asp

Name: **John H. Thomas**
Spouse: **1st. Elizabeth 2nd Sophia L.**
Birth date: **1833**
Birth place: **Virginia**
Home in 1870: **Franklin, Portage, Ohio**
Home in 1930: **Franklin, Portage, Ohio**
Father's name **William**
Mother's name: **Susannah**
Occupation: **Teamster**
Enlistment date: **July 27, 1862**
Enlistment place: **Pulaski County, Virginia**
Side served: **Virginia - Confederate**
Service record: **Va. 30th Sharpshooters Battalion Co. D**
Description: **5'6" Dark Complexion gray eyes dark hair**
Death date: **1934**
Death place: **Franklin, Ohio**
Cemetery: **Standing Rock Cemetery Franklin, Ohio**

Name: **Morris Ullman**
Spouse: **Lenche Abraham**
Birth date: **1835**
Birth place: **Baden—Wurtenberg, Germany**
Ancestry birth place: **Germany**
Father's name: **Leopold Ullman**
Mother's name: **Klara Einstein**
Occupation: **Founder of The Black Cat Whiskey Co. Cleve. Ohio**
Enlistment place: **Selma, Alabama**
Side served: **Confederate**
Service record: **Corp. Co. K 4th Militia Infantry Alabama**
Description: **5'3 ¾ tall, brown eyes**
Death date: **1908**
Death place: **Cleveland, Ohio**
Cemetery: **Mayfield Jewish Cemetery Cleveland Hts. Ohio on Mayfield Rd.**
P. O.W. **Alton Prison March 22nd. 1863**

Ullman family memorial stone at Mayfield Rd. Jewish Cem. Below: Ullman & Einstein Co Invoice Apr. 2, 1902

DISTILLERS AND DISTRIBUTORS OF
SPRING GARDEN
MARYLAND
PURE RYE.

ULLMAN, EINSTEIN & CO.
WHISKIES.

BLENDERS OF
FINE OLD WHISKIES.
OHIO GRAPE BRANDY
A SPECIALTY.

154-156-158 SHERIFF ST.
OPPOSITE NEW MARKET HOUSE

CLEVELAND.

Terms

Sold to Messrs. Frantz & Bealdt, City.

Ordered through

4	gals. Alcohol	2 56	10 24
1	gal. Spirits	1 53	1 53
2	" Rum Punch	1 50	3 00
			$14 77
			9 32
			5 45

May 7/1902

Confederate Soldier
Alabama

Tracking Cleveland's Black Cat
By Jack Sullivan

A young immigrant and former Confederate soldier came to a Northern city shortly after the Civil War to market a product named after a well known symbol for a bad luck. We might assume that his failure was swift and certain. But not if the Johnny Reb' was Morris Ullman, the city of Cleveland, and the product Black Cat Whiskey. Ullman and his extended family can be tracked through more than 50 years as they rose to wealth and business prominence in Northern Ohio.

A distant relative of the renown physicist Albert Einstein, Morris Ullman was born in 1835 in Baden-Wurtemberg, Germany, and emigrated to the United States in 1851 at the age of 16. According to newspaper accounts, he first settled in Alabama and then moved to Guilford County, North Carolina, where he became a naturalized citizen in 1857. In 1860, like hundreds of thousands other Southern boys, he joined the Confederate Army and served for the duration of the Civil War..

The role of Jewish soldiers in the Confederate Army generally has been overlooked by historians. Shown here is a caricature of one from *Jewish* Magazine. More than 10,000 fought for the South, Gen. Robert E. Lee allowed his Jewish soldiers to observe all holy days. Northern generals, including William Sherman and Ulysses S. Grant, by contrast would not.

The Founding of Ullman Brothers

Morris came North after Lee's surrender and settled initially in Franklin, Pennsylvania, about 50 miles northeast of Youngstown, Ohio. There he met his wife, Lenche, a year older than he. They married in 1866 and their son, Monroe, was born in Franklin later that year. Soon after, Morris and his new family moved to Cleveland. There he was reunited with an older brother, Emanuel Ullman, who already may have been engaged in the liquor trade.

The company they founded dated its origins to 1866, but Ullman Brothers & Co. first showed up in Cleveland business directories three years later, in 1869, located at 69-71 Michigan St. in the Tower City area. From the beginning the brothers demonstrated a marketing flair. They had a highly decorated, etched shot glass with the "U" initial, designating the firm.

In 1873 their eighteen-year-old cousin, Herman Einstein, emigrated from Germany to Cleveland and was hired by the Ullmans as a clerk, bookkeeper and salesman. Herman's older brother, Leopold had come to Cleveland earlier and also likely was in the whiskey business. After Emanuel Ullman's untimely death in 1881, the two families merged their efforts and created Ullman, Einstein & Co. Herman and Leopold became partners in the firm with Morris Ullman as the managing partner.

Enter the Black Cat

Almost immediately the partners began to merchandise throughout Northern Ohio and beyond its Black Cat Whiskey. The label featured the feline and declared the liquor to be "pure" and "old." How old is open to question. Ullman-Einstein were not distillers. They obtained their product from a number of sources, probably in Maryland and Kentucky. The firm may have been involved in "rectifying," that is, mixing a number of lines of straight whiskey into a blend to achieve a consistent taste, then putting its label on the bottle.

However they arrived at the Black Cat, the Ullman-Einsteins advertised it widely. They also featured it on a range of giveaway items. The Black Cat was depicted on a variety of shot glasses. With its distinctive whiskers and eyes, the cat projects real personality. Ullman-Einstein also issued several Black Cat highball glass, including one without a picture. I particularly like an inlaid cloisonné porcelain watch fob in black, white, gold, red and blue that features the cat and the Cleveland municipal flag. Even though the item was not cheap to produce, the back of the fob indicates that it too was a giveaway.

Unlike popular superstition, the Black Cat brought the cousins good luck and, more important, prosperity. Outgrowing their Michigan Street quarters, in 1892 they moved to Sheriff Street, now known as 4th Street SE. The firm inhabited a building three stories high and more than a half block long. It stood across from Cleveland's New Market House, a hub of the city's mercantile trade. Signs on its building declared that rye and bourbon whiskies were among its specialties. Its letterhead claimed the company, in addition to being a whiskey distributor and "blender," was a distiller, with a Baltimore facility.

Beyond the Cat

Although the Black Cat was the flagship of the company, Ullman, Einstein presented a wide variety of brands to its clientele. The firm also was assiduous in registering many of them with the Federal Government to prevent trademark infringement. In 1905, it registered J. Gibbons, McGibben, Union Springs and Euclid Club whiskeys. In 1906, Black Cat, D.T. Gilmore and Son, UECO Old Nectar, and Wedding March. In 1907, Brook Trout and Walnut Creek, and finally in 1911, Mor Lee. No record exists of it's the firm having registered other known Ullman-Einstein brands like Elk Ridge, B.O.E., and Adalyn. U-E also carried labels from other whiskey dealers, notably Spring Garden, with Cincinnati origins, and James River, from Richmond, Virginia.

The firm issued shot glasses for many of these whiskeys, most of them bearing the distinctive etched U-E monogram. A giveaway tip tray for Elk Ridge Whiskey featured a famous British painting of a stag. For the most part, Ullman-Einstein marketed its products in bottles but from time to time used ceramic jugs.

Exclusion and Philanthropy

Two U-E brands tell a special story. During the later part of the 19th Century most Jews in Cleveland, like the Ullmans and the Einsteins, were immigrants from Germany. Numbering only about 3,500, they were generally accepted among the city's heavily German population. Leopold Einstein, for example strongly championed German cultural interests. In 1888 he was a leading fundraiser for the construction of a new Germania Hall in Cleveland.

Yet Jewish families faced discrimination from exclusive business and country clubs such as the Union Club of Cleveland and the Century Club. In 1872, twenty-two Jewish businessmen, Morris Ullman probably among them, founded the Excelsior Club. After meeting at several locations, in 1908 the club moved into a new home on Euclid Ave. in the Wade Park district. The building today is Thwing Hall at Case-Western reserve University. Both the Ullmans and Einsteins were active members of the club. Perhaps as a result, one of the company whiskey brands was named Excelsior Club. Another U-E whiskey brand, perhaps ironically, was named for one of the exclusionary organizations. Cleveland's Euclid Club.

Beyonf the remarkable business acumen of these cousins was their notable community involvement. The commitment to charitable work and preserving their religious heritage was strong among these early immigrants. In 1873, Morris Ullman was listed as a board member of the Union of American Hebrew Congregations. He was given special mention in the 1899 American Jewish Yearbook for his work on behalf of his fellow religionists. Herman Einstein was a board member of the Tifereth Israel Congregation. This group had broken away from a more conservative Cleveland synagogue to found their own "reformed" temple. He also served as treasurer of the Mt. Sinai Hospital, treasurer of the Hebrew Free Loan Assn., and was a member of the Federation of Jewish Charities.

The Firm Grows and Changes

As the firm grew and flourished, important events were occurring in the lives of two families. Monroe Ullman, educated in Cleveland schools, early joined U-E as a salesman and "traveling agent." In 1892, he married Florence Fuld in Albany, New York. They would have two children. In 1893, Lenche Ullman, mother of Monroe and wife of Morris, died at the age of 59. Jacob Einstein, a son of Leopold, joined the firm during this period.

In 1904, U-E incorporated for the first time. Morris Ullman and Leopold Einstein were its principal executives. Herman Einstein was named secretary and Monroe Ullman, a vice president. The next year the company name changed to Ullman-Einstein, the comma replaced by a hypen. In 1908 Morris died at the age of 73. The same year the firm moved to 657-659 Bolivar Ave. SE. Four years later Leopold Einstein died and Herman Einstein succeeded him as president and treasurer. Both Jacob Einstein and Monroe Ullman, sons of the founders, became company officers.

In 1914, the extended family received recognition from their community when all three of the Ullman-Einstein leadership were featured in a 1914 "Book of Clevelanders" that chronicled the city's leading businessmen. Jacob Einstein was singled out as a member of the board of the National Liquor Dealers Association and a trustee of the Ohio Wine and Spirits Assn. He clearly had become a state and national leader in the distilling industry.

This generation continued the philanthropic work of their parents. Monroe Ullman was a member of the Hebrew Relief Association, the Hebrew Free Loan Association, and the Wilson Avenue Temple. Jacob Einstein was a trustee of the Monteflor Home for the Old in Cleveland. In1903, he married Ruth Weiner, a local Cleveland woman. She became a well-known leader in the Jewish community for 50 years, responsible for initiating a number of successful charitable enterprises.

Demise of the Black Cat

Unlike those felines said to have nine lives, Ullman-Einstein's Black Cat had only one—or maybe two. Prohibition in Ohio and in the Nation dealt the kitty a death blow. Ullman-Einstein went out of business in 1919, taking with it the cat and all the other U-E brands.

Two family members did not live to see Repeal. Jacob Einstein died in 1919, young at 43. His uncle Herman followed in 1922. In the 1920s Monroe Ullman founded a security dealer and investment firm of which he was president. He continued to be recognized business figure in Cleveland until his death in 1938 at age 72. His wife, Florence, would live another 25 years as his widow, dying in 1963.

Black Cat Whiskey has had something of a second life. A labeled bottle sold recently on eBay for $160. That brand and other Ullman-Einstein products also live on in a multitude of collectible shot glasses, watch fobs, tip trays, bottles and jugs. They remind us of an immigrant family who rose to prominence in their adopted country and community through hard work and imagination. For them the Black Cat proved to be a symbol of fame and fortune.

Sherman House Museum – Lancaster, Ohio

The Sherman House was the birthplace of General William Tecumseh Sherman and his brother U.S. Senator John Sherman. Built in 1811. The Museum house artifacts, paintings, prints, maps, weapons and Gar memorabilia. The house is located 137 East Main St. Lancaster, Ohio 43130 Ph. # 740-687-5891 or 740-654-9923. Open April thru Mid- December. Tues. thru Sunday 1:00 to 4:00 PM. Closed Mondays & Holidays.

Website: Http://www.shermanhouse.org/shermanhouse.htm Fairfield Heritage Association.

Confederate Soldier
Virginia

Name: **Clifton Miller Walker**
Spouse: **1st. Mary E. 2nd. Mattie**
Birth date: **September 7, 1841**
Birth place: **Virginia**
Home in 1870: **Ohio** Home in 1880: **Wayne, Fayette, Ohio**
Father's Birth place: **Virginia,** Mother's Birth place: **Virginia**
Enlistment place: **Virginia**
Service record: **52nd Reg. Infantry Co. F 2nd Sergeant**
Death date: **April 18, 1907**
Cemetery: **Good Hope Cemetery, Fayette County, Oh Outside Greenfield, Oh**

Name: **Robert L. Watson**
Spouse: **Katherine**
Birth date: **Feb. 3, 1849**
Birth place: **North Carolina**
Father's name and Birth place: **John – North Carolina**
Mother's name and Birth place: **Nancy – North Carolina**
Service record: **62nd North Carolina Infantry Co. H. Pvt.**
Death date: **October 10, 1944**
Death place: **Guernsey County, Ohio**
Cemetery: **Senecaville Cemetery Senecaville, Guernsey County, Ohio**

He moved to Senecaville, Ohio somewhere after the 1880's.

62nd Regiment, North Carolina Infantry

62nd Infantry Regiment was formed at Waynesville, North Carolina, in July, 1862. Its members were raised in the counties of Haywood, Clay, Macon, Rutherford, Henderson, and Transylvania. The unit served in North Carolina, then in July, 1863, was assigned to General Gracie's Brigade and stationed at Cumberland Gap. Here many were surrendered in September, but a number escaped from being captured. They returned to the Asheville area and in April, 1864 had 178 men present. The records show 443 men of the 62nd were prisoners at Camp Douglas. It continued to fight under Generals Breckenridge, Vaughn, and Williams in East Tennessee, then became a part of Colonel J.B. Palmer's command at Asheville in March , 1865. Later it disbanded near the French Broad River. The field officers were Colonels George W. Clayton and Robert G. A. Love, and Lieutenant colonel Byron G. McDowell.

Cleveland Soldiers and Sailors Monument on Public Square

Confederate and Union soldiers in battle.

Name: **William M. Webb**
Spouse: **Lucy A.**
Birth date: **1839**
Birth place: **Tennessee**
Father's name and Birth place: **John - Virginia**
Mother's name and Birth place: **Elizabeth Ann Mayfield- So. Carolina**
Occupation: **Farmer**
Enlistment date: **July 16, 1861**
Enlistment place: **Camp Boone, Tenn.**
Side served: **Kentucky – CSA**
Service record: **Kentucky 2nd Infantry Regiment Co. F Pvt.**
Death date: **September 8, 1862**
Death Place: **On route to prison camp**
Cemetery: **Oak Street cemetery Coshocton, Coshocton County, Ohio**

2nd Regiment, Kentucky Mounted Infantry

2nd Infantry Regiment was organized in August, 1861, at Camp Boone, Tennessee, and became part of the Orphan Brigade or Louisville Legion. The men were from the counties of Hickman, Fayette, Bullitt, Jefferson, Graves, Franklin, Harrison, Scott, Owen, Bourbon, and Anderson. In October the unit contained 832 men and in the fight at *Fort Danelson* its force of 618 was captured. After being exchanged, it saw action at *Shiloh* and later was assigned to Hanson's, Helm's, and J.H. Lewis' Brigade. The 2nd was involved in the Battles of Murfreesboro and Chickamauga, and then participated in the Atlanta Campaign. During the fall of 1864 the unit served as mounted infantry and took part in the defense of Savannah and the campaign of the Carolinas. It reported 13 killed, 70 wounded, and 21 missing at *Murfreesboro,* lost fifty-two percent of the 302 engaged at *Chickamauga,* and totaled 293 men and 214 arms in December, 1863, .On April 26, 1865, it surrendered with the Army of Tennessee. The field officers were Colonels Roger W. Hanson, James M. Hawes, Robert A. Johnston, and James W. Moss: Lieutenant Colonels James W. Hewitt and Philip Lee: and Majors William P. Johnston and Harvey McDowell.

Name: **Thomas Witherspoon**
Spouse: **Cora Delia Ray**
Birth date: **1833**
Birth place: **Tennessee**
Father's name: **David Columbus**
Mother's name: **Katherine Blankenship**
Service record: **12th. Texas Infantry Co. F. Private**
Death date: **April, 1862**
Death place: **Camp Dennison**
Cemetery: **Spring Grove Cemetery Hamilton County, Ohio**

Witherspoon fought with his Regiment at the Battle of Belmont and then at the Battle of Shiloh. In April of 1862 he was wounded and captured by Union forces and taken as prisoner of war and sent to a military hospital at Camp Dennison near Cincinnati, Ohio. He died 5 and ½ weeks later. He was buried in Waldschmidt Cemetery at Camp Dennison and moved to Spring Grove Cemetery July 4, 1869 in Hamilton County, Ohio.

112th Regiment, Tennessee Infantry

12th Infantry Regiment was organized at Jackson, Tennessee, in May, 1861. Its members were recruited in Dyer and Gibson counties, and Company E contained men from Kentucky. The unit was assigned to B.R. Johnson's, P. Smith's, Vaughan's, and Palmer's Brigade. During June, 1862, the 22nd Regiment merged into the 12th, and in October, 1862, this command was consolidated with the 47th Regiment. It fought at *Belmont, Shiloh,* and Richmond, then joined the Army of Tennessee and served from *Murfreesboro* to *Bentonville.* This regiment was organized with 737 men, sustained 32 casualties at Richmond, and lost fifty-one percent of the 322 engaged at Murfreesboro. The 12th/47th had 87 disabled at *Chickamauga* and in December, 1863, totaled 373 men and 220 arms. It was included in the surrender on April 26, 1865. The field officers were Colonels Tyree H. Bell and Robert M. Russell; Lieutenant Colonels D.A. Outlaw and J.N. Wyatt; and Majors Robert P. Caldwell, James Purl, and J.N. Wyatt.

Civil War Museum

The 103rd Volunteer Infantry Civil War Museum is dedicated to perpetuating the heroic deeds and services of the men who served the Union during the Civil War from 1861-1865. The Museum Houses persevered and displays historic relics which has been inherited, collected or donated to the descendent of members of the 103rd Regiment Ohio Volunteers. Located at: 5501 E. Lake Road, Sheffield Lake, Ohio 44054. By appointment only. Ph.# 440-949-2790 website www.103ovi.org.

Farewell to the Army of Northern Virginia

After four years of arduous service, marked by unsurpassed courage and fortitude, the Army of Northern Virginia has been compelled to yield to overwhelming numbers and resources.

I need not tell the survivors of so many hard-fought battles who have remained steadfast to the last that I have consented to this result from no distrust of them; but feeling that valor and devotion could accomplish nothing that could compensate for the loss that would have attended the continuance of the contest, I determined to avoid the useless sacrifice of those whose past services have endeared them to their countrymen. By the terms of the agreement, officers and men can return to their homes and remain until exchanged.

You may take with you the satisfaction that proceeds from the consciousness of duty faithfully performed, and I earnestly pray that a merciful God will extend to you his blessing and protection. With an unceasing admiration of your constancy and devotion to your country, and a grateful remembrance of your kind and generous consideration of myself. I bid you all an affectionate farewell.

By: Robert E. Lee

CHAPTER III

JOHN HUNT MORGAN'S RAID INTO OHIO

This chapter is some history of John Hunt Morgan's famous raid thru Ohio and places of interest worth touring. The Wickerham Inn is where some of the Confederate soldiers slept. History Markers along the way, cemeteries that Morgan's men are buried in. The Battle of Buffington Island, the skirmish in Old Washington, the Rock that marked the spot that General Morgan and his remaining men surrendered, the location of the Ohio Penitentiary where Morgan was incarcerated and escaped from. A map of John Hunt Morgan's Raid thru Ohio on page 135.

The Longest Raid

Brigadier General John Hunt Morgan hoping to divert the attention of the Federal Army of the Ohio from Southern forces in Tennessee and 2,460 handpicked Confederate cavalrymen, along with a battery of horse artillery, rode west from Sparta, Tennessee, on June 11, 1863. Twelve days later, when a second Federal army (the Army of the Cumberland) began its Tullahoma Campaign, Morgan decided it was time to move northward. His column marched into Kentucky, fighting a series of minor battles, before commandeering two steamships to ferry them across the Ohio River into Indiana, where, at the Battle of Corydon, Morgan routed the local militia. With his path now relatively clear, Morgan headed eastward on July 13 past Cincinnati and rode across southern Ohio stealing horses and supplies along the way.

The Union response was not long in coming, as Maj. Gen. Ambrose Burnside, commanding the Department of the Ohio, ordered out all available troops, as well as sending several Union Navy gunboats steaming up the Ohio River to contest any Confederate attempt to reach Kentucky or West Virginia and safety. Brig. Gen. Edward H. Hobson led several columns of Federal cavalry in pursuit of Morgan's raiders, which by now had been reduced to some 1,700 men. Ohio Governor David Tod called out the local militia, and volunteers formed companies to protect towns and river crossings throughout the region.

On July 18, Morgan, having split his column earlier, led his reunited force towards Pomeroy, Ohio, a quiet river town near the Eight Mile Island Ford, where Morgan intended to cross into West Virginia. Running a gauntlet of small arms fire, Morgan's men were denied access to the river and to Pomeroy itself, and he headed towards the next for upstream at Buffington Island, some 20 miles to the southeast.

Arriving near Buffington Island and the nearby tiny hamlet of Portland, Ohio, towards evening on July 18, Morgan found that the ford was blocked by several hundred local militia ensconced behind hastily thrown up earthworks. As a dense fog and darkness settled in, Morgan decided to camp for the night to allow his jaded men and horses to rest. He was concerned that even if he pushed aside the enemy troops, he might lose additional men in the darkness as they tried to navigate the narrow ford. The delay proved to be a fatal mistake.

The US Navy's Mississippi Squadron was involved in Battle of Buffington Island. Morgan had brought field cannons with his column. A heavy river blockade and a means were realized early in the chase while Morgan's column traveled easterly towards Cincinnati, Ohio. Lt. Commander Leroy Fitch's fleet included the *Brilliant, Fairplay, Moose, Reindeer, St. Clair, Silver Lake, Springfield, Victory, Naumkeag Queen City* which were tinclads and ironclads. A few of these steamers lagged behind to zone-up protecting against a possible doubling back of Morgan's column. The forward vessels were each assigned a patrol zone along the Mason, Jackson and Wood counties of West Virginia by Fitch's instruction. *Naumkeag* patrolled from Point Pleasant, West Virginia to Eight Mile Island zone and *Springfield* guarded from Pomeroy, Ohio towards Letart Islands. It's patrol from Middleport, Ohio to Eight Mile Island along the West Virginia river bank. The *Magnolia, Imperial, Alleghany Belle,* and *Union* tinclads and armed packets which were privateers along with others documented under Parkersburg Logistics' command. The Army's "amphibious division" officer, Major General Ambrose E. Burnside at his Cincinnati headquarters, provided intelligence of Morgan's march and turned his flagship, *Alleghany Bell,* over to Fitch before the battle. The "amphibious division" tinclads had four to six large johnboats (side boats) used to fire rifles from, for landing to give chase and pickup prisoners.

Fitch's flagship was the ironelad U.S.S. *Moose,* USN. Moose and Fitch's dispatch privateer, *Imperial,* were tied up within earshot of the island the night before the battle. It has been written that Fitch had the boilers fired up and shooting its large cannons at the island on first rifle fire, slightly out of range before steam could make way. *Allegheny Belle* was a little farther down tied up along the Ohio side. Having heard *Moose's* cannons, it made steam and soon brought up Burnsides' "amphibious infantry".

The 9th West Virginia Infantry was delivered by packets working under Fort Union (Ft. Blair) to the high banked, tree lined crossings along the West Virginia shores. These were commanded by Colonel I.H. Duval under Federal Command at Wheeling, West Virginia. "The regiment was composed largely of refugees, who, having been driven from home, were fighting with a desperation that was not excelled by any troops in any army."

The river provided further impediment to the Confederate Cavalry during these skirmishes. It is unknown, how many horses and Confederate Cavalry Troopers drowned while facing West Virginia stationed sentry in several locations down shore stemming from the main battle. Some individuals did make the crossing without horse by foot evasion and was aided back south to home by sympathizers despite some of Col. RMJP Smith's 106th militia of Jackson and Mason counties Cavalry patrols behind the sentry line. One of several smaller shoal crossings was near Ravenswood, West Virginia. That sentry squad was provided a worn out cannon of which several earlier authors have anecdote. The "amphibious division" assaulted any Confederate squad found near the shores and pulled prisoners from the river.

Continuing upstream after the main battle broke into unit maneuver and skirmishes, USS Moose fired on a Confederate Artillery column trying to cross the river above the island at the next shoal crossing. Fitch dispatched Imperial to recover Confederate field Artillery left behind there. All along the river, spotty ironclad and field cannon fire with clusters of rifle fire was heard shooting at Morgan's scouts looking for another possible ford. Meanwhile, Parkersburg Logistics terminal had sent a local armed packet with 9th Infantry sentries below Blennerhassett Island on word of the Battle's gunfire some twenty mile below. These paralleled patrols opposite the Belpre, Ohio Union Army encampment below the Ohio side of the terminal. This steamboat river harbor and large land Debarkations Camp blocked Morgan's further attempt to ford the river upstream turning his retreat northerly and away from this Ohio River area. The local support vessels were busy hauling ammunition, rations and prisoners. Belpre, Ohio had a supply receiving dockage and depot.

General Morgan had missed his chance farther downstream as he approached this center. It was a direct rail route from the Washington D.C., Philadelphia and Baltimore region. The western states got their supplies from the east's rail depot and packet docks at the Union's Parkersburg Supply Center. Belpre and Parkersburg was also a huge Union embarkation center for union infantry being transported by conscript steam packet boats (privateers) to the Kentucky and Tennessee theatre. As a railroad Line from the East's factories, it had no bridges across the Ohio River. There were no railway bridges across the Ohio River at this time. Railroad bridges would be built across the Mississippi and Ohio rivers after the Civil War. Clearly, before Gen. Morgan left the South, he lacked detailed intelligence of the Union's logistics system on the upper Ohio Valley as some military historians have figured.

On the foggy morning of July 19, two Federal brigades under August Kautz and Henry M. Judah finally caught up with Morgan and attacked his position on the broad flood plain just north of Portland, nearly encircling the Confederates as another column under James M.

Shackelford arrived on the scene. In the spirited early fighting, Maj. Daniel McCook, the 65 year old patriarch of the famed Fighting McCooks, was mortally wounded. Nearly 3,000 Federals were soon engaged with Morgan's outnumbered and exhausted men. In Addison, two Union gunboats, the U.S.S. Moose and the U.S. /S. Allegheny Belle, steamed into the narrow channel separating Buffington Island from the flood plain and opened fire on Morgan's men, spraying them with shell fragments. Soon they were joined by a third gunboat.

Morgan, his way to the Buffington Island ford now totally blocked, left behind a small rear guard and tried to fight his way northward along the flood plain, hoping to reach yet another ford. It proved to be an exercise in futility, as Morgan's force was split apart by the converging Federal columns and 52 Confederates were killed, with well over one hundred badly wounded in the swirling fighting. Morgan and about 700 men escaped encirclement by following a narrow path through the woods. However, his brother in law and second in command, Col. Basil W. Duke, was captured, as were over 750 of Morgan's cavalrymen, including his younger brother John Morgan. Duke formally Surrendered to Col. Isaac Garrard of the 7th Ohio Cavalry.

Morgan's beleaguered troops soon headed upstream for the unguarded ford opposite Belleville, West Virginia, where over 300 men successfully crossed the Ohio River to avoid capture, most notably Col. Adam "Stovepipe" Johnson and famed telegrapher George Ellsworth. General Morgan, who was halfway across the ford, noted with dismay that his remaining men were trapped on the Ohio side as the Federal gunboats suddenly loomed into view. He wheeled his horse midchannel and rejoined what was left of his column on the Ohio riverbank. Over the next few days, they failed to find a secure place to cross the river, and Morgan's remaining force was captured on July 26 in Northern Ohio following the Battle of Salineville.

John Hunt Morgan and 364 troops surrendered. Confederate Brigadier General John Hunt Morgan and his cavalrymen were captured during their daring raid into Ohio. Conditions for Confederate soldiers housed in the Ohio State Penitentiary in Columbus improved after General Morgan sent a written complaint to the Buckeye State's governor, David Todd. The Confederates were placed in the dark, dank stone prison, where they were subject to harsh punishment and forced to live on bread and water. Todd visited the prison after receiving Morgan's letter, and soon afterward reforms were instituted to improve living conditions. Morgan did not stay to savor the improvements, through. In November 1863, he and six other Confederate officers escaped. After climbing a wall of the Ohio State Penitentiary, John Morgan and his men separated to have a better change to escape. Morgan went to a train station and bought a ticket south. A gentlemen that sat beside Morgan started a conversation and ask Morgan if he heard the news of General Morgan escaping from the penitentiary. Morgan and his officers made it back to Kentucky safely.

Many of those captured at Buffington Island were taken via steamboat to Cincinnati as prisoners of war, including most of the wounded.

General John Hunt Morgan in a raid in Greenville, Tennessee was killed by Federal soldiers on September, 1864

Wickerham Inn

The Wickerham Inn is the oldest brick building in Adams County, Ohio and was one of the earliest taverns to exist in the Northwest Territory.

In 1797, Peter Wickerham moved to the Northwest Territory. Like many veterans of the American Revolution. Wickerham hoped to improve his fortunes on the frontier. He eventually settled in Adams County, in modern day Peebles, Ohio. He built a cabin along Zen's Trace, an important road during the late eighteenth and early nineteenth centuries. In 1800, Wickerham decided to build a brick tavern, which he completed in 1801. Known as Wickerham Inn, the tavern remained in operation until the 1850s. During the War Between the States Confederate soldiers, commanded by General John Hunt Morgan slept in the Inn on the night of July 15, 1863, when passing through Adams County. Wickerham Inn is Located on Route 41 North of Peebles, Ohio

According to legend, the Wickerham Inn is haunted. Purportedly, a stagecoach driver was murdered and beheaded in the tavern. Supposedly his body was not found for approximately one hundred years. In 1922, the Inn was remodeled, and construction workers found a headless skeleton buried in the limestone floor. The body was purportedly buried, but the inn remained haunted.

OHIO
HISTORICAL
MARKER
MORGAN'S RAID
In July 1863, Confederate General John H. Morgan led a force of 2,000 cavalrymen across southern Ohio. Morgan's force entered Ohio from Indiana on July 13. A chase ensued as Union cavalry pursued Morgan's men across twenty Ohio counties. Most of Morgan's troops were captured in Meigs County at the Battle of Buffington Island. Morgan, with several hundred cavalry, managed to escape. They raced northeast, fighting skirmishes along the way, and forded the Muskingum at a point near Rokeby Lock on July 23, 1863. As they went, the soldiers raided local farms for food and replacement horses. They were finally captured in Columbiana County on July 26. The raid marked the northern-most point ever reached by Confederate forces. Across southern Ohio, frightened residents burned bridges over fordable streams and buried silver and jewelry to hide them from the marauders.
MUSKINGUM RIVER PARKWAY
AND
THE OHIO HISTORICAL SOCIETY
1996
4-58
OHIO
HISTORICAL
MARKER
MORGAN'S RAID ROUTE
General John Hunt Morgan of Kentucky led a force of Confederate cavalrymen into Meigs County during a forty-six-day raid north of the Ohio River. The advance forces burned Benjamin Knight's carding mill and sawmill, the Shade River Bridge, and pillaged local businesses in Chester on July 18, 1863, while waiting for the rest of the column to catch up. This two-hour halt delayed General Morgan's arrival at the ford at Buffington Island until after dark, allowing Union troops to arrive before he could make his escape. General Morgan surrendered eight days later near West Point in Columbiana County, the northernmost point ever reached by Confederate forces during the Civil War.
MEIGS COUNTY HISTORICAL SOCIETY
OHIO TRAVEL AND TOURISM
THE OHIO HISTORICAL SOCIETY
1997
5-53

The Battle of Buffington Island is located on St. Rt. 124 in Meigs County, Ohio

At the battle of Buffington Island around sixty Confederate soldiers were killed and are buried in unmarked graves near the battlefield.

THE BATTLE OF
BUFFINGTON ISLAND
JULY 19, 1863
DEDICATED TO UNION FORCES AND LEADERS

Shackelford's Brigade - Brig. Gen. James M. Shackelford
3rd Kentucky Cavalry (Maj. Lewis Wolfley)
8th Kentucky Cavalry (Lt. William A. Sasseen)
9th Kentucky Cavalry (Maj. George W. Rue)
12th Kentucky Cavalry (Col. Eugene W. Crittenden)
22nd Indiana Battery (Capt. Benjamin F. Denning)
Ohio Militia - Capt. D.L. Wood
Athens County Militia (Capt. J. Stedman)
Marietta Militia (Maj. Bloomfield)
Harmar Battery (Lt. J. Young)
U.S. Navy - Lt. Cmdr. LeRoy Fitch
U.S. Gunboat *Moose* (Lt. Cmdr. LeRoy Fitch)
U.S. Steamer *Imperial* (Master T.J. Oakes)
U.S. Steamer *Allegheny Belle* (Master Nat Pepper)
Kanawha Division - Brig. Gen. Eliakim P. Scammon
12th Ohio Infantry (Col. Carr B. White)
23rd Ohio Infantry (Maj. James M. Comly)
91st Ohio Infantry (Col. John A. Turley)
13th West Virginia Infantry (Col. William R. Brown)
McMullin's Independent Battery (Capt. J. McMullin)

MEIGS COUNTY HISTORICAL SOCIETY
MEIGS COUNTY COMMISSIONERS
OHIO TRAVEL AND TOURISM
THE OHIO HISTORICAL SOCIETY

St. Rt. 285, N. High St. in Senecaville, Ohio
Unknown Confederate Soldier who was with Gen. John Hunt Morgan, he was killed in Senecaville, and is buried in the cemetery. There is believed to be one or two more in the residence yard nearby.

Old Washington, Ohio

"On July 23, 1863, General John Hunt Morgan entered Guernsey County with 600 Confederate cavalrymen, the remnant of a 2,000 man diversionary raiding force that had traversed Kentucky, Indiana, and southern Ohio. Morgan's forces halted in Old Washington on the morning of July 24 for rest and provisions. Three pursuing Union cavalry units under Brigadier General James M. Shackelford (1st and 3rd Kentucky, 14th Illinois) assembled on Cemetery Hill to the south and began firing on the Confederates in town. The raiders returned fire. In the exchange three Confederates were killed and several wounded, Eight were captured. Outflanked, Morgan proceeded northeast to Columbiana County, where he surrendered two days later. The three Confederate casualties are interred in the cemetery behind this site."

Old Washington, Ohio
Wills Township, Guernsey County, Ohio

HERE WAS LAID TO REST BY THE CITIZENS OF WASHINGTON UNDER PUBLIC AUTHORITY. THE BODIES OF THREE CONFEDERATE CAVALRYMEN KILLED DURING THE BATTLE OF WASHINGTON JULY 24, 1863, WHEN A FORCE IN COMMAND OF CONFEDERATE GENERAL JOHN MORGAN, WAS OVERTAKEN AND DEFEATED BY FEDERAL CAVALRYMEN IN COMMAND OF GENERAL JAMES M. SHACKELFORD.

General John Hunt Morgan skirmish with the Union army in Old Washington, Oh. left 3 unknown Confederate soldiers dead.
Old Washington Cemetery, Old Mill Rd. Wills Twp. Guernsey County, Oh.

Old Washington Cemetery is a very old cemetery. This is a must to see for anyone who loves history. The town itself has some historic buildings.

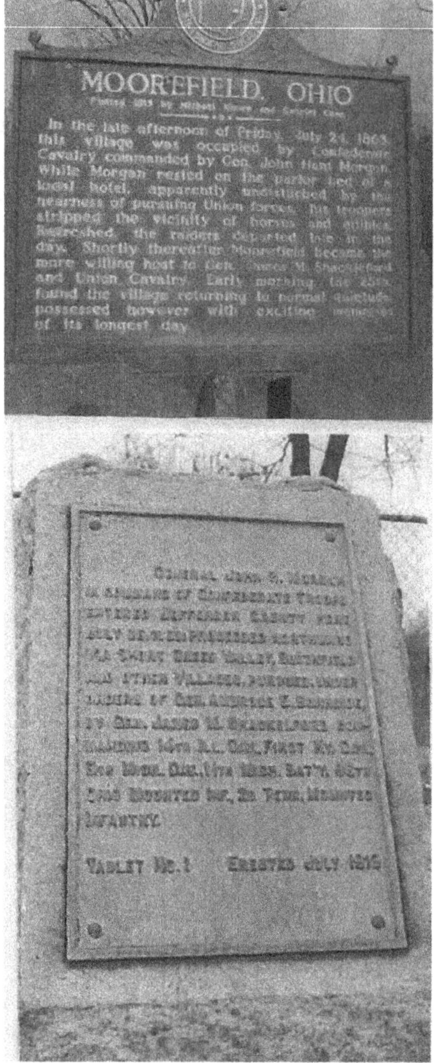

Moorefield, Ohio

While Morgan rested on the parlor bed of a local hotel, apparently undisturbed by the nearness of pursuing Union forces, his troopers stripped the vicinity of horses and edibles. Refreshed, the raiders departed late in the day. Shortly thereafter Moorefield became the more willing host to Gen. James M. Shackleford and Union Cavalry. Early morning, the 25th, found the village returning to normal quietude possessed however with exciting memories of its longest day
No. 4 Harrison County Historical Society 1965

Harrisville

Gen. Morgan of Confederate troops passed through this village July 25, 1863; proceeded northward via New Alexandria.

Tablet No. 1 Erected July 1913

Dillonvale, Ohio

John Hunt Morgan's Raid through Ohio.
This plaque is missing.

Smithfield, Ohio

General Morgan's troops entered Jefferson County here July 25, 1863; proceeded northward via Short Creek Valley, Smithfield and other villages.

Tablet No. 4 Erected July 1913

New Alexandria, Ohio

Gen. Morgan's troops passed through this village July 25, 1863; proceeded northward via McIntire and Cross Creek Valleys and Wintersville.

Tablet No. 5 Erected July 1913

Wintersville, Ohio

Gen. Morgan's troops passed here July 25, 1863; Engagement here militiaman Henry L. Parks was wounded, died July 27, 1863. Miss Margaret D. Daugherty in Thomas Maxwell's house was severely wounded.

Tablet NO. 8 Erected July 1913

Two Ridge, Ohio

General Morgan's troops passed here "Two Ridges Church" July 25, 1863; proceeded northward via Richmond. The 9th Michigan Cavalry, wounded, died August 27, 1863.

Tablet No. 9 Erected July 1913

Richmond, Ohio

General Morgan's troops passed through this village July 26, 1863; proceeded northward via Circle Green and Nebo (now Bergholz.

Tablet No. 10 Erected July 1913

East Springfield, Ohio

General Morgan's Confederate troops passed through this village July 26, 1863; proceeded northward via Circle Green and Nebo (now Bergholz).

Tablet No. 11 Erected July 1913

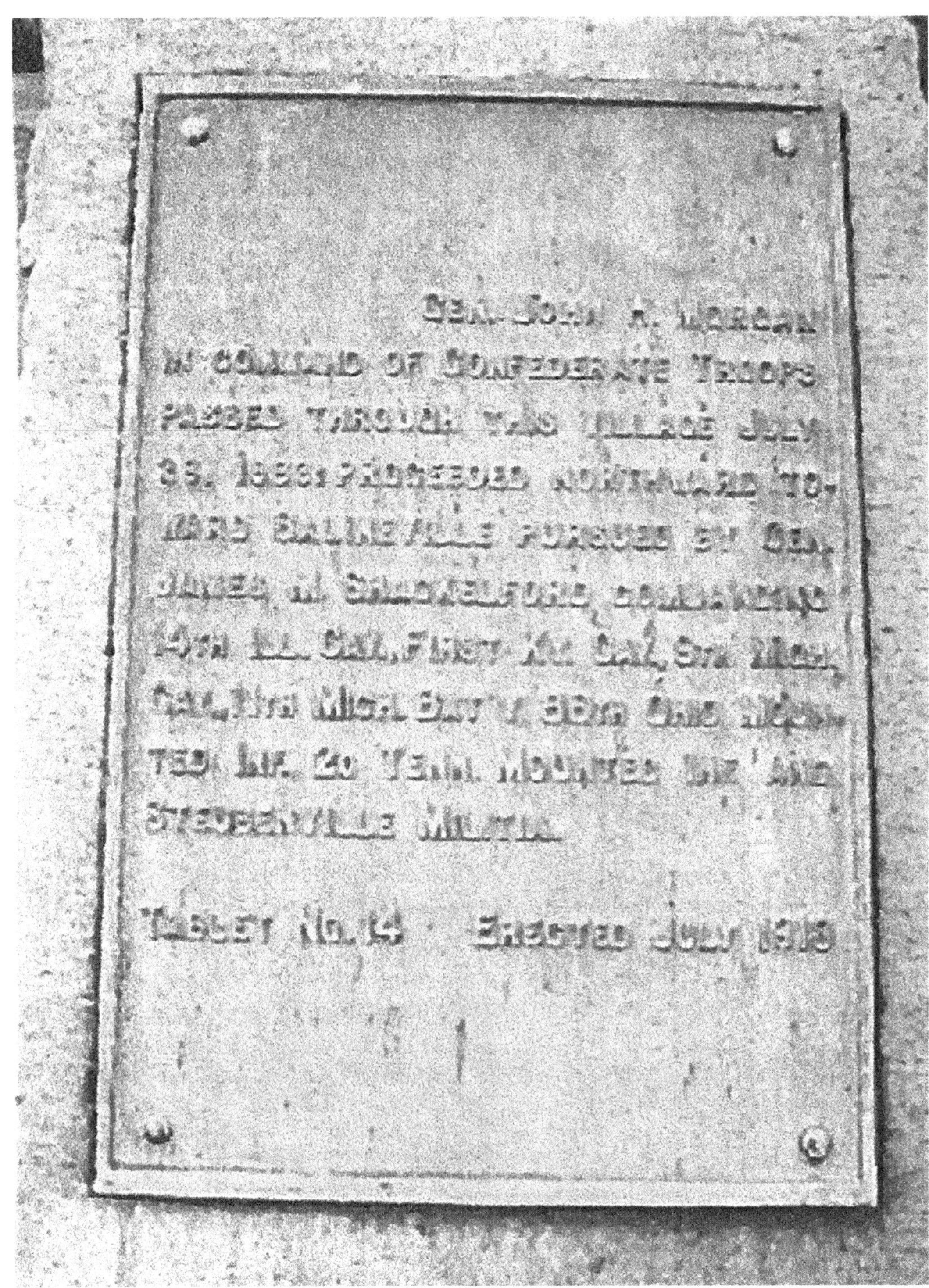

Monroeville, Ohio on Rt. 644

General John H .Morgan in command of Confederate Troops passed through this village July 26, 1863; proceeded northward toward Salineville.

Tablet NO. 14 Erected July 1913

The raid of the rebel Morgan into Indiana, which he seems to be pursuing with great boldness, has thoroughly aroused the people of that State and of Ohio to a sense of their danger. On 13th General Burnside declared martial law in Cincinnati, and in Covington and Newport on the Kentucky side. All business is suspended until further orders, and all citizens are required to organize in accordance with the direction of the State and municipal authorities. There is nothing definite as to Morgan's whereabouts; but it is supposed that he will endeavor to move around the city of Cincinnati and cross the river between there and Maysville. The militia is concentrating, in obedience to the order of Governor Tod.

—*Harper's Weekly, July 25, 1863*

Near West Point, Columbiana County, Ohio

This stone marks the spot where the confederate raider Gen. John H. Morgan surrendered his command to Major George W. Rue July 26, 1863 and is the farthest point north ever reached by any body of Confederate troops during the Civil War.

Morgan's Raid at this spot on July 26, 1863 General John Hunt Morgan with 336 of his Confederate raiders surrendered to Major George W. Rue after spreading panic across southern Ohio for twenty-three days.

Erected by Will L. Thompson East Liverpool, Ohio 1909

A group of Morgan's Men at Camp Douglas in August 1863

It would not be impolite to describe Camp Douglas as a hell hole. From 1862-1865, more than 6,000 Confederate prisoners died from disease, starvation, and the bitter cold winters. Camp Douglas had not been designed as a prison rather; it began as training grounds for Federal troops. As a prison, it operated much like a miniature city behind walls. Prisoners, guards, and sometimes paroled troops awaiting return to the front were all force to reside in appalling conditions. Situated in a bizarre location, Camp Douglas sat on swampy soil nest to the University of Chicago. This land had been owned by Stephen Douglas and was donated to the city of Chicago upon his death.

Columbus, Capital of Ohio

McPherson Park on Spring St., N. Spring and E. Neil, Arena District

On this site once stood the Ohio Penitentiary, which was built in 1834 and operated through 1984. Incarcerated here in July 1863 was Confederate General John Hunt Morgan a cavalry commander known as the "Thunderbolt of the Confederacy." and about 70 of his officer. Morgan's Raiders brought the Civil War to the North with a spectacular raid through Kentucky, Indiana and Ohio in the summer of 1863. The raid ended with Morgan's capture in far eastern Ohio.

Morgan surrendered the remnant of his command on July 26, 1863, near West Point in Columbiana County, the northernmost point reached by any significant force of armed

Confederates during the war. He and his officers were sent to the Ohio Penitentiary rather than to a prisoner of war camp because of reports that captured Union officers had received similar treatment. This proved to be to Morgan's advantage in November 1863, he and six of his officers escaped by tunneling from an air shaft beneath their cells into the prison yard and scaling the walls. Only two escapes were recaptured. Morgan returned to Confederate service and was killed in 1864.

John Hunt Morgan

June 1, 1825 – September 4, 1864 (aged 39)

John Hunt Morgan

Engraving by George Edward Perine (1837–85)

Nickname	Thunderbolt
Place of birth	Huntsville, Alabama
Place of death	Greeneville, Tennessee
Place of burial	Lexington Cemetery
Allegiance	United States of America Confederate States of America
Service/branch	United States Army Confederate States Army
Years of service	1846–1847 (USA) 1857–1861 (Kentucky Militia) 1861–1864 (CSA)
Rank	First Lieutenant (USA) Captain (Kentucky Militia) Brigadier General (CSA)

Battles/wars	Mexican-American War
	▪ Battle of Buena Vista
	American Civil War
	▪ Battle of Shiloh
	▪ Battle of Hartsville
	▪ Morgan's Raid
	  ▪ Battle of Buffington Island
	  ▪ Battle of Corydon
	  ▪ Battle of Salineville

General John Hunt Morgan's raid through Ohio estimated and location of Confederate dead. Buffington Island about 60 men, Senecaville one to three, Goshen Township Cemetery Clermont County, Private W. M. Frazier 12th Kentucky Cavalry Co. B., Dillonvalle, Meigs County, Langsville, Meigs County unmarked, unknown on private property now under water. North of Connellsville, Confederate soldier shot and died in a skirmish along the Muskingum River near Eagle Port. Athens, Ohio, the Ridges Asylum Cemetery near the campus of Ohio University has one grave. Old Washington, Ohio 3 unknown.

CHAPTER IV

JOHNSON ISLAND WAS A PRISON CAMP FOR MAINLY CONFEDERATE OFFICERS.

Camp Chase was a Union training camp turned into a prison camp for Confederate soldiers.

Camp Dennison was a Union training camp and medical post for Union and Confederate soldiers.

31 Confederate soldiers died here, their bodies were removed in 1869, 9 taken to Spring Grove cemetery in Hamilton, Ohio, the other 22 were reburied at Camp Chase.

Confederate Prisoners of War Camp, Johnson's Island, Sandusky Bay, Ohio, Ohio's most significant Civil War sight. 1861—1865

This photograph was taken at the dedication ceremony of the Bronze Monument to Confederate Soldiers in Johnson's Island, Ohio, Stockade Cemetery, .on June 8, 1910. Courtesy of M. Demattia.

Johnson's Island has an historic interest that makes it dear to patriotic Americans. The island is about one mile in length and half a mile in breadth, and rises to a height of fifty feet above the lake level, containing about 300 acres. In its original state it was covered with a heavy growth of oaks, and is said to have been a favorite resort of the Indians. It was formerly owned by a man named Bull, and was then known as Bull's Island, and was the site of the old custom-house of the port, removed here from Port Marblehead. L.B. Johnson, of Sandusky, purchased the property in 1852, and rented it to the government in 1861 as a depot for Confederate prisoners, Company A. Hoffman Battalion, taking possession January, 1, 1862. Companies B, C, and D were shortly after added, and in 1863 six more—all known as the One Hundred and Twenty-eight Regiment, Ohio Volunteer Infantry. The first prisoners were brought here in April, 1862. The prison was eventually used almost exclusively for Confederate officers, the number varying from 2,000 to 3,000. During the full period of its occupancy about 15,000 prisoners were confined here, nearly all of whom were at one time or another exchanged. Two were shot in retaliation for executions in the South, one was hanged as a spy, and one was shot in an attempt to escape. One was also shot by a guard for getting over the "dead line." On September 7, 1865, the last prisoners on the island were sent to Fort Lafayette by order of the War Department, and the place was abandoned as a military post. The most striking memento of these sad days is the little cemetery on the north shore, where 206 Confederates were buried. Twenty of the bodies have been removed, and doubtless many others would be taken away if friends and relatives knew the resting place of the missing ones. Here a complete and correct list of the prisoners buried at Johnson's Island for the purpose of assisting friends in the South to locate dead comrades, the following, compiled from the report of the commissary-general of prisoners, is herewith subjoined. Several of the graves are marked "unknown," but as far as possible the full names have been obtained.

For many years the graves were only marked by rough, wooden headstones cut out and inscriptions carved upon them with jack-knives by comrades of the dead Confederates. Those letters were skillfully engraved and usually gave the name, rank, birth, and date of death, in fact, being the chief authority from which the official list was made up. A short time ago, however, a party of Georgia journalists visited the little cemetery, noted that the wooden headstones were fast going to decay, and, in order to rescue from oblivion the identity of their soldier dead, the newspapermen, upon their return home, raised by popular subscription in the South enough money to defray the expense of erecting a marble tombstone at the head of each grave. Only a few of the original wooden headboards are now in existence and these are kept as souvenirs the love that the soldiers bore for their dead friends.

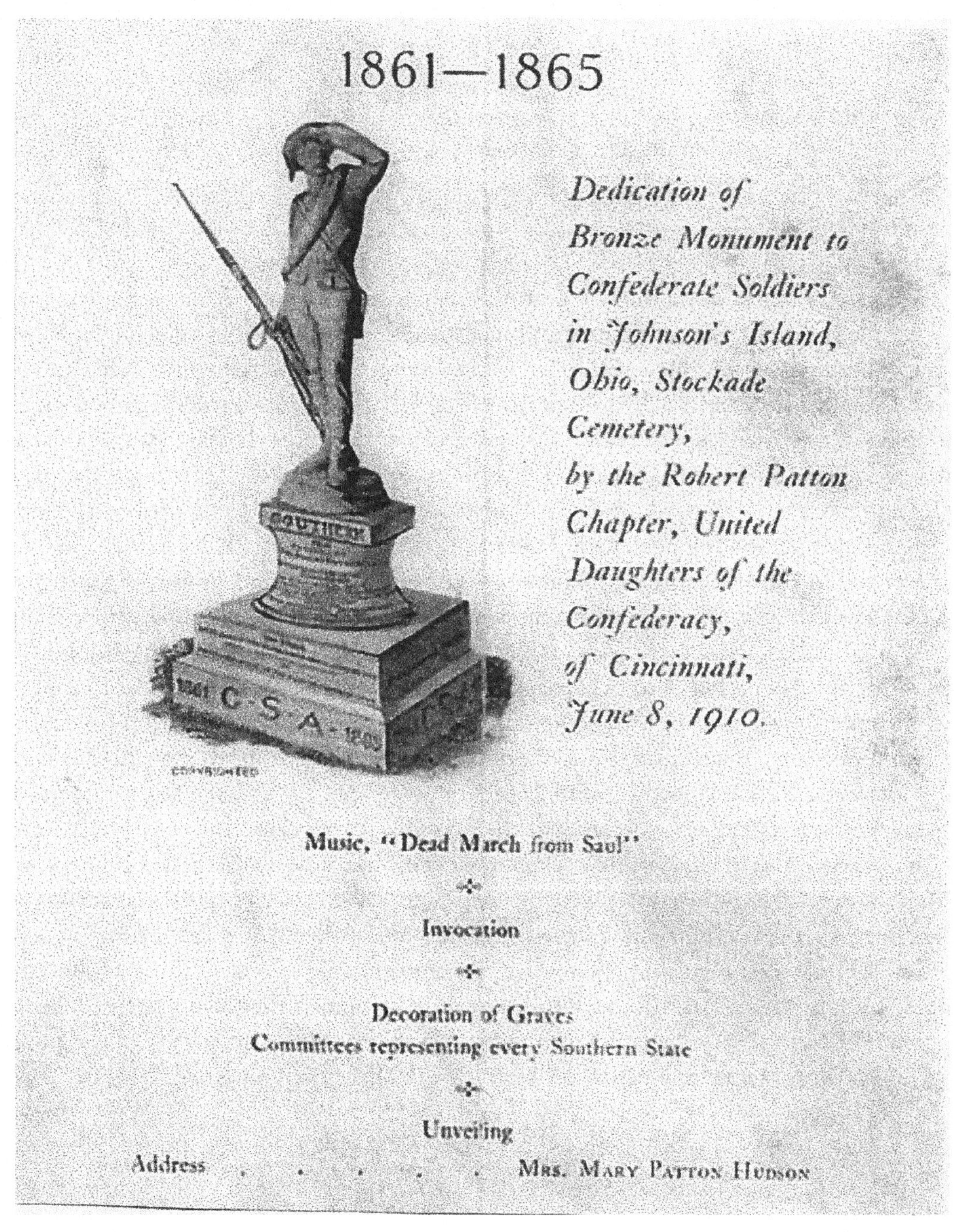

1861—1865

Dedication of Bronze Monument to Confederate Soldiers in Johnson's Island, Ohio, Stockade Cemetery, by the Robert Patton Chapter, United Daughters of the Confederacy, of Cincinnati, June 8, 1910.

Music, "Dead March from Saul"

Invocation

Decoration of Graves
Committees representing every Southern State

Unveiling

Address . . . . . Mrs. Mary Patton Hudson

<u>The following is the list of graves:</u>

J. E. Cruggs, Colonel Eighty-fifth Virginia
E. M. Tuggle, Captain Thirty-fifth Georgia Infantry
A. E. Upchurch, Captain Fifty-fifth North Carolina Infantry
J. P. Peden, Second Lieutenant Hamilton's Battery
Joel Barnett, Lieutenant-colonel Ninth Battalion, Louisiana Cavalry
William J. Hudson, Lieutenant Second North Carolina Infantry
D. E. Webb, Captain First Alabama Cavalry
J. W. Nullins, Lieutenant First Mississippi Infantry
W. E. Hansen, First Georgia Infantry
H. D. Stephenson, Captain Fifteenth Arkansas Infantry
R. K. Copass, Lieutenant Sixth Tennessee Infantry
J. D. Caraway
C.B. Jackson, Virginia
J. Huffstetter, Lieutenant First Battalion Arkansas Infantry
L. B. Williams, Lieutenant Sixty-third North Carolina Infantry
W.P. Harden, Lieutenant North Carolina Infantry
J. M. Dotson, Lieutenant Tenth Tennessee Cavalry
D.D. Keller, Private Second Tennessee Cavalry
S.G. Jetter, Alabama Infantry
C.W. Gillespie, Captain North Carolina Cavalry
B. Anderson, Private Missouri S.C.
W.W. Veasey, Lieutenant Tenth Kentucky Cavalry
J.W. Gregory, Captain Ninth Virginia Infantry
Peter Cole, Private Sixtieth Virginia Infantry
William Johnson, Private Poindexter's Missouri Cavalry
E.L. More
Daniel Herrin, Poindexter's Missouri Cavalry
J. W. Collier, Lieutenant Eighteenth Kentucky Infantry
John M. Kean, Captain Twelfth Louisiana Artillery
L. W. McWhirter, Captain Third Mississippi Infantry
John Dow, Pulaski, Ohio
H. Hodges, Memphis, Tennessee
E. Gibson, Lieutenant Eleventh Arkansas Infantry
D. Christian, One Hundred and Twenty-eighth Virginia Infantry
L. Raisins, Forth-sixth Virginia Infantry
Samuel Fox, Colonel
J. Ashbury, Kentucky
J. Reaves, First Georgia Cavalry
J. A. McBride, Lieutenant Sixtieth Tennessee Infantry
S.R. Graham, First Lieutenant Third Texas Cavalry
S.W. Henry, Captain Nineteenth Tennessee Cavalry
E.M. Orr, Lieutenant Sixty-second North Carolina Infantry
Mark Bacon, Captain Sixtieth Tennessee Infantry
J.B. Hardy, Captain Fifteenth Arkansas Infantry
Hugh Cobble, Private Fifth Kentucky
J.B. Cash, Lieutenant Sixty-second North Carolina Infantry
J.W. Johnson, Captain Green's R. Missouri S. G's
J.U.D. King, Captain Ninth Georgia Infantry
M.R. Handy, citizen, Hopkins County, Ky.
E. Morrison, Private Eighth Alabama Infantry
Charles H. Matlock, Colonel Fourth Mississippi
W.W. Davis, Private Thirty-fifth Mississippi Infantry

Confederate Soldiers Buried at Johnson's Island, Ohio

**W.N. Swift, Lieutenant Thirty-fourth Georgia Infantry
A. Kelly, Lieutenant Tenth Arkansas Infantry
J.D. Conaway, Private Nineteenth Virginia Cavalry
J. Middlebrooks, Captain Fortieth Georgia Infantry
J.B. Hazzard, Captain Twenty-fourth Alabama Infantry
J.P. Vance, Captain Bell's R., Arkansas Infantry
D.H. McKay, Lieutenant Forth-sixth Alabama Infantry
John R. Jackson, Captain Thirty-eighth Alabama Infantry
H.B. Dawson, Lieutenant Seventeenth Georgia Infantry
D.D. Johnson, Lieutenant Forty-eighth Tennessee Infantry
J.B. Hardy, Captain Fifth Arkansas Infantry
W.T. Skidmore, Lieutenant Fourth Alabama Cavalry
M.D. Armfield, Captain Eleventh North Carolina Infantry
E.W. Lewis, Captain Ninth Battalion Louisiana Cavalry
J.N. Williams, Lieutenant (or Captain) Sixth Mississippi Infantry
J.T. Ligon, Lieutenant Fifty-third Virginia Infantry (or Twenty-third Arkansas)
F.G.W. Coleman, Lieutenant Seventh Mississippi Artillery
J.E. Threadgill, Lieutenant Twelfth Arkansas Infantry
J.G. Shuler, Captain Fifth Florida Infantry
B.J. Blount, Lieutenant Fifty-fifth North Carolina Infantry
J.D. Arrington, Lieutenant Thirty-second North Carolina Infantry
Joseph Lawske, Lieutenant Eighteenth Mississippi Cavalry
John C. Holt, Lieutenant Sixty-first Tennessee Infantry
Samuel Chormley, Blount County, Tennessee
J.W. Moore, Lieutenant Twenty-fifth Alabama Infantry
D.L. Scott, Second Lieutenant Third Missouri Cavalry
William Peel, Lieutenant Eleventh Mississippi
J.L. Land, Lieutenant Twenty-fourth Georgia Infantry
N.T. Barnes, Captain Tenth Confederate Cavalry
John F. McElroy, Lieutenant Twenty-fourth Georgia Infantry
John Q. High, Lieutenant First Arkansas Battalion Infantry
J.C. Long, Lieutenant Sixty-second North Carolina Infantry
B.C. Harp, Lieutenant Twenty-fifth Tennessee Infantry
W.S. Norwood, Lieutenant South Carolina Infantry
R.K.C. Weeks, Second Lieutenant Fourth Florida Infantry
S.P. Sullins, Captain First Alabama Infantry
P.J. Rabeman, Captain Fifth Alabama Infantry
R.H. Lisk, citizen
F.F. Cooper, Captain Fifty-second Georgia Infantry
W.E. Watson, Adjutant First Tennessee Infantry
Albert F. Frazer, Fifteenth Mississippi
W.E. Killem, Lieutenant Fourth Virginia Infantry
F.T. Coppeye, Lieutenant Tennessee Infantry
J.L. Dungan, Private Twenty-second Virginia
S.T. Moore, Second Lieutenant King's Regiment, Alabama Infantry
John J. Gobeau, Lieutenant Tenth Mississippi Infantry**

Confederate Soldiers Buried at Johnson's Island, Ohio

In late 1861, Federal officials selected Johnson's Island as the site for a prisoner of war camp to hold up 2,500 captured Confederate officers. The island offered easy access by ship for supplies to construct and maintain a prison and its population. Sandusky Bay offered more protection from the elements than on other nearby islands, which were also closer to Canada in the event of a prison break. Woods of hickory and oak trees could provide lumber and fuel. The U.S. government leased half the island from a private owner Leonard B. Johnson for $500 a year, and for the duration of the war carefully controlled access to the island.

The 16.5 acre prison opened in April 1862. A 15 foot wooden stockade surrounded 12 two-story prisoner housing barracks, a hospital, latrines, sutler's stand, three wells, a pest house, and two large mess halls (added in August 1864). More than 40 buildings stood outside the prison walls, including barns, stables, a limekiln, forts, and barracks for officers, and a powder magazine. They were used by the 128th Ohio Volunteer Infantry, which guarded the prison. Among the prominent Confederate generals imprisoned on Johnson's Island were Isaac R. Trimble and James J. Archer (both captured at the Battle of Gettysburg), William Beall, Thomas Benton Smith, Edward "Allegheny" Johnson and Missouri cavalrymen M. Jeff Thompson. Prisoners had a lively community, with amateur theatrical performances, publishing, and crafts projects.

After the war, the prison camp was abandoned and control reverted to the owner. Most auctioned off by the Army, and some were razed after falling into disrepair. Efforts in 1897 to turn the island into a resort (as with nearby Cedar Point) failed, and the land was used for farming and rock quarrying. Many lakeside homes have since been built, and are now quite developed with two subdivisions. Most of the Civil War related sites have since been destroyed and built over.

In 1990 Johnson's Island was designated a National Landmark. A causeway was built to connect it with the mainland. Only the Confederate cemetery is open to the public. Ground-penetrating radar studies have proved that several graves lie outside its fence. Heidelberg College conducts yearly archeology digs at the prison site.

Confederate Prisoners at Johnson's Island

Dedicated on June 21, 2003 by the Ohio Div. United Daughters of the Confederacy and the Lt. General James Longstreet Camp 1658 Sons of Confederate Veterans

Dedicated on June 21, 2003 by the Ohio Div. United Daughters of the Confederacy and the Lt. General James Longstreet Camp 1658 Sons of Confederate Veterans

John Wates Beall, Jan. 1, 1835- Feb. 24, 1865

Place of Birth: Jefferson County, Va. now West Virginia; Place of Death; Governors Island, New York. Military service: Confederate States Navy.
1861 to 1865. Rank: Acting Masters

He attended the Univ. of Virginia and studied Law.
This picture was on the day of his execution.

Virginian John Beall began his Civil War career at 26 as a private in the 2nd Virginia Infantry Regiment fought in the 1st Battle of Bull Run as a part of the Stonewall Brigade. He then led a company of General Turner Ashby's cavalry in the Shenandoah Valley until he was severely wounded in the chest while leading a charge on October 16, 1861. Beall was given a medical discharge from the army during his long convalescence, but he was not ready to stop fighting.

In spring 1863, Beall won the War Department's approval of a daring plan for raiding Union shipping vessels in the Chesapeake Bay. He was appointed an acting master in the Confederate navy and was authorized to raise a hand of partisan raiders. The group would have to provide its own ship, and the raiders' only payment would be a share of the booty they captured from Northern vessels.

On the evening of September 17, 1863, Beall and 18 men set out into the bay in two ships and quickly captured a Union sloop and two fishing scows. The next night, Beall's men captured a Yankee sloop carrying $200,000 worth of sutler's stores that was bound for Port Royal, S.C. Three more ships were captured by September 21, and then the raiders returned safely to their Mathews County base. Union response to the first raid was slow and ineffectual. But When Beall's crew set out again in November, they were quickly captured, strapped in irons in old Fort McHenry, Md., and held as pirates. Southern authorities ordered the same number of Union Prisoners to be held in similar conditions, eventually forcing the federals to great the raiders as prisoners of war.

After being exchanged on May 5, 1864, Beall found approval to continue his partisan activities slow to come and went to Canada to look for other opportunities to strike the enemy. The commander of Confederate secret operations in Canada, Jacob Thompson, recruited Beall to form a force of refugees and escaped Confederate prisoners who were in Canada to disrupt Northern trade on Lake Erie.

Specifically, Beall was to free Confederate prisoners of war being held on Johnson's Island, off Sandusky in Lake Erie, as well as those at Camp Chase in Columbus, Ohio. If successful, the enterprise was supposed to result in the establishment of a Confederate Department of the Army on Lake Erie. With the aid of Charles H. Cole, fresh from Nathan Bedford Forrest's cavalry, Beall made plans to capture two Union ships. He hoped to use the ships to overpower the USS Michigan, which was protecting the area, free the Rebel prisoners on Johnson's Island, and begin an overland route to Columbus by commandeered train. Meanwhile, in preparation, Cole had endeared himself to some Union officers and became a guest aboard the Michigan, from which he intended to send important signals to guide Beell's attack.

On September 18, 1864, Beall and his men captured the passenger ship Philo Parsons, which was on a trip from Detroit to Sandusky, Ohio. Then, Beall and his crew quickly took the Island Queen and moved into position near the Michigan, close to Johnson's Island, to await the signals from Cole.

At night fell, Beall's crew peered through the darkness, looking for Cole's messages, but none came. Unknown to the raiders, Cole had been discovered and word had been sent to the Michigan's captain, who arrested Cole. As time passed, Beall's crew became increasingly concerned, until they mutinied and forced Beall to pull back and to destroy the Philo Parsons at Sandwich, Canada.

While Beall's plan had failed, his mere attempt, along with his reputation, sent shock waves through Lincoln's cabinet and left Secretary of War Edwin Stanton in a state of "excited panic." News traveled to Buffalo, where the locals were expecting "piratical craft sailing boldly in and firing upon their defenseless houses."

Ship on top of page is the "Philo Parsons", Ship on bottom is the "Island Queen". Both ships operated out of Lake Erie in the 1860's

Camp Chase

Camp Chase was a military staging, training and prison camp in Columbus, Ohio, during the American Civil War. All that remains of the camp today is a Confederate cemetery containing 2,260 graves. The cemetery is located in what is now the Hilltop neighborhood of Columbus, Ohio.

History

Champ Chase was a Civil War camp established in May 1861, on land leased by the U.S. Government. It served as a replacement for the much smaller Camp Jackson. Four miles west of Columbus, the main entrance was on the National Road. Boundaries of the camp were present-day Broad Street (north), Hague Avenue (east), Sullivant Avenue (south), and near Westgate Avenue (west). Named for former Ohio Governor and Lincoln's Secretary of the Treasury Salmon P. Chase, it was a training camp for Ohio volunteer army soldiers, a parole camp, a muster out post, and a prisoner-of-war camp. The nearby Camp Thomas served as a similar base for the Regular Army.

As many as 150,000 Union soldiers and 25,000 Confederate prisoners passed through its gates from 1861-65. By February 1865, over 9,400 men were held at the prison. More than 2,000 Confederates are buried in the Camp Chase Cemetery (located at 2900 Sullivant Avenue, Columbus, and is open from 8 a.m. to 5 p.m. daily).

Four future Presidents passed through Camp Chase --- Andrew Johnson, Rutherford B. Hayes, James Garfield, and William McKinley. It also held Confederates captured during Morgan's Raid in 1863, including Col. Basil W. Duke. Early in the war, the prison section held a group of prominent western Virginia and Kentucky civilians suspected of actively supporting secession, including former 3-term United States Congressman Richard Henry Stanton. The camp was closed in 1865, and by September 1867, dismantled buildings usable items, and 450 patients from Tripler Military Hospital (also in Columbus) were transferred to the National Soldier's Home in Dayton. In 1895, former Union soldier William H. Knauss organized the first memorial service at the cemetery, ad in 1906 he wrote a history of the camp. The Memorial Arch was dedicated in 1902. From 1912 to 1904, the United Daughters of the Confederacy held annual services. The Hilltop Historical Society now sponsors the event on the second Sunday in June.

The Lady in Gray

The Lady in Gray is purportedly an apparition that haunts Camp Chase Cemetery. The story goes that the ghost is looking for her lost love, and cannot find him in the cemetery. The woman is described as young, in her late teens or early twenties, dressed entirely in gray, and carrying a clean white handkerchief. The legend of the Lady in Gray dates back to just after the Civil War, when visitors to Camp Chase spotted the woman walking through the cemetery, trying to read the carved names on the mock grave markers. She was seen quite often for several years, before disappearing completely.

View of Confederate soldiers and their housing units at Camp Chase, Ohio

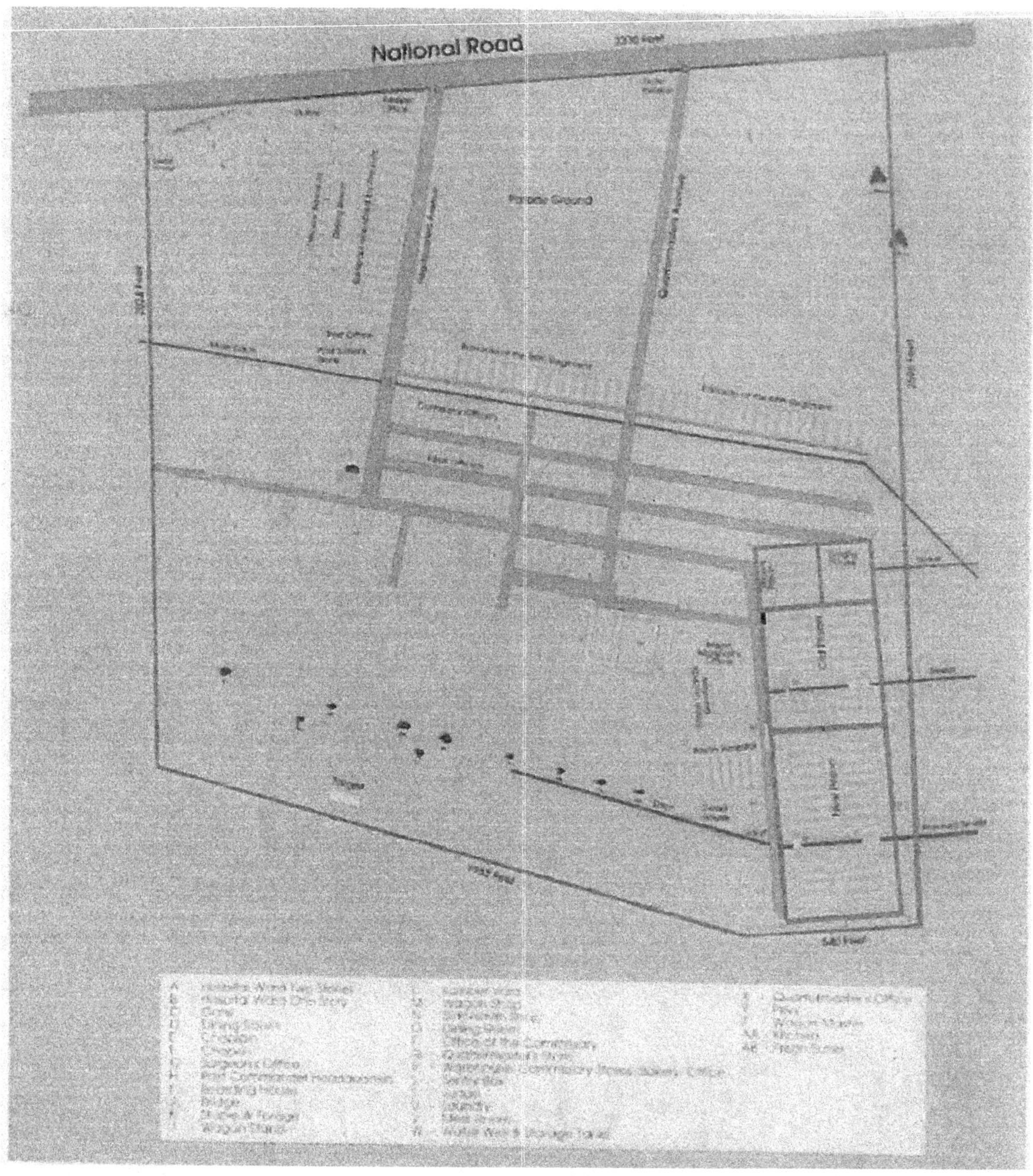

Take a walk between the graves at the Camp Chase Cemetery and you'll find yourself among many soldiers who died in the smallpox epidemic of 1863. Overcrowding forced two or three men to share single-occupancy bunks, and led to severe shortages in food and medicine, as well as clothing and blankets. The men were malnourished and cold, and therefore highly susceptible to disease. In February of 1863 alone, 499 men died from smallpox.

Not to Be Forgotten: Camp Chase Confederate Cemetery

Many, many Confederates were captured whose families have never known their fate, although prayerful diligence was exercised as long as there was a ray of hope. May this list of thousands of names give consolation to mourning hearts, as it will when found that husband, brother or son, having stood by their colors until overwhelming numbers compelled capitulation, and that whatever opportunities for freedom that my have come to him, all were rejected, and he went down to death a faithful Confederate soldier!

Quote from Confederate Veteran magazine, Nashville, Tennessee Jan. 1898, in reference to the list of the Confederate prisoners of war buried in Ohio.

Today as you pass through the entrance in the stone wall surrounding Camp Chase cemetery, the bustle of Columbus fades behind. Camp Chase encompasses less than two acres, so it is easy to appreciate the entire landscape. More than 2,000 headstones stretch out before your eyes, some so close together they nearly touch. Throughout the cemetery, large old trees with broad canopies offer cool shade on even the hottest summer days. It is hard to imagine that this cemetery was one of the largest Union Civil War prisoner-or-war camps for thousands of captured troops who served in the Army of the Confederate States of America (CSA).

Camp Chase, Ohio

2, 260 Confederate Soldiers are buried here. 1861-1865
2900 Sullivant Avenue,
Columbus, Ohio

Camp Dennison, Cincinnati, Ohio 1861-1865

Camp Dennison was a military recruiting, training and medical post for the United States Army during the American Civil War. It was located near Cincinnati, Ohio, not far from the Ohio River. The camp was named for Cincinnati native William Dennison, Ohio's governor at the start of the war.

With the outbreak of the Civil War in 1861, George B. McClellan, commander of Ohio's state militia, was charged by Governor Dennison with selecting a site for a recruitment and training center for southern Ohio, a possible target for the Confederate States Army due to its Ohio River location and proximity to slave states such as Kentucky and Virginia, from which invasions could be launched. McClellan was joined by Joshua H. Bates and another member of the militia in preparing the plans for the new camp. The site was actually chosen by then Captain William S. Rosecrans, who chose a level tract of land near Indian Hill, Ohio, 17 miles from Cincinnati. The land was on both sides of the Little Miami Railroad tracks, which ended at Cincinnati's Public Landing.

There are variable area listed, but 700 acres of land appears to have been rented from the Buckingham and Nimrod Price families. They were offer $12 to $20 per acre per month, a figure named without negotiation, and considered generous. Rosecrans laid out the camp via survey around April 24, 1861, and a large contingent of recruits from Camp Chase, numbering about 1,500 men were sent by train. The first post commander was Melancthon Smith Wade, a Cincinnatian who was a former general in the Ohio Militia.

The LMR could transport volunteer from Central Ohio, and from areas along those tracks. The location had fresh water in the nearby Little Miami River but the recruits had to be trained to use latrines, for in 1862, the United States Sanitary Commission reported that man refused to use latrines, and instead used an area hillside, at the bottom of which was their water supply. It was the Little Miami Railroad which could transport troops quickly into Cincinnati in case of enemy threat. However, among the men initially sent, there were less than a dozen muskets among them, but presumably the Confederates, if they considered attacking Cincinnati, were not aware. One can view the land of Camp Dennison via Google. The Little Miami Railroad tracks are now a bicycle trail.

More than 50,000 Union soldiers were mustered in or out of service at Camp Dennison. As many as 12,000 occupied the camp at any one time. During Morgan's Raid in 1863, troops from Camp Dennison responded to the invasion by Confederate cavalry under Brig. Gen. John Hunt Morgan, as they had in 1862, when Cincinnati was briefly threatened by the cavalry of Albert G. Jenkins.

Within the first week, inclement weather made life very hard on those who were first there. They had no chance to build substantial structures, and the weather turned cold and accompanied by a lot of rain. The fields became a sea of mud. The camp hospital was established on the ground floor of the Waldschmidt barn, after horses were liveried elsewhere, the manure removed, and fresh straw laid down. Camp Dennison along with its surrounding cities of Indian Hill and Madeira have a curfew of 1 A.M., Many men contracted pneumonia, and then there was a measles epidemic. For a time, the "Hospital" was simply a shelter, although there was minimal bedding. At least one man died.

As the war progressed, shortly after the Battle of Shiloh a military hospital was established on the grounds of Camp Dennison, with over 200 beds situated in a series of wooden barracks. These wooden barracks were originally used to house soldiers, but were converted into hospital wards. There were considerably more men sent there over the course of the war. The nearby Waldschmidt Cemetery served as the temporary gravesite for 340 Union soldiers and 31 Confederate soldiers who were prisoners of war. The bodies were re- interred at Spring Grove Cemetery or at Champ Chase in Columbus in 1869.

The end of the Civil War in 1865 eliminated the need for Camp Dennison, which was deactivated in Sept. A small community, Camp Dennison, sprang up around the camp and hospital. Many of the later barns and homes used lumber & materials from the abandoned army camp.

Camp Dennison Civil War Museum/Christian Waldschmidt Homestead
7509 Glendale Milford Rd. Camp Dennison, Ohio 45116

In 1794, Christian Waldschmidt, a veteran of the American Revolution, moved his family to a site on the Little Miami River and built a new community called New Germany. In 1804, he built his home, which included a store. Waldschmidt was a businessman and encouraged new settlement, staffing a church and helping to found a school, and beginning industries vital to the survival of his new home, such as Ohio's first paper mill, a cooperative distillery, woolen mill, sawmill, and a blacksmith shop.

During the Civil War, the house and surrounding grounds were part of Camp Dennison, used primarily as a general training center, recruiting depot, and hospital post, and named in honor of Governor William Dennison. The main house, now know as Waldschmidt House, served as the headquarters for General Joshua Bates.

Chapter V

Six Ohio Born Confederate Generals and one born in Pennsylvania and then Resided in Ohio

Charles Clark
Born in Ohio
Brigadier Gen. & Governor of Mississippi 1811-1877

"I am the duly and constitutionally elected Governor of the State of Mississippi, and would resist, if in my power, to the last extremity..."

Gov. Charles Clark to Union Gen. E.D. Osband, 1865

Charles Clark was born in Lebanon, Warren County, Ohio, May 24, 1811. He received his education in Kentucky, and moved to Mississippi about 1831, where he taught school for a time. Later a planter and staunch Whig adherent of Henry Clay, he served in the State Legislature in from 1838-1844, and in the Mexican War as Colonel of the Second Mississippi Infantry. In 1860, Clark choose to switch political parties, and become a Democrat, and a delegate to the conventions in Charleston and Baltimore in 1860, where he supported John Cable Breckinridge for the presidency. He was early appointed Brigadier General , and later Major General of Mississippi State Troops. After the acceptance of the Mississippi Regiments into Confederate Service, he was appointed Brigadier General to rank from May 22, 1861

General Clark commanded a Brigade in General Albert Sidney Johnston's army in Kentucky, and at the battle of Shiloh, where he was severely wounded in the shoulder at the opening of the battle. Clark returned to command in time to participate in the battle of Baton Rouge where he lead a Div. Clark was again severely wounded, his hip being shattered by a mini ball. Captured on the field, and thinking the wound to be mortal, the Federals allowed Clark to be taken to New Orleans to his personal physician. Clark would live, but was made a permanent invalid, having to use crutches or a cane for the rest of his life. General Clark returned to Mississippi, and was elected Gov. in the fall of 1863. He served in office until arrested by Federal authorities in the Spring of 1865. He was imprisoned for a time in Fort Pulaski, Georgia but returned to Mississippi upon his release. Denied any role in politics for the time being, Clark returned to the practice of law and the management of his plantation "Doro" in Bolivar County, Miss. Clark served as Chancellor of his district from 1876 until his death Dec. 18, 1877, at his plantation where he is buried

Johnson Kelly Duncan
Born: Mar. 19, 1827 Pennsylvania
Moved to Findlay, Ohio when he was twelve
Death: Dec. 18, 1862

Civil War Confederate Brigadier Gen. He was born in York, Pennsylvania. He graduated 5th in the West Point class of 1849. He then served against the Seminoles in Florida, and explored possible railroad routes in the Northwest. He left the U.S. Army in 1855 to supervise government construction in New Orleans. By 1861 he considered himself a Louisianan and sided with the South when the Civil War began. His first assignment was as a Colonel of Artillery defending Forts Jackson and St. Philip below New Orleans. He was commissioned a Brigadier Gen. on Jan. 7, 1862, and had about 500 men and 80 guns at his disposal when Union Capt. David G. Farragut brought up his fleet and mortar boats to attack the forts. On the first day of firing, April 18, 1862, Farragut's mortars lobbed close to 3000 rounds at Fort Jackson in a 10-hr bombardment. He and his men held out until April 24. On that day Farragut successfully ran with his fleet past the fort's guns, landing infantry behind the fort. He surrendered on April 28, and was taken prisoner. After being exchanged on Aug. 27, 1862, he was given charge of an infantry brigade during the operations in Kentucky. He briefly commanded a division, and then became General Braxton Bragg's staff chief in Tennessee but died of typhoid fever in Knoxville.

Robert Hopkins Hatton
Born: Nov. 26, 1826
Steubenville, Ohio
Death: May 31, 1862
Buried at: Initially Knoxville, Tennessee, Reburied at Cedar Grove Cemetery, Lebanon, Tenn.
Allegiance: United States of America and Confederate States of America
Year of Service: 1861-1862 CSA
Brigadier General

Robert Hopkins Hatton (Nov. 2, 1826-May 31, 1861) was a lawyer, politician, U. S. Congressman, and Confederate officer during the American Civil War. Hatton was born in Steubenville, Ohio, but, early in his life, his family moved to Tennessee. He graduated from Cumberland University, then studied law there at Cumberland School of Law and established a successful practice in Lebanon, Tennessee, after passing the bar exam in 1850. He joined the Whig Party and was elected to the State Legislature in 1855. He unsuccessfully ran for governor in 1857. He was elected to the Thirty-sixth Congress in 1858 as an Opposition party candidate (the Whig party had collapsed), where he served as chairman of the Committee on Expenditures in the Dept. of the Navy. Hatton believed that the Union should be preserved and initially opposed secession. However, after President Lincoln called for volunteers to invade the Southern states, Hatton reversed his position and formed a Confederate military unit, the Lebanon Blues, which became a part of the 7th Tenn. Hatton was soon elected as colonel of the Regiment, which was sent to western Va. in July 1861. In 1862, Hatton and his men were ordered to the Richmond area to stop Federal Maj. General George B. McClellan's drive on the Confederate capital.

During the resulting Peninsula Campaign, Hatton served with distinction, and on May 23, 1862, he was promoted to Brigadier General of the 4th Brigade, 1st. Division, Army of Northern Virginia; this appointment was not confirmed by the Confederate Congress. Just eight days later, he was shot in the head and killed while leading his Tennessee Brigade at the Battle of Fair Oaks.

His body was returned to Tennessee for burial, but because Middle Tennessee was occupied by Federal troops, he was temporarily buried at Knoxville. On March 23, 1866, he was reburied in Lebanon's Cedar Grove Cemetery. A statue of him was erected in Lebanon's Town.

Statue of Robert H. Hatton on the City Square in Lebanon, Tennessee

Bushrod Rust Johnson
Birth: Oct. 7, 1817 in Norwich, Ohio.
Died: Sept. 12, 1880 Brighton, Ill. Re-interred in 1975 Old City Cemetery, Nashville, Tenn.
Allegiance: U.S.A. & CSA
Years of service: 1840-1847 & 1-1875 Rank: Maj. Gen.
Commands Held: Seminole War And the Mexican American War.

Bushrod Rust Johnson was a teacher, university chancellor, and Confederate General in the American Civil War.

Johnson was born in Norwich, Ohio on Oct. 7, 1817. He graduated from West Point and was appointed second lieutenant in the Third infantry. He served in the Seminole War, and was on frontier duty at Fort Leavenworth, Kansas, when he was promoted to first lieutenant in Feb. 1844. He was forced to resign from the Army in 1847 and become a teacher after being accused of selling contraband goods. He was professor in the Western Military Institute of Kentucky from 1848 to 1851, when he became its superintendent. Four years later he became superintendent of the Military College of the University of Nashville, Tenn., a position he held until the outbreak of the Civil War. He was also at that time colonel of Tennessee Militia. During his stay in Kentucky he had been lieutenant-colonel of Militia.

He was appointed colonel of engineers in the provisional army of Tennessee on June 28, 1861. When the Tennessee troops were turned over to the Confederate States, he was assigned to the army acting in Tennessee & Kentucky under the command of Gen. Albert Sidney Johnston. In 1861, he joined the Confederate Army and as a Brigadier Gen. fought at the Battle of Stones River, Battle of Chickamauga, and Battle of Knoxville.

Daniel Harris Reynolds
Born: Dec 14, 1832 in Centerburg, Ohio
Died: March 14, 1902
Lake Village, Arkansas
Buried at Lake Village Cemetery.
Rank: Confederate Brigadier General

Daniel Harris Reynolds was a lawyer, Confederate Gen. and state Senator who ranks as one of Arkansas's most talented and dedicated citizen-soldier during the Civil War.

Reynolds was born on Dec. 14, 1832, in Centerburg, Oh, to Amos and Sophia (Houck) Reynolds. He studied at Ohio Wesleyan Univ. in the town of Delaware, where he joined the Masonic order in 1853. He studied law privately in Louisa County, Iowa, and Somerville, Tenn., where he befriended fellow future Confederate Gen. Otho French Strahl. Admitted to the bar in 1858, he established a legal practice in Lake Village (Chicot County).

At the outset of the Civil War, Reynolds raised a cavalry company, the "Chicot Rangers," and entered Confederate service as a captain in command of Co. A of the First Arkansas Mounted Rifles. The regiment mustered in at Fort Smith (Sebastian County) on June 14, 1861. Serving initially in the Trans-Mississippi Theater, the regiment saw its first action at the Battle of Wilson's Creek, Missouri, on August 10, 1861; although injured in this engagement in a fall from his frightened horse, Reynolds stayed in the field and also fought at Pea Ridge March 7-8, 1862. Dismounted shortly after the Battle of Pea Ridge, the Mounted Rifles served thereafter as infantry, producing lingering resentment among the regiment's officers and enlisted men. The regiment soon transferred to the Army of Tennessee and served in the Western Theater (that is, east of the Mississippi River) for the rest of the war.

Despite a lack of military training or experience, Reynolds proved a natural leader, both in camp and in battle. Highly respected by superiors and subordinates alike, he advanced consistently through the ranks of regimental command, earning promotion to Major on April 14, 1862; Lieutenant Colonel on May 1, 1862; and Colonel of the First Arkansas Mounted Rifles on November 17, 1863 (retroactive to September 20). With the impending promotion of Brigadier General Thomas James Churchill, Reynolds' colleagues petitioned the Confederate secretary of war for his promotion to Brigadier General, even though he was not the Brigade's ranking

Colonel. He was promoted to Brigadier General on March 12, 1864, retroactive to March 5. For the rest of the war, he commanded "Reynolds's Arkansas Brigade," composed of the First Arkansas Infantry Regiments and the Fourth Arkansas Infantry Battalion.

Reynolds had little patience for ineffective commanders and voiced his displeasure after several unsuccessful campaigns. As a result of one personality conflict, Maj. Gen. Samuel Gibbs French placed him under arrest in Jan. 1864; although the charges were quickly dismissed, Reynolds refused to serve under French and transferred his brigade to the command of Maj. Gen. Edward Cary Walthall, with whom he enjoyed a close friendship and mutual respect.

In the Atlanta campaign, Reynolds defeated Brigadier Gen. Hugh Judson Kilpatrick at the Battle of Lovejoy Station on Aug. 20, 1864, helping temporarily maintain Conf. supply lines to Atlanta.

Reynold's left leg was amputated because of a wound received in the Battle of Bentonville, N.C. on Mar. 19, 1865. After the war, he returned to Lake Village, reestablished his law practice, and received a presidential pardon from Andrew Johnson. From 1866 to 1867, he served as a state senator for Ashley, Chicot, and Drew counties until Federal Reconstruction policy forced the removal of former Confederates from elected office.

He married Martha Wallace on November 24, 1868, and raised five children. He died in Lake Village on March 14, 1902, and is buried in Lake Village Cemetery.

Brigadier General
Roswell Sabine Ripley
(Commanding Brown's Div)
Confederate
Born: March 14, 1823
Worthington, Ohio
Died: March 29, 1887
New York City, N.Y.

Brigadier-General Roswell Sabine Ripley was born at Worthington, Ohio, March 14, 1823. He graduated at the U.S. military academy, number 7 in the class of 1843, of which Gen. U.S. Grant was twenty-first. With promotion to brevet second Lieutenant, Third artillery, he served until 1846 on garrison duty, and for a few months as assistant professor of mathematics at West Point. In 1846, being commissioned second Lieutenant, he was on the coast survey until ordered to Mexico, where he fought at Monterey in Sept. Then being promoted first Lieutenant, Second artillery, he took part in the siege of Vera Cruz, and at the battle of Cerro Gordo won the brevet of captain. At Contreras, Churubusco Molino del Rey, Chapultepec and the capture of the Mexican capital he won new honors and came out of the war with the brevet rank of major. After service as aide-de-camp to General Pillow to July, 1848, he prepared and published a history of the war in 1849, and subsequently was engaged in the Indian hostilities in Florida and in garrison duty until March, 1853, when he resigned and engaged in business at Charleston, the home of his wife. At the organization of the South Carolina army he received the rank of Lieutenant-colonel, commanding the First artillery battalion; R.S. was named to command the artillery battalion by

Gov. Pickens (S.C). in early 1861. At the opening of the bombardment of Fort Sumter on April 12, 1861, he commanded the artillery on Sullivan's island with his headquarters at Fort Moultrie under the command of Brig. Gen. Dunovant. At the bombardment of Fort Sumter he was highly commended by the generals commanding for his services in charge of the batteries on Sullivan's island. In August following he was commissioned Brigadier-General in the provisional army of the Confederate States, and was put in command of the department of South Caroline, and when that was merged in a larger department under Gen. R.E. Lee, he was given charge Of the Second military district of the State. Joining the army of Northern Virginia in June, 1862, he commanded a brigade of D.H. Hill's division, composed of Georgia and North Carolina regiments, in the battles of Mechanicsville, Gaines' Mill, Malvern Hill, South Mountain and Sharpsburg. In the latter engagement he was shot in the throat, but returned to the fight after his wound was dressed. About a month later he took command of the First military district of South Carolina, including Charleston and its defenses, and was in immediate command during the memorable attacks of the Federal fleets and army in 1863 and 1864. In January, 1865, he was ordered to report to General Hood, and at the last was assigned to command of a division of Cheatham's corps of the army of North Carolina. Then going abroad he resided in Paris several years, and upon his return resumed his business operations at Charleston. He died at New York, March 26, 1887.

Ref: Confederate Military History Vol. 5 pg. 418

Historic Organizations

Anyone with an ancestor who served honorably in the War Between the States can join any number of these organizations.

Sons of Confederate Veterans Founded in 1896

Sons of Union Veterans Founded in 1881

United Daughters of the Confederacy founded in 1894

Daughter of Union Veterans founded in 1885

Or you can join the Order of Confederate Rose founded in 1993. This is a way for you to support Confederate heritage, true history and southern pride. The organization is open to all ten years of age and older.

The Civil War Round table is another excellent group to join.

For information on the web just type in any of the names above.

Ripley House – 623 High Street Worthington, Ohio

The Ripley House is a gable-ended structure built for both home and business with a front entrance facing the main street for the shop. One important feature remaining today is the Adam style mantel that has diminutive fluted columns and a delicate elliptical sunburst medallion. Historically, it is the 1823 birthplace of Roswell Sabine Ripley, who attended West Point, married and settled in Charleston, South Carolina, and became a Confederate general during the War Between the States.

Brigadier General
Otho F. Strahl
Born: June 3, 1831 in
Elliotts Cross Roads, Ohio
Died: Nov. 30, 1864
In Franklin, Tennessee
Re-interred in Old City Cemetery
in Dyersburg, Tenn.

Otho French Strahl (June 3, 1831 – November 30, 1864) was an attorney and a Brigadier General in the Confederate States Army during the American Civil War. He was one of a small number of Southern generals who were born in the North.

Strahl was born near Elliotts Cross Roads, Ohio, and raised in nearby Malta, both in rural Morgan County. Strahl, one of the choicest sprits that embraced the cause of the South, and finally offered all upon her alter, was a native of Ohio, who had settled in Tennessee and was practicing law at Dyersburg when the great war of States began. Although of Northern birth, both of his grandmothers were Southern women, and perhaps had much to do with molding their sentiments which made him such an ardent sympathizer with the South. When Tennessee was making ready to cast in her lot with the Southern Confederacy, the young lawyer entered the Fourth Tennessee regiment as a captain (May, 1861). Early in 1862 he became lieutenant colonel of the regiment. As such he shared in the hardships of the regiment. As such he shared in the hardships and glories of the campaign of Shiloh, Bentonville, and Murfreesboro, in which he so conducted himself as to be promoted to colonel early in 1863, and then to the rank of brigadier-general., July 28, 1863. In the hundred days' campaign from Dalton to Atlanta in 1864, he and his men added to their already magnificent record. Mr. S.A. Cunningham, who was a boy soldier in his brigade at Franklin, November 30, 1864, has given in his magazine a graphic account of the conduct and death of his commander that fateful day. Mr. Cunningham Being that day right guide to the brigade, was near Strahl in the fatal advance, and was pained at the extreme sadness in his face, he was surprised, too, that his general went into battle on foot. The account of Mr. Cunningham continues: "I was near General Strahl, who stood in the ditch and handed up guns to those posted to fire them. I had passed to him my short Enfield (noted in the regiment) about the sixth time. The man who had been firing, cocked it and was taking deliberate aim when he was shot, and tumbled down dead into the ditch upon those killed before him. When the men so exposed were shot down, their places were supplied by volunteers until these were exhausted, and it was necessary for General Strahl to call for others. He turned to me, and though I was several feet back from the ditch, I rose up immediately, and waling over the wounded and dead took position, with one foot upon the pile of bodies of my dead fellows and the other upon the embankment, and fired guns which the general himself handed up to me, until he, too, was shot down." The general was not instantly killed, but soon after received a second shot and then a third which finished the fearful work. . "General Strahl was a model character, and it was said of him that in all the war he was never known to use language unsuited to the presence of ladies." While the army was camped at Dalton on the 20th of April, 1864, services were held in the Methodist church by Bishop Charles Todd Quintard, of the Episcopal church. On this occasion Bishop Quintard baptized General Strahl and presented him to Bishop Stephen Elliott for confirmation, with three other generals of the Confederate army—Lieutenant General Hardee and Brigadier-Generals Shoup and Govan.

Chapter VI

Historic Morgan's meeting house
Ohio Moon Sister's Confederate spies
Incidents in Ohio

Morgan Township House (1858) Okeana, Butler County, Ohio

Where the first Copperhead Society in Southern Butler County was organized on July 17, 1863.

Morgan Township, positioned along the southern border of Butler County in southwest Ohio, is a quiet, rural region that has not changed much from its Civil War days. Sprawling farms, many graced with buildings dating back to the early nineteenth century, still dominate the landscape. Residents here are faithful and active stewards of their heritage. Even in the midst of encroaching urbanization from Cincinnati and Hamilton suburbs, the people of Morgan Township have worked hard to preserve their historical treasures.

One such treasure lies within the small town of Okeana, Ohio, where stands the Morgan Township House in a lot opposite 6463 Okeana-Drewersburg Road. Built in 1858, this structure is the only surviving antebellum-era public building in Butler County that is still located on its original site. On April 20, 1857, the township trustees met in Okeana to purchase land for their new meeting place. With the aid of a tax levy, they were able to buy a %50 lot in the center of town lying within the narrow V-shaped strip of land between the Okeana-Drewersburg Road and the heavily traveled Cincinnati-Brookville Turnpike. The trustees ordered a "township house" to be built on the lot. Construction of the house was completed in 1858 at a cost of $650 for the building, $41 for fencing, $12.60 for twelve chairs, and $10.25 for one table. Official township meetings and unofficial local gatherings were held in the building until 1972. The building also served the community as a school, concert hall, voting precinct, bank, and township garage.

The most dramatic event in the history of the 1858 Morgan Township House occurred during the upheaval of the American Civil War (1861-65). Although Ohio was a steadfast pro-Union state, by 1863 many Unionist citizens in Ohio, and throughout the North, had become disenchanted by the lengthy and bloody war. Many sons and fathers had already fallen for a cause that some persons felt was not worth dying for anymore. Those dissatisfied with the long war felt that President Abraham Lincoln had overstepped his constitutional bounds granted to the executive branch of the U.S. government, and those violations were infringing upon the rights of Union citizens. They believed the war they had signed up to fight was no longer about keeping the Union together, but about freeing the slaves, as implied by Lincoln's Emancipation Proclamation of January 1863. The institution of national conscription (mandatory drafting of citizens to fill the ranks of the Federal armies) in March 1863 was the final straw for the Copperheads, who were lead by an outspoken Ohio politician named Clement L. Vallandigham from Dayton, Ohio. They called for Lincoln's immediate removal from office and for a cessation to hostilities.

The most detested of Lincoln's self-extended powers was his suspension of the writ of habeas corpus(a lawful order that allows the plaintiff to appear before a court to contest his imprisonment). The habeas corpus decision was tested by Clement Vallandigham. A lawyer and former Ohio representative to the U.S. House of Representatives, he was arrested on May 5, 1863, for speaking out against the Lincoln administration and the war. Vallandigham was a firm believer that it was time for the Union to cease fighting and issue for peace with the Confederacy. In 1862 he had risen to be a clear leader among the growing opposition to the war, a grass-roots group of people known by their political enemies as "the Copperheads." Their motto was "To maintain the Constitution as it is, and to restore the Union as it was." Although his beliefs were a minority opinion, Vallandigham was considered a threat to the United States government. Union Major-General Ambrose Burnside ordered the arrest of Vallandigham on charges of violating General Order No. 38, which stated that those who were in the "habit of declaring sympathies for the enemy" would be jailed. Vallandigham was denied a writ of habeas corpus. He was subsequently tried by a military court from May 5-6, 1863, was convicted of "uttering disloyal sentiments," and was sentenced to 2 years in Federal prison. Out of retaliation, Copperhead supporters in Dayton, Ohio burned the office of the pro-Republican newspaper *Dayton Journal.* Lincoln calmed the situation by commuting Vallandigham's sentence from imprisonment to banishment to the Confederacy. The Copperhead leader was sent under guard to Tennessee, where he was released behind Confederate lines on May 26.

Southwest Ohio was bitterly divided over the arrest and trial of Clement Vallandigham, and political tensions increased. A substantial anti-war sentiment had grown in the southern townships of Butler County, with Morgan Township being the epicenter of the unrest. Morgan Township's voting majority was composed of anti-Republican households. In the Election of 1860, only 152 of 401 voters in the township had cast their ballots in support of Lincoln. The Copperhead movement peaked in Butler County during the Summer of 1863. When Confederate Brigadier-General John Hunt Morgan and his 3,400-man cavalry division invaded Ohio at Harrison on July 13, the Copperheads in southern Butler County sought cooperation from the famous Southern raider. However, having been disgruntled by the Copperheads' lack of military support for the Confederacy, Morgan offered no assistance to these Northerners. In fact, Morgan's men often treated the Copperheads with less respect than the pro-Union residents along his path. After the swift departure of Morgan's Raiders on July 14th, the Copperheads of Butler County decided that they had to take matters into their own hands. On July 17, 1863, Copperhead citizens from Morgan, Ross, Reily, and Hanover Townships of Ohio and from neighboring Franklin County, Indiana, met at the Morgan Township House. There they organized themselves into a group called the "Butler County Mutual Protection Company." This political society would not last long.

From his sanctuary in the Confederate States, Clement Vallandigham escaped to Canada in early July of 1863. At the June 11th Ohio Democratic Convention he won the candidacy for the Democratic ticket for Governor of Ohio, in absentia. However, in the ensuing October 1863 gubernatorial election, Vallandigham lost by a landslide to pro-Union Republican John Brough. This sound defeat of the Copperhead in the Ohio elections spelled the death knell for the Butler County Mutual Protection Company. The organization ceased to meet after this event. Other Copperhead organizations in southwest Ohio continued to maintain a strong presence in politics, but the anti-war political movement in southern Butler County petered out.

Cynthia Charlotte (Lottie) Moon Virginia Bethel (Ginnie) Moon (Clark)

Lottie and Ginnie Moon: Confederate Spies Cynthia (Lottie) born in 1828 in Virginia, and Virginia (Ginnie) was born in 1844 in Oxford, Ohio and the daughters of a doctor. In 1830's the family moved to Oxford, Ohio, in the southwestern corner of the state. One of Lottie's suitors was a young man from nearby Indiana named Ambrose Burnside, and sources say that she jilted him at the altar. She finally settled down with Jim Clark, who soon became a judge.

After Dr. Moon's death, Mrs. Moon enrolled Ginnie in the Oxford Female College and moved to Memphis. One of the teachers criticized Ginnie for her Confederate leanings. She dropped out of school and went to live with Lottie and Jim, who were also pro-Southern. When the Civil War began, Lottie was 31 years old, and Ginnie only 16. Their two brothers promptly enlisted in the Confederate army.

Southwestern Ohio had a small but vocal group on Confederate sympathizers. Judge Clark became active in the Knights of the Golden Circle, a Confederate spy ring. Its operatives sometimes visited the Clarks when they were carrying secret messages back and forth. On one occasion, a courier arrived with important dispatches for Confederate General Edmund Kirby Smith in Kentucky.

Lottie volunteered to carry the messages, her first act as a Confederate spy. She disguised herself as a old woman, and headed for Lexington, Kentucky, by boat. She delivered her dispatches to a Rebel officer, and then threw off her costume. Using her acting talents, she tearfully enlisted the aid of a Union general, who helped her return home by train.

By this time, Ginnie had moved to Memphis with her mother. They wrapped bandages and nursed wounded soldiers, as the Yankees got closer to Memphis. In June of 1862, the Union took over the city. Ginnie soon began her own spying activities, carrying messages and supplies to the Rebels, boldly passing through Union lines on the pretext of meeting a beau.

In 1863, Ginnie and her mother carried messages to the Knights of the Golden Circle, pretending they were only visiting Lottie and Jim. But the Yankees knew that women were being used as Confederate spies. The Moons were preparing to return to Memphis from Cincinnati by boat, but at the last minute an officer entered their cabin with orders to search them.

As Ginnie explained the situation in her memoir; "There was a slit in my skirt and in my petticoat I had a Colt revolver. I put my hand in and took it out., backed to the door and leveled it at him across the washstand. If you make a move to touch me, I'll kill you, so help me God!"

Her tactics did no good, but she pulled the message she carried from her bosom, "dipped it in the water pitcher and in three lumps swallowed it."

In the provost marshal's office, Union officers searched Ginnie's trunks. Inside one of them, they found a very heavy quilt. They ripped it open and found that it was filled with opium, quinine, and morphine, medicines that were badly needed in the Confederate Army.

What happened next is in dispute, but apparently a Federal officer pushed Ginnie's hoop skirts aside so he could close the door, and noticed that her skirts were also quilted. The officer called for a housekeeper, who searched the spy and found more drugs quilted into her skirts, on her person, and in a large bustle in the back of her dress.

The Moons were taken to a hotel, where they were put under house arrest. Ginnie immediately requested to see her "Friend," Union General Ambrose Burnside, the same Ambrose Burnside who had courted Lottie all those years ago. He was the new commander of the Union Department of the Ohio in Cincinnati, and was busily prosecuting Confederate sympathizers in the area. He issued an order that anyone showing Southern leanings were to be tried for treason and that anyone caught helping the Rebels would receive the death penalty.

The following morning, General Burnside sent word that he would see Ginnie. Holding out both hands, Burnside said, "My child, what have you done this for?" "Done what?" she asked. "Tried to go South without coming to me for a pass. They wouldn't have dared stop you."

Since General Burnside was so understanding, the other officers sought to gain Ginnie's favor. "I was asked down to the parlors every evening to meet some of the staff officers," she wrote. "The Yankee woman in the parlor looked very indignant to see these officers being so polite to a Secesh woman."

Lottie arrived at Burnside's headquarters, dressed in disguise, and tried to convince her old beau to release her mother and her sister, but he supposedly said, "You've forgotten me, but I still remember with pleasure the hours I used to spend with you in Oxford." And he put her under house arrest, too.

For weeks, the women were kept under surveillance. Ginnie had orders to report daily at 10 a.m. to Federal General Hurlburt, hoping this would curtail her spy activities, but apparently it didn't After three months, Ginnie was ordered to leave Union territory and stay gone!

There is no record of what she did for the next eight months. Then, in 1864, she surfaced in Danville, Virginia, with her sister-in-law. Ginnie's brother was ill and had traveled to the south of France to await the end of the war. He asked his wife, children. And Ginnie to join him there. The two women received passes and started for Newport News.

But Union General Ben Butler spoiled their plans. They wouldn't be allowed to continue their journey, he said, unless they took the Union oath. Ginnie refused, but her sister-in-law felt she had to go to her husband. Later, Ginnie asked her how she could take an oath she despised. The woman said, "I didn't hear a word that man talked about. I kept saying the multiplication tables as hard as I could."

General Butler kept Ginnie in custody for a while, but in the end allowed her to return to Confederate territory. The war soon ended, but not for Ginnie. She lived another 61 years, and never accepted defeat for a single moment. Lottie became a novelist and newspaper correspondent, covering stories all over the world. That couldn't have been an easy job for a woman at that time.

They were classy ladies!

In 1861 when the Civil War broke out James Clark was head of the Knights of the Golden Circle, a secret order of southern sympathizers known as Copperheads. Because they wore copper pennies in their kepis. James Clark, one of the ablest men at the bar ever here, and well remembered as a judge, died at the Magnetic Springs House, in Statesville, New York, December 28, 1881, aged about fifty seven. He was a native of this State, and severed two terms as a judge of the Supreme Court. He was here for twelve or fifteen years. He was a man of marked ability as a lawyer, Judge and scholar. His range of reading was very wide, and he collected a fine library. For a few years he contributed to the New York Ledger and other journals. He left Hamilton, Ohio about 1864 to go to New York, and afterwards resided there.

Lottie Moon House

220 High Street Oxford, Ohio on North West corner of High St. & University Avenue

Confederate Park
Memphis, Tennessee

("Ginnie") Bethel Moon, 1844-1926. The daughter of a Confederate sympathizer. Ginnie Moon was a noted Southern Civil War spy. Born in Ohio, Ginnie moved to Memphis with her mother in 1862. She was arrested for spying soon after the Federal Army occupied the city, but escaped to continue her work elsewhere. Ginnie returned to Memphis after the war and was a heroine of the yellow fever epidemics of the 1870's. She died in New York City.

Incidents in Ohio during the Civil War:

Battle of Fort Fizzle

The **"Battle of Fort Fizzle"** (also called the **Holmes County Draft Riots and the Holmes County Rebellion)** is the name given to a skirmish that took place during the American Civil War in Holmes County, Ohio, between Federal troops and local draft resisters opposed to the Conscription Act of 1863.

Adopted by Congress on March 13, 1863, the Conscription Act authorized President Abraham Lincoln to draft men into military service in states that did not meet their volunteer quotas. When Federal officials tried to enforce the act in Holmes County in June, about 900 to 1000 locals built a makeshift fort, equipped with four artillery pieces, to prevent the act's enforcement. After a brief encounter in which two resisters were wounded, a force of 420 Federal troops dispersed the resisters, giving the place the name "Fort Fizzle" because the rebellion had "fizzled out".

The episode ended when the last four resisters who had assaulted a Federal draft official turned themselves in.

Ben McCulloch

Ben McCulloch, a small river steamer built in 1860 at Cincinnati, Ohio was impressed into Confederate Army transport service. Early in 1863 she conveyed supplies on the Tallahatchie and Sunflower Rivers and on Tehula Lake.

Following the capture of Yazoo City by the Federals, she was one of the four remaining Confederate vessels that escaped up the Tallahatchie and Yalobusha Rivers. In July 1863 she was burned on Tehula Lake by Confederate cavalry to avoid capture.

CSS Ohio Belle (1862)

CSS Ohio Belle, a 406-ton side-wheel river steamer built at Cincinnati, Ohio, in 1855, was used by the Confederate Army as a watch boat on the Mississippi River. She was captured at Island Number Ten on 7 April 1862. In 1864, Ohio Belle was employed as a U.S. Army transport. Following the Civil War, she operated briefly under the name *Alabama Belle* before being broken up in 1867.

CHAPTER VII

MT. VERNON, DAN EMMITT, SHOWDEN FAMILY AND CLEMENT VALLANDIGHAM ANTI -WAR PROTEST

Mound View Cemetery, Mount Vernon, Ohio
Grave site of Daniel Decatur Emmett

Honor of Daniel Emmett there is a Dan Emmett Music and Arts Festival in Mount Vernon, Ohio that is held in Mid-August.
For Information call 740-392-Fest (3378) or e-mail Festival@danemmettfestival.org

For Travel & Visitors Information visit Knox County Convention and Visitors Bureau at www.visitknoxohio.org
Call 1.800-837-5282 or 740-392-6102

Dan Decatur Emmett
Author of the song Dixie

Dan Emmett's House

Born: 1815 Mt. Vernon, Ohio
Died: 1904 Mt. Vernon, Ohio

This house once stood on South Mulberry Street near Ohio Avenue. It is now located off South Main St. just West of the Senior Citizen's Center and next to the Kokosing River. It is open for tours during special events or by appointment with the Knox County Historical Society.

Daniel Decatur Emmett, is remembered today chiefly for a song he wrote in 1859... Dixie. Born in Mount Vernon, Ohio of Irish ancestry, on October 29, 1815. Emmett grew up in the rough frontier community, hearing church hymns, the fife and drums of the militia and the jolly tunes of the fiddler. He taught himself to play the fiddle and began composing his own tunes at an early age. Dan first performed his song *Old Dan Tucker* at the age of 15 during a Fourth of July celebration on the village green in Mount Vernon. At 17 he joined the United States Army, becoming the leading fifer at Jefferson Barracks, Missouri. He was discharged on July 8, 1835, after the Army learned he had falsified his age in order to enlist. Afterwards he traveled with various circus bands, where he learned the technique of Negro impersonation.

In the winter of 1842-43, four stars of the minstrel profession formed a novel ensemble, consisting of the fiddle, bones, banjo and tambourine. Calling themselves the 'Original Virginia Minstrels", the four men, Dan Emmett on the fiddle, Frank Brower on the bones, Billy Whitlock on the banjo and Dick Pelham on the tambourine, first performed in public at the Bowery Amphitheatre on February 6, 1843, in New York. This unique ensemble, along with their song Old Dan Tucker, swept the entire minstrel world. Wearing ill-assorted garments, oddly shaped hats and gaudy pants and shirts, the four Virginia Minstrels were an often rowdy, fun-loving group. Within a few short months scores of similar minstrel bands were performing throughout the country. The Original Virginia Minstrels had a short life. After a financially disastrous tour of the British Isles in 1844, the group disbanded. All of the minstrels eventually returned to the United States, except Dick Pelham who remained in England.

Emmett composed Dixie with the help of the Snowden family in the spring of 1859, while with Bryant's Minstrels in New York. The tune, written as a walk around, became popular almost immediately and at the outbreak of the Civil War was popular in both the North and South. In the beginning of the war the troops of both armies marched to war to the tune of Dixie but by the end of 1861 Dixie had become identified as a Southern tune.

Dan Emmett was married to Catherine Rives in 1853 in New York. She died in 1875. In 1879 he married Mary Louise Bird, a widow with two daughters.

In addition to Dixie and Old Dan Tucker , Dan Emmett also wrote Turkey in the Straw, Old Zip Coo, The Blue Tail Fly, High Daddy, Polly Wolly Doodle, The Boatman's Dance, The road to Richmond, Walk along John, Early in the Morning, and many other popular songs of the 1800's.

In 1881 and 1882, now a man in his 60's Emmett hit the road with Leavitt's Gigantean Minstrels, playing Dixie to stand ovations, for which he was to receive $35.00 a week, board and railroad fare. He was in Chicago 1888. At the age of 80, in 1895, he took his last tour with Al Field's troupe, principally in the South, Emmett retired to Mount Vernon And lived here until his death, June 28, 1904. He is buried here in Mound View Cemetery, where his monument is surrounded by an iron fence. A stone and plaque are located on South Mulberry Street near Ohio Avenue where his birth place once stood. A memorial tribute presented to the city of Mount Vernon by the Ohio Division of the Daughters of the Confederacy in 1831 is located at the Knox County Historical Society on Harcourt Road.

Emmett was inducted into the songwriters Hall of Fame in 1970.

Seville Historical Society Museum, Seville, Ohio

This museum holds not only the history of Seville, Ohio but also a "Giant" collection of historical information on Captain and Mrs. Martin Van Buren Bates, giants of their time!

Captain Bates was a Confederate soldier from Kentucky.

The museum is only open once a month, but you can get an appointment just about anytime. Give them a call when you are going to be in the area.

330-769-4056

The museum is located at 70 West Main Street, Seville, Ohio

Seville Historical Society & Museum. Across from Triangle Park (Ask anybody for directions).

Ben Snowden Lew Snowden

Ben and Lew Snowden composing (or helping to compose) the song "Dixie"

The Snowden Family Band was an 19th century African American musical group. The children of the Snowden family of Clinton, Knox County, Ohio comprised the ensemble. The band's career stretched from before the American Civil War into living memory; no other African Americana band of their type lasted as long.

The Snowden's made their living by farming. However, through their music, they integrated themselves into their predominantly white community and entertained, corresponded with, and even taught their white neighbors. A long Knox County tradition credits them with composing (or helping to compose) the famous song "Dixie."

The Snowden children began touring sometime around 1850. Friends and contacts in other towns often invited them to perform. Their concert tours lasted for several days and brought them to settlements across rural Ohio. They traveled in a vehicle that one contemporary described as a "sort of stage coach carriage", and they typically stopped in a village or town for a one-night engagement.

Sometimes, offers come to play in more lucrative markets farther a field. Friends wrote from Missouri that "Ben if you and Lew would come out here you could make a fortune holding concerts." Nevertheless, the band rarely strayed from within a 75-mile radius of Clinton.

The band consisted of five regular members from among the seven Snowden children: Sophia, Ben, Phebe, Martha, Lew (or Lou), Elsie and Annie. Their instruments were common for the mid-19th century, and most were store-bought. Sophia and Annie played the fiddle, possibly the only females at the time known today to have done so. The band's handbills advertised this curiosity; one from the 1860s reads, "**They Have Two Female Violinists...Come And See The Violin Mastered By Females.**" Where they were well known, they often stayed with some distinguished resident for the night. The next morning, they moved on to the next settlement, usually about ten miles away. Their itinerary always remained flexible, and tours had no set duration. One friend wrote: "I suppose you have got home bouy this time...we have all putt off writing to you so as to bee shure that you may bee at home we though you may bee gone longer than you expected."

Original compositions made up some portion of the Snowden band's repertoire, although they rarely wrote these down. As a result, "We Are Goin to Leave Knox County", written in the

1860's is the only surviving song of undeniable Snowden origin. Its first verse and refrain bid the Snowden home farewell:

We are goin to leave Knox County
To lands We Nevre Sean
With nothing But our violins
To make the music ring

Fare Well knox conty
farewell fore a Whyle
fare well knox conty Dear
an friends that on ous Smile

Still, a Mount Vernon, Ohio, tradition credits the Snowden's with at least one other well-known work: "Dixie". The story, now in its third generation, dates to the 1910s or 1920s. It even prompted the local black American Legion post to place a new grave marker on Ben and Lew Snowden's final resting site in 1976, reading, "They taught 'Dixie' to Dan Emmett." However, the notion is implausible. Ben and Lew Snowden were only small children when Dan Emmett and Bryant's Minstrels first performed the now-famous walk around in New York City. Howard L. Sacks and Judith Rose Sacks propose that the writers of "Dixie" were not Ben and Lew Snowden but their parents, Thomas and Ellen Snowden. The idea also appears in a 1978 genealogy of the Greer family of Ohio, which states that "After the Greers had settled in Knox Co., Ellen (Cooper) stayed with them until she married Tom Snowden, an entertainer whose musical gifts inspired Daniel Emmett to write "Dixie".

The Snowden's made little distinction between music they wrote and music they played, so the idea that they might have collaborated or even given a song to Dan Emmett is therefore not surprising. Evidence does place Emmett where he might have encountered, or even played with, the Snowden's: His grandparents' farm neighbored the Snowden', his father may have shoed the Snowdens' horses, and his birthplace late became the Snowdens' church. Thomas Snowden, a freed slave, and Ellen Cooper, a house servant, met and married in Knox County. They had nine children, of whom seven survived infancy. Although Thomas and Ellen Snowden were both illiterate, the children attended white schools and learned to read and write.

The Snowden's were primarily farmers by trade, with their homestead located at Clinton, Ohio, a small village north of Mount Vernon. In July 1856, the 39year old Ellen Snowden became the head of household upon the death of Thomas Snowden, 53. The family soon had trouble paying the mortgage on their farm, prompting them by 1859 to add a line to their handbills proclaiming that they were trying "to secure means to pay back indebtedness upon their homestead." In 1864, the bank foreclosed on two of their farm's 8 acres. Ellen Snowden paid the rest of the mortgage the following year.

Their music allowed the Snowdens to integrate into their mostly white community. Music and the Snowdens were synonymous in the area; the 1860 census for Morris Township in Knox County lists their "Profession, Occupation, or Trade" as "Snowden Band", and in 1876 city directory for Mount Vernon lists them as "Snowden Minstrels". The Snowdens played local events, or received invitations telling them, for example, the "Snowden & Mrs. Snowden Are Respectfully

Invited to attend a Birthday Party At Mr. Samuel Alberts of their daughter on Monday Evening. Please bring your music."

Socially the Snowdens professed conservative values, praising in their letters and music such concepts as women's virtue, temperance, and piety. They attended the African Methodist Episcopal Church, one of the few in the United States at the time that used instruments during the worship service.

By 1900, Ben and Lew Snowden were the last remaining members of the family. They took up racehorse driving as a hobby and continued to farm, but it was still their music that defined them. They performed from their home's gable, and the next generation of fiddlers most likely sought them. Out. Though there is no hard evidence to prove such meetings occurred, both John Balzell and Dan Emmett likely knew the Snowdens and played with them on occasion. Ben Snowden died in 1920, and Lew Snowden in 1923. They left no know heirs.

From the book: **Way Up North in Dixie** by Harold L. Sacks and Judith Rose Sacks

Clement Vallandigham
Leader of Ohio Democratic Party
and an opponent of the American Civil War

Born: July 29, 1820 New Lisbon, Ohio
Died: June 17, 1871
Buried: Woodland Cemetery, Dayton, Ohio

Clement Vallandigham was born on July 29, 1820, in New Lisbon, Ohio. His father was a Presbyterian minister and educated his son at home. In 1837, Vallandigham enrolled at Jefferson College in Pennsylvania. He entered as a junior due to his father's previous tutoring. Vallandigham remained at the college for only a year. In 1838, he accepted a position as a teacher at a private school in Maryland. He returned to Jefferson College in 1840 as a senior, but he never graduated. He left school early to take up the study of law and was admitted to the Ohio bar in 1842.

Vallandigham went into politics in 1845 and served as a member of the Ohio legislature from Columbiana County. He served a single term and then moved to Dayton, Ohio. He took a position as the editor of a newspaper that supported the Democratic Party. Vallandigham also remained involved in politics and sought the Democratic nomination to be Ohio's lieutenant governor in 1851. The party refused to nominate him. In 1852 and 1854, Vallandigham ran for a seat in the United States House of Representatives against Fusion Party candidate Lewis Campbell. Vallandigham lost both elections. Undaunted, Vallandigham campaigned against Campbell again in 1856. Although Campbell was originally declared the winner by nineteen votes, Vallandigham won the election by twenty-three votes after a recount. In 1858, Vallandigham won reelection against Campbell by 188 votes, and in 1860, he won by 134 votes over the Republican Party's candidate. After Vallandigham's victories , the Republican-controlled Ohio legislature redrew Vallandigham's district in 1861. When Vallandigham sought reelection in 1862, Republican military hero Robert Schenck defeated him by nearly 1,250 votes.

In the years leading up to the American Civil War, Vallandigham was a staunch opponent to war to settle the differences between the North and the South. He believed that President Abraham Lincoln should let the South secede rather than use violence to keep the nation together. Vallandigham was one of Lincoln's most outspoken critics and the leading Peace Democrat in Ohio.

In April 1863, General Ambrose Burnside, commander of the Department of the Ohio, issued General Order No. 38. Burnside placed his headquarters in Cincinnati. Located on the Ohio River, just north of the slave state of Kentucky, Cincinnati had a number of residents sympathetic to the Confederacy. Burnside hoped to intimidate Confederate sympathizers with General Order No. 38.

General Order No. 38 stated:
The habit of declaring sympathy for the enemy will not be allowed in this department.
Persons committing such offenses will be at once arrested with a view of being
Tried…or sent beyond our lines into the lines of their friends. If must be understood
That treason, expressed or implied, will not be tolerated in this department.

Burnside also declared that, in certain cases, violations of General Order No.38 could result in death.

Most Peace Democrats in Ohio objected to General Order No. 38. They believed that the order was a clear violation of civil liberties, most notably the right to freedom of speech. Vallandigham helped organize a rally for the Democratic Party at Mount Vernon, Ohio, held on May 1, 1863. Peace Democrats Vallandigham, Samuel Cox, and George Pendleton all delivered speeches denouncing General Order No. 38. Vallandigham was so opposed to the order that he allegedly said that he "despised it, spit upon it, trampled it under his feet." He also supposedly encouraged his fellow Peace Democrats to openly resist Burnside. Vallandigham went on to chastise President Lincoln for not seeking a peaceable and immediate end to the Civil War and for allowing General Burnside to thwart citizen rights under a free government.

In attendance at the Mount Vernon rally were two army officers under Burnside's command. They reported to Burnside that Vallandigham had violated General Order No. 38. The general ordered his immediate arrest. On May 5, 1863, a company of soldiers arrested Vallandigham at his home in Dayton and brought him to Cincinnati to stand trial. Burnside charged Vallandigham with the following crimes;

Publicly expressing, in violation of General Orders No. 38, from Head-quarters Department of Ohio, sympathy for those in arms against the Government of the United States, and declaring disloyal sentiments and opinions, with the object and purpose of weakening the power of the Government in its efforts to suppress an unlawful rebellion.

A military tribunal heard the case, and Vallendigham offered no serious defense against the charges. He contended that military courts had no jurisdiction over his case. The tribunal found Vallandigham guilty and sentenced him to remain in a United States prison for the remainder of the war.

Vallandigham's attorney, George Pugh, appealed the tribunal's decision to Humphrey Leavitt, a judge on the federal circuit court. Pugh, like his client, claimed that the military court did not have proper jurisdiction in the case and had violated Vallandigham's constitutional rights. Judge Leavitt rejected Vallandigham's argument. He agreed with General Burnside that military authority was necessary during a time of war to ensure that opponents to the United States Constitution would not succeed in overthrowing the Constitution and the rights that it guaranteed United States citizens.

As a result of Leavitt's decision, authorities were to send Vallandigham to federal prison. President Lincoln feared that Peace Democrats across the North might rise up to prevent Vallandigham's detention. The president commuted Vallandigham's sentence to exile in the Confederacy. On May 25, Burnside sent Vallandigham into Confederate lines.

While Burnside clearly objected to Vallandigham's views, it does not appear that the general was attacking him personally. Numerous Ohioans, especially those with family members living in Southern states, openly objected to the war. Other Northern military commanders issued orders similar to General Order No. 38. Burnside attempted to restrain all Confederate sympathizers residing in the Department of Ohio.

Vallandigham remained in the South for only a few weeks. He traveled to Canada, where he sought the Democratic nomination to be Ohio's governor in June 1863. At the Democratic Party's state convention, delegates endorsed Vallandigham's efforts. They also demanded that President Lincoln allow Vallandigham to return to the United States. Lincoln agreed to do so but only if Vallandigham swore to support the Union war effort. Vallandigham refused to do so. Due to his controversial views and Union battlefield victories at Gettysburg and Vicksburg during the summer of 1863, Vallandigham lost the election to the Union Party candidate, John Brough, by nearly 100,000 votes.

Vallandigham remained active in politics and the Democratic Party for the rest of the war. He returned to the United States in 1864, violating the military court's order. Federal government officials did not seek to arrest Vallandigham for ignoring the ruling. Vallandigham encouraged Democratic Party to nominate George McClellan unanimously as its candidate in the presidential election of 1864. In February 1864, Vallandigham was elected supreme commander of the Sons of Liberty or the Order of American Knights. Members of this organization resided primarily in Northern and Border States during the Civil War and opposed the Union war effort. Many members of the Sons of Liberty were Peace Democrats and called for the immediate end to the Civil War. They also opposed the draft. Ohio government officials estimated that between eighty thousand and 110,000 Ohioans belong to these organizations, but most historians discount these numbers as being dramatically higher than the group's actual numbers.

Rumors circulated throughout the North during 1864 that Confederate sympathizers intended to free Southern prisoners at several prison camps, including Johnson's Island and Camp Chase, in Ohio. These freed prisoners would form the basis of a new Confederate army that would operate in the heart of the Union. Supposedly, General John Hunt Morgan, who had raided Ohio the previous year, would return to the state and assist this new army. The plot never materialized. General William Rosecrans, assigned to oversee the Department of Missouri, discovered the planned uprising and warned Northern governors to remain cautious. John Brough, Ohio's governor, sent out spies to infiltrate the groups of sympathizers. These men succeeded and stopped the uprising before it could occur. Confederate supporters hoped to capture the *Michigan*, a gunboat operating on Lake Erie near Sandusky. They would then use the gunboat to free Confederate prisoners at Johnson Island. Union authorities arrested the plot's ringleader, Charles Cole.

Following the Civil War, Vallandigham emerged as a leader of Ohio's Democratic Party. He served as the chairman of the Ohio Democratic Convention in 1865. He also encouraged the Democrats to adopt his "new departure" resolution. Vallandigham came to believe that the Democratic Party had to support slavery's end and equal rights for African Americans with whites if the party was ever to regain power from the Republicans.

Vallandigham's political career ended with his untimely death on June 17, 1871. While preparing the defense of an accused murderer, Vallandigham enacted his view of what occurred as the crime scene. Thinking that a pistol that he was using as a prop was unloaded, Vallandigham pointed it at himself and pulled the trigger. The gun discharged, and Vallandigham was mortally wounded.

Clement Vallandigham is buried in Woodland Cemetery in Dayton, Ohio.

Chapter VIII

Giant of Seville and Huntley Submarine

Martin Van Buren Bates **Anna Hannon Bates**

1st Lieutenant Co. A 7th Battalion
Virginia Cavalry, Confederate States of America

A baby boy was born in Letcher County in 1837 who was to emblazon his name in history as one of the most unusual men who ever lived.

Martin Van Buren Bates was of normal size at birth, was the son of normal parents and his brothers and sisters were of average height and weight. Yet Martin Bates grew into a man seven feet and nine inches tall, and for years his weight was 470 pounds. But his phenomenal physique does not by any means exhaust this amazing man's attributes and accomplishments. Although of peace loving nature, he was a courageous and fearless officer in the Civil War, gaining his commission for bravery on the battlefield. At a time when 75% of Americans lived out their careers within fifty miles of their homes, Captain Bates toured much of the world. He gained fame in the United States, Canada, England, and Europe.

These achievements would seem sufficient for any mortal in the slow-paced days of a century ago. But Bates had such a gregarious personality, such genuine liking for humanity, that he knew President Garfield, was a personal friend of President McKinley and was honored in London by Queen Victoria.

Bates acquired many nicknames, including "Baby" and Giant of the South, but his first nickname was given to him when he was eleven years of age and weighed 170 pounds. Seeing the astonishing dimensions of the boy on his eleventh birthday, his uncle said,

"That's a mighty big boy, by heck."

Martin's mother was deceived by his rapid elongation and came to the natural conclusion that he must be delicate. She forbade him to help with the household chores until she became convinced he was stronger than his older brothers.

While yet a young man Bates, journeyed to the county seat and took the examination for a school teacher, received his certificate and embarked on a teaching profession. "Well," said one of his former students many years later, "I never did care about obeying a teacher, but that "Big Boy Bates' was a fellow none of us boys ever sassed! We didn't dare. Why, he was so big his voice just sort of rumbled like a bull bellowing." Fact of the matter is, though, all the students liked Bates.

In the Civil War Bates chose the cause of the "Rebels" and enlisted in the Confederate Army as a private. Once into the conflict, Bates forsook his habitual good nature and became a fierce and capable fighter. He soon won a battlefield promotion and became Captain before the end of the war. He engaged in battles to over much of the south, and his fame spread among the "Yankees" who talked a great deal about "that Confederate Giant who was as big as five men and fights like fifty." He was severely wounded in a battle around the Cumberland Gap area and also captured, although he later escaped. After the Civil War Bates returned to his native Kentucky. He spent months renewing old friendships. But restlessness was upon him. The hectic life he had known in combat made him reluctant to settle down to a commonplace and uneventful existence. Also he was sensitive enough to foresee the coming of the feuds which had their actual beginning in the hatreds engendered by the Civil War.

"I don't want any part of the trouble that's coming to these hills." Martin Bates confided to his nephew John Wright. "I've seen enough bloodshed. I didn't want any more."

When Bates left Kentucky after selling his property, he traveled to Cincinnati and joined a circus. He immediately became one the stars of the show. Soon after he became a trooper, the circus took a preliminary swing into the eastern part of the United States, and then departed for a tour of Canada. In Halifax, Nova Scotia, Bates figured in one of the strangest encounters that ever occurred outside the pages of a fairy story. A personable young woman visited the circus at Halifax. Her name was Anna Hannon Swan, but her meeting with Bates was one of the oddest coincidences on record. Incredibly she was eight feet tall, one inch taller than Bates. The elated circus manger knew a natural attraction when he saw one. He hired Miss Swan, and when the circus left Canada for an extended stay in Europe the "giantess" was with the cast. Romance followed as the two "super people" found themselves drawn to each other. This love affair was culminated in London when Anna Hannon became Mrs. Martin Van Buren Bates.

Half of London tried to be present at the wedding. Queen Victoria found the "giants" as charming as the common people found them to be. She presented the newlyweds with a watch for each of them. At her order the watches had been made of a size to correspond with the proportions of the recipients. The watches were as large as ordinary saucers. Moreover, they were gold, studded with diamonds, and worth $1,000.00 each—a fabulous sum in that day.

Fresh from this royal welcome in England, the Bates were the stellar attraction in every city the circus played in Europe. All the acts drew applause, but the overgrown man and woman with such warm smiles were the darlings of the people. Their magnetic personalities transcended all barriers of race, custom, and language and endeared them to the spectators everywhere.

Back in the United States, Captain and Mrs. Bates remained with the circus for many years. They repeatedly criss-crossed the United States. The fame they had gained and their personal qualities combined to make them as popular in their own country as they were in Canada, England, and Europe. When the circus swung through Kentucky it was like "old home week" except that now the affable Bates had a wife to introduce to his many friends.

Quoting now from Mr. Bates' autobiography after they had toured England, Scotland and Ireland. "At Glasgow, we exhibited at the Argoyle Rooms; after a most successful season we re-crossed the River Tay. This was before the bridge was completed, and returned to our London residence.

"It was on the 18th day of May, 1872, that our first child was born only to die at birth. Doctors Cross and Buckland were the physicians in charge. It was a girl weighing eighteen pounds and being twenty-seven inches tall. This loss affected us both, and by the advice of the doctors I took my wife upon the continent. There we traveled for pleasure, only giving receptions when requested to do so by Royal Command.

"After a short tour in Ireland we decided to return to American. We left England on the second day July, 1874, upon the City of Anwerp. We journeyed west for pleasure. While in Ohio, I purchased a farm in Seville, Medina County. It consisted of 130 acres of good land. I built a house upon it designed especially for our comfort. The ceilings have a height of fourteen feet; the doors are eight and one half feet in height. The furniture was all built to order and to see our guests make use of it recalls most forcibly the good Dean Swift's traveler in the land of Brobdignag. "I had determined to become a farmer, so I stocked my farm with the best breeds of cattle, most of them being full-blooded and short horns. My draught horses are of the Norman bread. Carriage horses eighteen hands high with a couple of Clydesdale mares constitute my home outfit. I am thus specific because I am continually asked as to these matters.

"My rest was not to last long, for yielding to the soliciations of managers, I consented to again travel. The seasons of 1878, 1879 and 1880 found us leading attractions of the W.W. Cole circus.

"While we have during these years been blessed with many things, affliction again visited us in the loss of a boy, born on the 19th day of January, 1879. He was 28 inches tall, weighed twenty-two pounds and was perfect in every respect. He looked at birth like an ordinary child of six months. With this exception our lot has been one of almost uninterrupted joy."

Anna Haining Bates, born Anna Haining Swan (August 6, 1846- August 5, 1888),
Was a Canadian from Mill Brook, New Annan, (near present-day Tatamogouche), Colchester County, Nova Scotia, famed for her great height, believed to be 7'111/2" at the peak of her stature. Her parents were of average height and were Scottish immigrants.

At birth Anna weighed approximately 18 pounds. Anna was the third of 13 children, all also of around average height. From birth she grew very fast. On her 4th birthday she was 4 feet 6 inches tall. On her 6th birthday she was measured again, and she stood 5 foot 2 inches tall, an inch or two shorter than her mother. On her 10th birthday she measured at 6 feet 1 inch. By her 15th birthday Anna Swan was measured at just over seven feet tall. She would reach her full height two years later, which was 7 feed 11inches tall.

Anna excelled at literature and music and was considered to be very intelligent. She also excelled at her studies of acting, piano and voice. She played Lady Macbeth in one play.

The remaining years of Anna's life were spent quietly on the farm that she and her husband owned, in Seville, Ohio.

Anna Bates died suddenly and unexpectedly in her sleep, at her home on August 5, 1888 just one day before her 42nd birthday. She succumbed to heart failure after struggling with a thyroid goiter for some time previously.

After his wife's death, Captain Bates wired Cleveland, Ohio, for a coffin. A standard size coffin was sent as they believed that the wire was a mistake. Furious about this, he contacted them again to say that his first wire was correct. The funeral had to be delayed as it took the coffin three further days to arrive. Anna was finally buried on Monday 13th of August. Martin ordered a statue of her from Europe for her grave, sold the oversized house, and moved into the town.

In 1897 he remarried, this time to a woman of normal stature, and lived a mostly peaceful and uneventful life until his death in 1919 of nephritis. The Bates' and their son are buried in Mound Hill Cemetery in Seville, Ohio.

Anna Haining Bates

The Statue is in the Mound Hill Cemetery, Seville, Ohio.

Ohio Historic Marker in Seville, Ohio

Martin Van Buren Bates, gravestone in Mound Hill Cemetery in Seville, Ohio

Giant Fest is a "Giant of a Festival" with two local parks in Downtown Seville, Ohio. This festival has been created to commemorate the world's tallest couple, Captain Martin Van Buren Bates and his wife Anna Swan Bates. The Bates were a unique and special couple, who led extraordinary lives. Through the creation of Giant Fest, we can better publicize their life stories, both now and for years to come. A native of Kentucky, the captain stood 7-feet, 9 inches and weighed 470 pounds, Anna who was born in Nova Scotia, was 7-feet, 11 inches tall and weighed 413 pounds. **Giant Fest** is held in September. For more information contact: Velvet Eby at 330-769-9131 or contact Giant Fest P.O. Box 264 Seville, Oh. 44273. Website http://www.giantfest.com/

Artwork by R.G. Skerrett
Confederate Hunley built by Port Lavacans

According to their paper, the group was founded in Mobile, Alabama by Lavacans Edgar Collins Singer, an Ohio-born engineer; Dr. John R. Fretwell, a physician born in Mississippi; James Jones, a jeweler born in Kentucky; J.D. Braman, a merchant born in Connecticut; C.E. Frary, a Canadian-born carpenter; David Bradbury, a contractor born in Mains; Robert W.; Dunn, a trader born in Kentucky; B.A. Whitney, a merchant born in Massachusetts (who died in Charleston while Hunley was operating there) and William Longnecker, who was in the livery business in Lavaca and was born in Ohio. "The group got their start as artillerymen attached to Shea's Battalion of Texas Light Artillery, stationed at Lavaca," according to the Rhodes/Ragan paper. "In early 1863 E.C. Singer and Dr. Fretwell invented an underwater contact mine that was quickly patented in Richmond.

"All the above mentioned Lavaca men (who were associated with Singer and Fretwell), were transferred to the Engineering Department and quickly ordered to Mine Mobile Bay (Alabama) with their newly invented underwater mines (known as torpedoes during the Civil War). It was during the manufacture and deployment of these mines that the group absorbed New Orleans Inventors Horace L. Hunley, James McClintock and Baxter Watson, who had built a rather crude submarine some months earlier. The Texans decided to invest in another submarine, and the four aforementioned Lavaca men (and Horace Hunley) invested in the underwater project.

"Upon the submarine's completion it was transferred to Charleston, South Carolina by rail aboard two flat cars. E. C. Singer, J.D. Braman, R.W. Dunn, William Longnecker And B.A. Whitney (all citizens of Lavaca) are know to have been part of the original crew. Within weeks after the submarine's arrival in Charleston (and three unsuccessful nocturnal attempts against the union ironclads anchored past Fort Sumter), the vessel was seized by the Confederate Navy. Two crews were killed during operations in Charleston, and a third died on the night of February

17, 1864, following the successful attack on the USS Housatonic, the first vessel in history to fall victim to a submarine.

"Although the submarine was seized by the Confederate military, it was still owned by the Singer Submarine Corps., who received a substantial bounty for their efforts from the Confederate Government.

"The group was obviously a secret organization (hence one of the groups names 'Singer's Secret Service Corps'), and it is documented that the partners not only built and deployed underwater mines (several of which found their mark against union ships), and were engaged in railroad sabotage, but also may have built four late war submarines in Shreveport, Louisiana, and one in Galveston, Texas (surviving documentation indicates a modified Hunley design).

Ragan writes at the end of the Hunley paper, "I feel that it is my duty to inform the citizens of Port Lavaca as to their Hunley history and have thus co-authored this article with Calhoun County Historical Commission Chairman George Fred Rhodes, in the hope of finding living relatives of the men mentioned above.:

H. L. Hunley was a submarine of the Confederate States of American that played a small part in the American Civil War, but a large role in naval warfare. The Confederate States Ship (CSS) *Hunley* demonstrated both the advantages and the dangers of undersea warfare. The CSS *Hunley* was the first submarine to sink an enemy warship, although the vessel was also lost following the successful attack. The Confederate lost 32 crewmen in CSS Hunley's career. The submarine was renamed after the death of her inventor, Horace Lawson Hunley, and some time after she had been taken into the Confederate forces at Charleston, South Carolina.

H.L. Hunley, almost 40 feet long, was built at Mobile, Alabama, launched in July 1863, and shipped by rail to Charleston, South Carolina on August 12, 1863. On February 17, 1864, Hunley attacked and sank the 1240-short ton screw sloop USS *Housatonic* in Charleston harbor, but soon after, Hunley also apparently sank, drowning all eight crewmen. Over 136 years later, on August 8, 2000, the wreck was recovered, and on April 17, 2004, the DNA- identified remains of the eight *Hunley* crewemen were interred in Charleston's Magnolia Cemetery with full military honors.

Hunley, McClintock, and Watson first built a small submarine named *Pioneer* in New Orleans, Louisiana. *Pioneer* was tested in February 1862 in the Mississippi River and was later towed to Lake Pontchartrain for additional trials, but the Union advance towards New Orleans caused the men to abandon development and scuttle *Pioneer* the following month. The poorly documented *Bayou St. John* Confederate submarine may have been constructed about the same time as Pioneer.

The three inventors moved to Mobile and joined with machinists Thomas Park and Thomas Lyons. They soon began development of a second submarine, *American Diver*. Their efforts were supported by the Confederate States Army; Lieutenant William Alexander of the 21st Alabama Infantry Regiment was assigned oversight duty for the project. The men experimented with electromagnetic and steam propulsion for the new submarine, before falling back on s simpler hand-cranked propulsion system. American Diver was ready for harbor trials by January 1863, but it proved too slow to be practical. One attempted attack on the Union blockade was made in February 1863 but was unsuccessful. The submarine sank in the mouth of Mobil Bay during a storm later the same month and was not recovered.

Confederate Navy Lieutenant John A. Payne of *CSS Chicora* volunteered to be *Hunley's* skipper, and a volunteer crew of seven men from *Chicora* and CSS *Palmetto State* was assembled to operate the submarine. On august 29, 1863, Hunley's new crew was preparing to make a test dive to learn the operation of the submarine when Lieutenant Payne accidentally stepped on the lever controlling the sub's diving planes while the crew were rowing and the boat was running. This caused Hunley to dive with hatches still open, flooding her. Payne and two other men escaped; the remaining five crewmen drowned.

On October 15, 1863, Hunley failed to surface during a mock attack, killing its inventor and seven other crewmen. In both cases, the Confederate Navy salvaged the vessel and returned her to service.

Hunley was originally intended to attack by means of a floating explosive charge with a contact fuse (a torpedo in Civil War terminology) towed behind it at the end of a long rope. Hunley would approach an enemy vessel, dive under it, and surface beyond. As she continued to move away from the target, the torpedo would be pulled against the side of the target and explode. However, this plan was discarded as impractical due to the danger of the tow line fouling Hunley's screw or drifting into Hunley herself.

The floating explosive charge was replaced with a spar torpedo, a cask containing 90 pounds of gunpowder attached to a 22-foot long wooden spar, as seen in illustrations of the submarine made at this time. The spar was mounted on Hunley's bow and was designed to be used when the submarine was some 6 feet or more below the surface. The spar torpedo had a barbed point, and would be stuck in the target vessel's side by ramming. The spar torpedo as originally designed used a mechanical trigger attached to the attacking vessel by a cord, so that as the attacker backed away from her victim, the torpedo would explode. However, archaeologists working on Hunley have discovered Evidence, including a spool of copper wire and components of a battery, that it may have been electrically detonated. Following Horace Hunley's death, General Beauregard issued an order that the submarine was no longer to attack her target underwater. In response to this order, an iron pipe was attached to the bow of the submarine and angled downwards so the explosive charge would still be delivered under sufficient depth of water to make it effective. This was the same method developed for the earlier "David" type surface craft so successful against the USS New Ironsides. The Confederate Veteran of 1902 printed a reminiscence authored by an engineer stationed at Battery Marshall who, with another engineer, made adjustments to the iron pipe mechanism before Hunley left on her last mission on the night of February 17, 1864. A drawing of the iron pipe spar, confirming its "David" type configuration, was published in several early histories of submarine warfare.

Hunley made her first and only attack against a live target on the night of February 17, 1864. The vessel was the USS Housatonic. Housatonic, a 1240-ton steam-powered sloop of war with 12 large cannons, was stationed at the entrance to Charleston, South Carolina harbor, about 5 miles out to sea. In an effort to break the naval blockade of the city, Lieutenant George E. Dixon and a crew of seven volunteers attacked Housatonic, successfully embedding the barbed spar torpedo into her hull. The torpedo was detonated as the submarine backed away, sending Housatonic and five of her crew to the bottom in five minutes, although many survived by boarding two lifeboats or by climbing the rigging until rescued.

After the attack, Hunley failed to return safely. Convincing evidence that Hunley survived as long as an hour after the attack, which took place approximately 8:45 p.m. The commander of Battery Marshall reported the day after the attack that he had received "the damn signals" from the submarine indicating she was returning to her base. The signal, from a blue carbide gas signal lantern, was received at around 9:00 p.m. at Fort Moultrie on Sullivan's Island. The signal was also seen by crew members of Housatonic who were in the ship's rigging awaiting rescue. The reports are quoted in the official enquiries of both Federal and Confederate Governments and in the Official Records of the war. This type of lantern cannot be seen at distances beyond about one and a half miles, indicating that the submarine had come fairly close to shore after the attack on Housatonic.

After signaling, Dixon would have taken the sub underwater to try to make it back to Sullivan's Island. What happened next is unclear.

One possibility is that the torpedo was not detonated on command, but rather malfunctioned due to damage incurred during the attack. It was intended that the torpedo be detonated approximately 150 to 175 feet from the target, to minimize damage to the sub. However, witnesses aboard Housatonic uniformly stated that it detonated at no more than about 100 feet, and possibly as close as 75 feet from the target. If the torpedo did not explode as planned, then shock damage from the torpedo and from Housatonic's Magazine explosion might have opened the sub's seams, slowly filling her with water. Her crew may have failed to realize that the submarine was slowly going under. Submerging again would have put enough water aboard that her crew would likely have driven her directly into the shallow bottom, blocking the ballast intakes and making it impossible to pump her back out. Cold and immersion would have killed the crew relatively quickly.

In October 2008, scientists reported that they had found that Hunley's crew had not set the pump to remove water from the crew compartment, which might indicate that it was not being flooded. "It now really starts to point to a lack of oxygen make (the crew) unconscious, "the chairman of the South Carolina Hunley commission said, "They may have been cranking and moving and it was a miscalculation as to how much oxygen they had. "Her crew perished, but H. L. Hunley had earned a place in the history of undersea warfare as the first submarine to sink a ship in wartime.

The Hunley discovery was described by Dr. William Dudley, Director of Naval History at the Naval Historical Center as "probably the most important (American underwater archaeological) find of the 20th century. The tiny sub and its contents have been valued at over $40 million, make its discovery and subsequent donation one of the most important and valuable contributions ever to South Carolina.

Diver Ralph Wilbanks found the wreck in April 1995 while leading a NUMA dive team funded by novelist Clive Cussler, who announced the find as a new discovery and said that it was in about 18 feet of water over a mile inshore of the Housatonic. Wilbanks located the submarine buried under several feet of silt, which had concealed and protected the vessel for over a hundred years. The divers exposed the forward hatch and the ventilator box (the air box for the attachment of a snorkel) to identify, her. The submarine was resting on her starboard side at about a 45-degree angle and was covered in a ¼ to ¾ inch encrustation of rust bonded with sand and seashell particles. Archaeologists exposed part of the ship's port side and uncovered the bow dive plane. More probing revealed an approximate length of 40 feet, with all of the vessel preserved under the sediment.

Archaeological investigation and excavation culminated with the raising of Hunley on August 8, 2000. A large team of professionals from the Naval Historical Center's Underwater Archaeology Branch, National Park Service, the South Carolina Institute of Archaeology and Anthropology, and various other individuals investigated the vessel, measuring and documenting it prior to removal. Once the on-site investigation was completed harnesses were slipped underneath the sub and attached to a truss designed by Oceaneering, Inc. After the last harness had been secured, the crane from the recovery barge *Karlissa* B hoisted the submarine from the harbor bottom.

On August 8, 2000, at 8:37 A.M., the sub broke the surface for the first time in over 136 years, greeted by a cheering crowd on shore and in surrounding watercraft. Once safely on her transporting barge, Hunley was shipped back to Charleston. The removal operation concluded when the submarine was secured inside the Warrren Lasch Conservation Center, at the former Charleston Navy Yard, in a specially designed tank of fresh water to await conservation.

The crew was composed of Lieutenant George E. Dixon(Commander), Frank Collins, Joseph F. Ridgaway, James A. Wicks, Arnold Becker, Corporal J. G. Carlsen, C. Lumpkin, and Miller, who first name is still uncertain.

Apart from the commander of the submarine, Lieutenant George E. Dixon, the identities of the volunteer crewmen of the Hunley had long remained a mystery. Douglas Owsley, a physical anthropologist working for the Smithsonian Institution's National Museum of Natural History, examined the remains and determined that four of the men were American born, while the four others were European born, based on the chemical signatures left on the men's teeth and bones by the predominant components of their diet. Four of the men had eaten plenty of maize, and American diet, while the remainder ate mostly wheat and rye, a mainly European one. By examining Civil War records and conducting DNA testing with possible relatives, forensic genealogist Linda Abrams was able to identify the remains of Dixon and the three other Americans: Frank Collins, Joseph Ridgaway, and James A. Wicks, Identifying the European crewmen has been more problematic, but was apparently solved in late 2004. The position of the remains indicated that the men died at their stations and were not trying to escape from the sinking submarine.

On April 17, 2004 the remains of the crew of H. L. Hunley were interred in Charleston's Magnolia Cemetery with full military honors. A crowd estimated at between 35,000 and 50,000, including 10,000 period military and civilian re-enactors, were present for what some called the "Last Confederate Funeral."

Hunley remains at the Lasch Conservation Center for further study and conservation. Continued study has led to unexpected discoveries, including the complexity of the sub's ballast and pumping systems, steering and diving apparatus, and final assembly.

Tours of the Hunley

Visitors can obtain tickets for guided tours of the conservation laboratory in Charleston, South Carolina that houses the Hunley at the Warren Lasch Conservation Center on Weekends. The Center includes artifacts found inside the Hunley, exhibits about the submarine and a video.

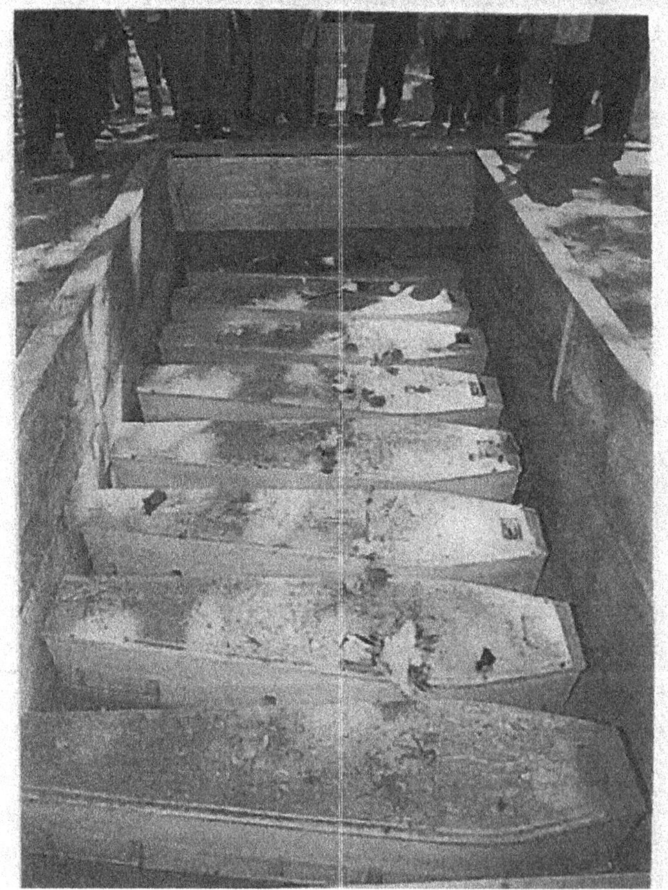

The burial of the 3rd Hunley crew Charleston, S. Carolina, April 2004

The crew men are buried at Magnolia Cemetery

Chapter IX

Ethnic groups that made up the Confederate Army:

Blacks
Jewish
Indians
Hispanics
Irish
Germans
Englishmen
Canadian
French
Swiss
Scottish
Swedes
And other groups of people that made up the greatest Army the world has ever known

Confederate soldier on the left unidentified. Confederate soldiers on right is Andrew and Silas Chandler, Co. F. 44th Mississippi Infantry posing with D- Guard.

This Chapter is in tribute of these brave Slaves and Freemen of Color who supported and fought for the Confederate States of America, and believed in the cause of Southern Independence.

In 1861 at the Battle of Manassas, Virginia noted black abolitionist Frederick Douglass Said: "There are many colored men in the Confederate Army as real soldiers, having muskets on their shoulders, bullets in their pockets, ready to shoot down loyal troops and doing all that soldiers may do to destroy the Federal government."

It has been estimated that over 65,000 Southern blacks were in the Confederate ranks. Over 13,000 of these, "saw the elephant" also known as meeting the enemy in combat. These Black Confederates included both slave and free. The Confederate Congress did not approve blacks to be officially enlisted as soldiers (except as musicians), until late in the war. But in the ranks it was a different story. Many Confederate officers did not obey the mandates of politicians, they frequently enlisted blacks with the simple criteria, "Will you fight?" Historian Ervin Jordan, explains that "biracial units" were frequently organized "by local Confederate and State militia Commanders in response to immediate threats in the form of Union raids". Dr. Leonard Haynes, an African-American professor at Southern University, stated, "When you eliminate the black Confederate soldier, you've eliminated the part of the history of the South."

1ST LOUISIANA NATIVE GUARD
1861

Tennessee in June 1861 became the first Southern State to legislate the use of free blacks as soldiers. Governor Ishiam Harris was authorized to enroll blacks between the ages of 15 to 50, who were to be paid $18 per month with the same rations and clothing as their white counterparts. By Sept. 1861 two black regiments had been mustered into Confederate service in Memphis.

The South was the only home most of the slaves and Freemen knew and some sixty thousand of them were willing to risk their lives to protect their way of life against the unknown dangers of defeat by the Union Forces. Black historian, Roland Young, says he is not surprised that blacks fought. He explains that "some, if not most, Black southerners would support their country" and that by doing so they were "demonstrating it's possible to hate the system of slavery and love one's country." Some would ask, "Why would they serve; why would they fight?" They served and fought for the same reasons as their white counterparts. They felt that the South was their home, too. Whether slave or free, each had a stake in the society and each had a home they felt endeared to. For example, many Charleston negroes actually cheered at the possibility that they would be able to shoot Yankees shortly after the outbreak of War. This is the very same reaction that most African Americans showed during the American Revolution, where they fought for the colonies, even though the British offered them freedom if they fought for them.

1. The "Richmond Howitzers" were partially manned by black militiamen. They saw action at 1st Manassas (or 1st Battle of Bull Run) where they operated battery no. 2. In addition two black "regiments", one free and one slave, participated in the battle on behalf of the South. "Many colored people were killed in the action", recorded John Parker, a former slave.

2. At least one Black Confederate was a non-commissioned officer. James Washington, Co. D 35th Texas Cavalry, Confederate States Army, he became it's 3rd Sergeant. Higher ranking black commissioned officers served in militia units, but this was on the State militia level (Louisiana) and not in the regular C.S. Army.

Top Left: Jerry Perkins - Top Right: Bill Yopp - Lower Left: Unknown Confederate Veteran – Lower Right: Ex-Confederates Buchanan, W.L. Drake, & Uncle Lewis Nelson (1920)

3. Free black musicians, cooks, soldiers and teamsters earned the same pay as white confederate privates. This was not the case in the Union army where blacks did not receive equal pay. At the Confederate Buffalo Forge in Rockbridge County, Virginia, skilled black workers "earned on average three times the wages of white Confederate soldiers and more than most Confederate army officers ($350-$600) a year".

4. Dr. Lewis Steiner, Chief inspector of the United States Sanitary Commission while observing Gen. "Stonewall" Jackson's occupation of Frederick, Maryland, in 1862: "Over 3,000 Negroes must be included in this number [Confederate troops]. These were clad in all kinds of uniforms, not only in cast-off or captured United States uniforms, but in coats with Southern buttons, State buttons, etc. These were shabby, but not shabbier or seedier than those worn by white men in the rebel ranks. Most of the Negroes had arms, rifles, muskets, sabers, bowie-knives, dirks, etc... and were manifestly an integral portion of the Southern Confederate Army."

5. Black and white militiamen returned heavy fire on Union troops at the Battle of Griswoldsville (near Macon, Georgia). Approximately 600 boys and elderly men were killed in this skirmish.

6. In 1864, President Jefferson Davis approved a plan that proposed the emancipation of slaves, in return for the official recognition of the Confederacy by Britain and France. France showed interest but Britain refused.

7. The Jackson Battalion included two companies of black soldiers. They saw combat at Petersburg under Col. Shipp. "My men acted with utmost promptness and goodwill...Allow me to state sir that they behaved in an extraordinary acceptable manner."

8. Recently the National Park Service, with a recent discovery, recognized that blacks were asked to help defend the city of Petersburg, Virginia and were offered their freedom if they did so. Regardless of their official classification, black Americans performed support functions that in today's army many would be classified as official military service.

9. Confederate General John B. Gordon(Army of Northern Virginia) reported that all of his troops were in favor of Colored troops and that it's adoption would have "greatly encouraged the army". Gen. Lee was anxious to receive regiments of black soldiers. The Richmond Sentinel reported on 24 March 1864, "None will deny that our servants are more worthy of respect then the motley hordes which come against us." "Bad faith [to black Confederates] must be avoided as an indelible dishonor."

10. In March 1865, Judah P. Benjamin, Confederate Secretary of State, promised freedom for blacks who served from the State of Virginia. Authority for this was finally received from the State of Virginia and on April 1st, 1865, $100 bounties were offered to Black soldiers. Benjamin exclaimed, "Let us say to every Negro who wants to go into the ranks, go and fight, and you are free. Fight for your masters and you shall have your freedom." Confederate Officers were ordered to treat them humanely and protect them from "injustice and oppression."

11. A quota was set for 300,000 black soldiers for the Confederate States Colored Troops. 83% of Richmond's male slave population volunteered for duty. A special ball was held in Richmond to raise money for uniforms for these men. Before Richmond fell, black Confederates in gray uniforms drilled in the streets. Due to the war ending, it is believed only companies or squads of these troops ever saw any action.

12. Union General U.S. Grant in Feb. 1865, ordered the capture of "all the Negro men before the enemy can put them in their ranks." Frederick Douglass warned Lincoln that unless slaves were guaranteed freedom (those in Union controlled areas were still slaves) and land bounties, "they would take up arms for the rebels."

13. On April 4, 1865 (Amelia County, Va.), a Confederate supply train was exclusively manned and guarded by black infantry. When attacked by Federal Cavalry, they stood their ground and fought off the charge, but on the second charge they were overwhelmed. These soldiers are believed to be from "Major Turner's" Confederate command.

14. A Black Confederate, George______, when captured by Federáls was bribed to desert to the other side. He defiantly spoke, "Sir, you want me to desert, and I ain't no deserter. Down South, deserters disgrace their families and I am never going to do that."

15. Former slave, Horace King, accumulated great wealth as a contractor to the Confederate Navy. He was also an expert engineer and became known as the "Bridge builder of the Confederacy." One of his bridges was burned in a Yankee raid. His home was pillaged by Union troops, as his wife pleaded for mercy.

16. As of Feb. 1865 1,150 black seamen served in the Confederate Navy. One of these was among the last Confederates to surrender, aboard the CSS Shenandoah, six months after the war ended. This surrender took place in England.

17. Nearly 180,000 Black Southerners, from Virginia alone, provided logistical support for the Confederate military. Many were highly skilled workers. These included a wide range of jobs: nurses, military engineers, teamsters, ordnance department workers, brakemen, firemen, harness makers, blacksmiths, wagon makers, boatmen, mechanics, wheelwrights, etc. In the 1920's Confederate pensions were finally allowed to some of those workers that were still living. Many thousands more served in other Confederate States.

18. During the early 1900's, many members of the United Confederate Veterans (UCV) Advocated awarding former slaves rural acreage and a home. There was hope that justice could be given those slaves that were once promised "forty acres and a mule" but never received any. In the 1913 Confederate Veteran magazine published by the UCV, it was printed that this plan "If not Democratic, it is [the] Confederate" thing to do. There was much gratitude toward former slaves, which "thousands were loyal, to the last degree", now living with total poverty of the big cities. Unfortunately, their proposal fell on deaf ears on Capitol Hill.

19. During the 50th Anniversary of the Battle of Gettysburg in 1913, arrangements were made for a joint reunion of Union and Confederate veterans. The commission in charge of the event made sure they had enough accommodations for the black Union veterans, but were completely surprised when unexpected black Confederates arrived. The white Confederates immediately welcomed their old comrades, gave them one of their tents, and "saw to their every need." Nearly every Confederate reunion included blacks that served with them, wearing the gray.

20. The first military monument in the US Capitol that honors an African-American soldier is the Confederate monument at Arlington National cemetery. The monument was designed 1914 by Moses Ezekiel, a Jewish Confederate, who wanted to correctly portray the "racial makeup" in the Confederate Army. A black Confederate soldier is depicted marching in step with white Confederate soldiers. Also shown is one "white soldier giving his child to a black woman for protection".—source: Edward Smith, African American professor at the American University, Washington D.C.

21. Black Confederate heritage is beginning to receive the attention it deserves. For instance, Terri Williams, a black journalist for the Suffolk "Virginia Pilot" newspaper, writes: "I've had to re-examine my feelings toward the [Confederate] flag started when I read a newspaper article about an elderly black man whose ancestor worked with the Confederate forces. The man spoke with pride about his family member's contribution to the cause, was photographed with the[Confederate] flag draped over his lap that's why I now have no definite stand on just what the flag symbolizes, because it no longer is their history, or my history, but our history."

Resources:

Charles Kelly Barrow, et.al. Forgotten Confederates: An anthology about Black Southerners (1995). Currently the best book on the subject.

Ervin L. Jordan, Jr. Black Confederates and Afro-Yankees in Civil War Virginia(1995).Well researched and very good source of information on Black Confederates, but has a strong Union bias.

Richard Rollins. Black Southerners in Gray (1994). Excellent source.

Dr. Edward Smith, and Nelson Winbush, "Black Southern Heritage" An excellent educational video. Mr. Winbush is a descendent of a Black Confederate and a member of the Sons of Confederate Veterans (SCV)

This fact page is not an all inclusive list of Black Confederates, only a small sampling of accounts. For general historical information on Black Confederates, contact Dr. Edward Smith, American University, 4400 Massachusetts Ave., N.W., Washington, DC 20016: Dean of American Studies. Dr. Smith is a black professor dedicated to clarifying the historical role of African Americans.

Bill Yopp
A Southern Sympathizer

Excerpt from Forgotten Confederates, An Anthology about Black Southerners Compiled and edited by Charles Kelly Barrow, J.H. Segars & R.B. Rosenberg.

William H. "Ten Cent Bill" Yopp truly was a beloved veteran. He was born in a small slave cabin in Laurens County, Georgia. His master's family was one of the most prominent in the area, producing several members of the state legislature and one member of the Georgia secession convention of 1861. At the age of seven, Bill was bound as a body servant to young T.M. Yopp. The two boys were inseparable. They went everywhere together and became lifelong friends.

When the war broke out, T.M. Yopp, commissioned as a captain in Co. H. 14th Geo. Infantry, promptly went to Virginia. Along with him went "Ten Cent Bill." During the many battles of the Army of Northern Virginia, Bill was always by his master's side, twice nursing him back to health from severe wounds. Bill guarded the captain's belongings and consistently found needed provisions. In addition, he served as drummer for the company. When Captain Yopp was wounded at the Battle of Seven Pines, it was Bill who cleaned the wound and nursed the captain back to health. At the Battle of Fredericksburg, Captain Yopp was again severely wounded, and Bill was right there to care for him until, owing to exhaustion, he was sent home. Nevertheless, Bill soon rejoined his master in Virginia and remained at his side for the remainder of the War. He witnessed the surrender of the Army of Northern Virginia in April 1865.

As the outcome of the war became clear, slavery ended. During the earliest days of reconstruction, Bill set out to travel and to earn a living. Yet, many years later, Bill returned to the captain's family. In time, he came to care for his former master at the Georgia Confederate Soldiers' Home in Atlanta. While at the home, Bill gained the love and respect of the other veterans. He was admitted to the Atlanta U.C.V. Camp (United Confederate Veterans) and was prominent at all activities. His relationship with the home's chairman of the board of trustees, Col. R.D. Lawrence, was warm and long-lasting.

Bill was very effective in raising funds for the home. For several years he, with the help of the Macon Telegraph, raised enough money to give each veteran in the home a gift of $3.00 at Christmas. A book written by Bill concerning his exploits before, during, and after the war was also used for many years as a fundraiser for the home. The veterans at the home were so thankful that they took up a collection in 1920 to have a medal made for Bill, and the board of trustees voted to allow him to stay at the home as long as he lived. For years Bill was an attraction at both the soldiers' home and at the state fair on the day reserved for blacks who fought for and supported the Confederacy. He was one of the last surviving veterans in the home, which closed its doors to veterans in the 1940s.

At the age of 92, Captain Yopp died. Bill was the featured speaker at the memorial service, and it was a particularly emotional one. Not long afterward, Bill joined his longtime friend in the Confederate Cemetery in Marietta, Georgia, where several residents of the home were interred. Clearly, there was not a more beloved veteran than Bill Yopp.

"Indianapolis Daily Evening Gazette" August 7, 1863
C.S.A. "Colored Patriotism!"

"Everybody knows Bill Rawlings, the good-natured barber on Market street. His wife, Mary, is now engaged in making up uniforms for the troops. Her brother (Jim Dunge) is raising a company of free negroes to fight Lincoln's men, and Bill says if anybody will furnish him with a good leg, he can whip any ten Abolitionists, but even with one leg, he is willing to hobble out to the battle-field, if the Governor wants his service." So much for the first negro company in the Rock City. The editors of the Union and American, King Isham's organ, were evidently chuckling over the prospect of seeing the bloods of the "Rock City Guards" followed by colored Jim Dunge's Rock City—Black Guards, all bearing the Stars and Bars, playing Dixie and huzzahing for King Isham and Jeff Davis at the top of their lungs. They rather intimated that the African would do the best fighting, for while the white rebels could only whip five Abolitionists apiece, the black rebels could "whip any ten Abolitionists." In fact, the rebel organ hints that a one-legged darkey could fight as well as any two-legged rebel. It is well-know that Governor Harris recently favored the enlistment of slaves as well as free negroes, in the rebel service, and the General Pillow coincided with him."

Confederate Soldier Anthony T. Welters, is pictured in this late 1800's portrait.

Welters is one of at least two Black Confederate Soldiers buried in San Lorenzo Cemetary in Saint Augustine, Florida.

Anthony T. Welters, who served in Capt. John Lott Phillips' Company B, 3rd Florida Infantry Regiment, called the St. Augustine Blues, was also known under other names, such as Anthony Wetters, Tony Fontane and Antonio Huertas. A former slave, he was born in 1810 and enlisted as a fifer in 1861, when he was 51 years old.

He participated in the battles of Perryville, Murfreesboro, Vicksburg, Chattanooga, Chickamauga, Atlanta, Franklin and Nashville.

Returning to St. Augustine, Florida after the war, Welters lived at 79 Bridge St. and became active in politics and with the E. Kirby Smith Camp, United Confederate Veterans. He died in 1902 at 92 years old.

Dr. Winbush as a small boy and his Confederate Veteran Grandfather

From the St. Petersburg, Florida Times:

Nelson Winbush who finally recalled his grandfather, Mr. Nelson and his war tales" He used to say the Yankees were the dumbest, damned people you ever seen." Dr. Winbush says, "Telling a story about Union men marching straight at rebel guns." Dr. Winbush trove of mementos includes, pension papers, and newspaper clippings describing his grandfather service in the army. He also foraged for the Rebels and, fired rifles like everyone else. When asked he thought the role of blacks in the rebel army was any less than that of whites, he said. There lives were at risk, they served, that's all that matters. His grandfather, Dr. Winbush goes on, growes up playing with white boys on the plantation and felt it was only natural to" go along with his pals" to fight Yankees. After the war, he attended 39 Confederate reunions and became a minor celebrity in his native Tennessee.

Here is a little about Dr. Winbush's grandfather: it is the story of a young slave from a Tennessee plantation named Louis Napoleon Nelson, who went to war with the sons of his master. "They grew up together," Winbush says. At first his grandfather cooked and looked out after the others, but later he saw action, fighting with a rifle under the command of Confederate General Nathan Bedford Forrest, a slave trader and plantation owner.

At Shiloh, a two-day battle in 1862 in which more than 23, 000 American men were killed or wounded, the Confederate Army needed a chaplain. Louis Nelson couldn't read or write, but he had memorized the King James Bible. He stayed on as chaplain for the next four campaigns, leading services for both Confederate and Union soldiers, before they headed back to the battlefield. He also foraged for food. One time, he killed a mule cut out a quarter and hauled it back to his comrades. "When you don't have anything else, mule meat tastes pretty good." He would tell his grandson.

Over the years, the aging veteran Winbush went to 39 Confederate reunions, wearing a woolly gray uniform that Dr. Winbush still has. In photo on page 209 he stands next to two white men who accompanied him to solders' reunions until they were old men. Through the sepia gleams a dignity earned on the battlefield. "When he came back, that was storytelling time, " Dr. Winbush says. His grandfather died in 1934.

Dr. Nelson Winbush is a retired assistant principal with a master's degree. He is a member of the Sons of Confederate Veterans. He is a well known speaker on American History. He still resides in Florida.

Cornelius Holland **Claiborne Holland**

The Holland's' were black Confederate soldiers from Glade Farms, Virginia.

The "New York Times" reprinted a Union soldiers letter in Dec. of 1861 that said:

"A body of seven hundred Negro infantry opened fire on our men, wounding two lieutenants and two privates. The wounded men testify positively that they were shot by Negroes, and that not less than seven hundred were present, armed with muskets. This is, indeed, a new feature of the war. We have heard of a regiment of Negroes at Manassas, and another at Memphis, and still another at New Orleans, but did not believe it till it came so near home and attacked our men."

Confederate Reunion in Huntsville, Alabama (1928)

Black Confederates, Why haven't we heard more about them? National Park Service historian, Ed Bearrs, states, "I don't want to call it a conspiracy to ignore the role of Blacks both above and below the Mason-Dixon line, but it was definitely a tendency that began around 1910." Historian, Erwin L. Jordan, Jr., calls it a "cover-up" which started back in 1865. He writes, "During my research, I came across instances where Black men stated they were soldiers, but you can plainly see where 'soldier' is crossed out and 'body servant' inserted, or 'teamster' on pension applications." This is the very same reaction that most African Americans showed during the American Revolution, where they fought for the colonies, even though the British offered them freedom it they fought for them.

Charleston Mercury February 1, 1864

Wanted –The Highest Price will be paid for a NEGRO MAN to cook for a Mess of Officers in Wise's Brigade. Clothing will be furnished. Apply to Capt. Fellers, A.Q. 31, 4th Va. H. Artillery, Adams' Run South Carolina.

Confederate Monument at Arlington National Cemetery In Washington, D.C.

In 1900, a Confederate Section was authorized in Arlington National Cemetery. Confederate casualties from around the cemetery were gathered and re-interred in that Section. A circular frieze of 32 life sized figures shows Southern soldiers going off to war.

Black Confederate soldier depicted marching in rank with white Confederate soldiers. This is taken from the Confederate monument at Arlington National Cemetery. Designed by Moses Ezekiel, a Jewish Confederate, and erected in 1914. Ezekiel depicted the Confederate Army as he himself witnessed. As such, it is perhaps the first monument honoring a black American soldiers. (Photo by Bob Crowell)

From the Richmond Sentinel, 3/21/65

THE BATTALION from Camps Winder and Jackson, under the command of Dr. Chambliss, including the company of colored troops under Captain Grimes, will parade on the square on Wednesday evening, at 41/2 o'clock. This is the first company of negro troops raised in Virginia. It was organized about a month since, by Dr. Chambliss, from the employees of the hospitals, and served on the lines during the recent Sheridan raid.

Confederate Monument at Arlington National Cemetery depicting a Confederate soldier entrusting his children to a slave. While Confederate soldiers were away from their homes, Union soldiers frequently would victimize southern blacks in much the same ways as southern whites. Sometimes blacks experienced even worse treatment than whites, as Union officers often protected white women, but turned a blind eye when slave women were "ravaged" or abused. (Photo by Bob Crowell)

From the Richmond Enquirer, 3/23/1865

THE CORPS D'AFRIQUE - The appearance of the battalion of colored troops on the Square, yesterday afternoon, attracted thousands of our citizens to the spot, all eager to catch a glimpse of the sable soldiers. The bearing of the negroes elicited universal commendation. While on the Square, they went through the manual of arms in a manner which would have done credit to veteran soldiers, while the evolutions of the line were executed with promptness and precision. As an appropriate recognition of their promptness in forming the first battalion of colored troops in the Confederacy, we suggest to the ladies of Richmond the propriety of presenting the battalion with an appropriate banner.

The Confederate Monument at Arlington National Cemetery in Washington, D.C.

By the end of 1901 all the Confederate soldiers buried in the national cemeteries at Alexandria, Virginia, and at the Soldiers' Home in Washington were brought together with the soldiers buried at Arlington and re-interred in the Confederate section. Among the 482 persons buried there are 46 officers, 351 enlisted men, 58 wives, 15 southern civilians, and 12 unknowns. They are buried in concentric circles around the Confederate Monument, and their graves are marked with headstones that are distinct for their pointed tops. Legend attributes these pointed-top tombstones to a Confederate belief that the points would "keep Yankees from sitting on them."

Philadelphia Inquirer 7/24/1861 Taken from the Richmond Dispatch

Free Negro Operatives – Several hundred free men of color were enlisted at the City Hall yesterday, to serve in completing the fortifications now being erected below this city. We notice in our perambulations that many of the barber shops have been closed, the operatives therein having been withdrawn for the purpose above named – Richmond Dispatch

Sir Moses Ezekiel

Born: 1844, Richmond, Va
Cadet: Virginia Military Institute
Died: Italy, 1917
Brought back to U.S.
Buried in Confederate Section Arlington National Cemetery

Moses, the son of Jacob and Catherine (DeCastro) Ezekiel. He served as Sergeant of Company C of the Cadets, Virginia Military Institute during the Civil War. After that service, he graduated from VMI in 1866.

He then studied anatomy at the Medical College of Virginia. He moved to Cincinnati in 1868 and visited Berlin, Germany, in 1869 where he studied at the Royal Academy of Art under Professor Albert Wolf. Admitted into the Society of Artists in Berlin on the merits of his colossal bust of Washington, the first foreigner to win the Prize of Roam. The Jewish Order, Sons of the Covenant, commissioned him in 1874 to execute a marble group representing religious liberty for the Centennial Exhibition in Fairmount Park, Philadelphia, Pennsylvania, and a monument of Jessie Seligman for the Orphan Asylum in New York City. After 1886, his work became largely known.

Judah P. Benjamin

1811-1884
Born in: St. Croix,
West Indies
He was raised In S.C.
Where his English-Jewish parents settled, and entered Yale at 14. He moved to New Orleans and practiced law. During the War Between the States he served as Attorney General in the Provisional Confederate Government, Serving from Feb. 25, 1861 until Sept. 17, 1861
He then served as Secretary of War for the Confederate States of America

It is estimated that 15,000 Jewish men fought for the Confederacy, including, Mosses J. Ezekiel who also was commissioned by the United Daughters of the Confederacy to sculpture the Confederate monument at Arlington National Cemetery. Judah P. Benjamin, a Jewish American, also served under Jefferson Davis as Confederate Secretary of State and Secretary of War.

In Richmond, Virginia there is a cemetery to the brave war dead. It is called the only Jewish military cemetery in the world outside the state of Israel. The cemetery is located at Richmond's Shockroe Hill. Here lies the remains of Jewish soldiers who fought for the Confederacy.

A plaque was erected here by the Hebrew Ladies Memorial Association, whose organization was organized in 1866, and lists the names of the soldiers buried here.

General Robert E. Lee allowed his Jewish soldiers to observe all holy days, while General U. S. Grant and Wm. T. Sherman issued anti-Jewish orders.

Jewish Confederate Monument at Hollywood Cemetery, Richmond, Va.

Thomas Legion's Cherokee Battalion and Bodyguards

The *Thomas Legion's* Cherokee veterans posed for their last photograph during the New Orleans Confederate Reunion in 1903. Banner inscription: "Cherokee Veteran Indians of Thomas' Legion, 69th N. Caroling Regiment, Suo-Noo-Kee Camp U.C.V. 4th Brigade, N. Carolina, Division"

Pictured from left to right: Front row: Usai, Kimson Saunooke, Jesse Ross, Jesse Reed, Sevier Skitty. Back row: Bid Saconita, Dave Owl, *Lt. Colonel William Williams Stringfield*, Lt. Suatie (Suyeta) Owl (Owle), Jim Cag, Wesley Crow, Jessan, Lt. Calvin Cagle. (Cagle is often reported as a member of the Legion, but no records confirm it. However, his presence appears to connect him to the Legion). Names were furnished by the late James R. Thomas, son of William H. Thomas.

The fifteen thousand Confederate Indian troops of the Indian Territory, of whom no more than seven to eight thousand men were in the field at one given time. By the end of the war, organized into a division of two brigades. Brig. Gen. Douglas H. Cooper commanded the division. Col. Tandy Walker commanded the second, or Choctaw Brigade, composed of Choctaw and Chickasaw units. Brig Gen. Stand Watie, a Cherokee, commanded all the Indian unites not in the Choctaw Brigade.

The Confederate congress abandoned Richmond in the spring of 1865 without acting on Cooper's promotion to major general and Tandy Walker's promotion to brigadier general.

South Carolina Confederate Indian Soldier

Unlike the rest of the Confederacy, Indian Territory troops grew more and more successful after July 1863. The great majority of the Division, still in the field and undefeated in June of 1865, was finally surrendered at Doaksville, Choctaw Nation, on June 23, 1865, by Stand Watie, the last Confederate general in the field to surrender. General Cooper only surrendered his person in May 1865.

Winchester Colbert, governor of the Chickasaws, in surrendering his troops, became the last civil authority of the Confederacy to surrender on July 16, 1865, at Tishomingo, Indian Territory.

Maj. George Washington, hereditary chief of the White Band Caddos, was the last military officer to surrender, doing so immediately after Gov. Colbert at Tishomingo in July 1865. With the Caddo surrender, the last of the Indian Division, Army of the Trans-Mississippi, Confederate States Army passed into legend.

The red warriors of the Confederacy had performed their mission; except as prisoners of war, no Yankee ever crossed the Red River, Cooper's soldiers have kept the faith.

Refugio Benavides, Atanacio Vidauri, Cristobal Benavides, John Leyendecker

Over 13,000 Hispanics joined the Confederate army. At least 2,500 Mexican Texans joined the Confederate Army. The most famous was Santos Benavides, who rose to command the 33rd Texas Cavalry as a colonel, and thus became the highest ranking Tejano to serve the Confederacy. Though it was ill equipped, frequently without food, and forced to march across vast expanses of South Texas and northern Mexico, the 33rd was never defeated in battle. Colonel Benavides, along with his two brothers, Refugio and Cristobal, who became captains in the regiment, compiled a brilliant record of border defense and were widely heralded as heroes throughout the Lone Star State. The Benavides brothers defeated a band of anti-Confederate revolutionaries commanded by Juan N. Cortina at Carrizo(Zapata) in May 1861 and on three separate occasions invaded northern Mexico in retaliation for Unionist-inspired guerilla raids into Texas. The Benavides brothers were also successful in driving off a small Union force that attacked Laredo in March 1864.

Many Tejanos who enlisted in the Confederate Army saw combat far from home. A few who joined Hood's Texas Brigade marched off to Virginia and fought in the battle of Gaines" Mill, Second Bull run, Antietam, Fredericksburg, Gettysburg, the Wilderness, and Appomattox Court House. Thirty Tejanos who enlisted from San Antonio, Eagle Pass, and the Fort Clark are joined Trevanion T.Teel artillery co. and thirty-one more joined Charles L. Pyron co., both in John R. Baylor 2nd Texas mounted rifles, which marched across the deserts of West Texas to secure the Mesilla valley. These units were later incorporated into Gen. Henry Hopkins Sibley Confederate Army of N. Mexico and fought bravely at the battle of Val Verde.

Patrick Ronayne Cleburne Confederate Maj. General
1828-1864
Killed at the Battle of Franklin, Tennessee

Most prominent among Irish Confederate commanders was General Patrick R. Cleburne, and among the best-known Irish Confederates were the troops of the 10th Tennessee. Outfitted in new uniforms trimmed in red and equipped with British Tower Muskets from the war of 1812, they endured a regimental baptism of fire during the Fort Donelson Campaign of 1862.

At 1:25 pm on Thursday, February 13th, 1862, the 10th Tennessee engaged the enemy at Erin Hollow near Dover, Tennessee. It was the only combat the troops would experience as a full regiment. Shoulder to shoulder beneath their regimental flag of Irish Green, they poured fire into the Federal Flanks. Their well crafted uniforms had been supplied by one of their own. Into battle with him went McGavock's personal battle flag which served as a reminder to his troops that he was with them. They were the defenders of their Southern Homeland. *They Were The Rebel Sons Of Erin!*

The Irish Brigade at Harrison's Landing, Va. 1862

Photo from the Library of Congress

Over 40,000 Irishmen fought for the South. While Irish Americans were regarded as second class citizens in much of the North, they found full equality and acceptance in the ranks of the Confederate Army. In fact, one Irish immigrant, Patrick Ronayne Cleburne who enlisted in the army as a private, rose to the rank of Major General before being killed at the Battle of Franklin, Tennessee. Cleburne prior to the war was active in the Democratic Party and spoke out against the constitutionality of "discriminatory legislation against Catholics and foreigners."

On May 7, 1861 Cleburne stated, "...I believe the North is about to wage a brutal and unholy war on a people who have done them no wrong, in violation of the Constitution and the fundamental principals of the government. They no longer acknowledge that all government derives it's validity from the consent of the governed. They are about to invade our peaceful homes, destroy our property, inaugurate a servile insurrection, murder our men, and dishonor our women. We propose no invasion of the North, no Attack on them and only ask to be left alone." Three days later, Nathaniel Lyon's Federal forces illegally captured the Missouri State Guard at Camp Jackson in St. Louis, immediately followed by a massacre leaving men, women, and children dead. Facing this bleak outlook, Cleburne could have returned to Ireland but he declared he would stand up for his friends, as they "have stood up [for] me on all occasions." Cleburne became a hero to generations of Irish Americans and his statue stands in the American Museum of Immigration at the base of the Statue of Liberty.

Sons of Erin, 10th Tennessee Infantry CSA
An Irish Brigade formed in Nashville, Tennessee

"Southern Men, Ragged and Starving, were fighting for the Protection of their homes."
---Father John B. Bannon---

7th Louisiana Volunteer Infantry

The 7th Louisiana Volunteer Infantry, sometimes called the Pelican Regiment, was organized in May, 1861. Although composed mainly of laborers, clerks, and farmers from New Orleans, Baton Rouge, Donaldsonville, and Livingston, Louisiana, these men would later perform so well that Gen. Richard Taylor would refer to them as a "crack regiment." Muster roll records show that, though the ten companies were raised in and around New Orleans, only 373 men were native to Louisiana. An additional 331 men were born in Ireland along with 179 hailing from other states. There were also 50 Germans, 24 Englishman, and others including Canadians, French, Swiss, Scots, and Swedes.

The unit was mustered into Confederate service, for the duration of the war, at Camp Moore, Taugipahoa, Louisiana, on June 7, 1861. Later that month the 7th, numbering more than 850 men, was ordered to Virginia where it was brigaded, along with the 7th Virginia, Colonel Kemper and the 7th Mississippi, Colonel Humphreys, under General. Jubal Early. On July 17, 1861 the 7th was engaged in the skirmish at Blackburn's Ford with a loss of 9 killed and 15 wounded. Several days later the regiment fought at First Manassas.

Under the command of Col. Harry T. Hays, the 7th would play a prominent part in Jackson's Valley Campaign as part of Gen. Richard Taylor's famed Louisiana (Tigers) Brigade. Later the unit would serve from the Seven Days Battles to Cold Harbor, fight in Jubal Early's 1864 excursion to the Shenandoah Valley, and join in the retreat to Appomattox. After Col. Hays' promotion to Brig. Gen. the regiment came under the command of Col. Davidson Penn. Other field officers included Lt. Cols. Charles DeChoiseul and Thomas Terry, and Major J. Moore Wilson.

The 7th lost 132 men at Cross Keys and Port Republic in the spring of 1862. Later it would lose 68 during Seven Days and 69 during the Maryland Campaign. At Chancellorsville 80 were killed or wounded and 24 were casualties at Second Winchester. Of the 235 engaged at Gettysburg 24% were lost. In November, 1863, at Rappahannock Station 180 were captured.

Total casualties during the war were, from a total roll of 1.077 men; 190 killed, 68 died of disease, 2 died in an accident, and 1 murdered. About 53 deserted. When surrendered at Appomattox, the 7th numbered 42 men and no officers.

CHAPTER X

WHAT WAS GOING ON BEFORE, DURING AND AFTER THE WAR BETWEEN THE STATES?

Black Code, White Slavery, The Hidden History of Slavery in New York, 200 Years of Northern Slavery, Black Slave Owners, Slavery in Canada, Jefferson Davis Inaugural Address, Town Line, New York Seceded, Confederate and Union Letters, Death in Union contraband camps, Confederate Soldiers Odds against them, Carpetbaggers, Women in Confederate Army and Jim Limber Davis.

In this chapter I would like the readers to make up their own mind on what happened before, during and after the War. By giving you facts that most people don't know about. It was never a Civil War; the U.S. Congress officially named it "The War Between the States". In the back of the book you will find a list of books I strongly recommend you to read. Everyone should find out what really happened in America that led up to the War Between the States. There were more white slaves brought to America than Black slaves and they weren't indentured servants. They were slaves and they died by alarming amount on their way to America and in America as slaves.

What was going on before, during and after the War Between the States?

Lincoln Quote:
"I am not now, nor ever have been in favor of bringing about in any way the social or political equality of the white and black races. I am not now nor ever have been in favor of making voters or jurors of Negroes, nor of qualifying them to hold office, nor of intermarriages with white people. There is a physical difference between the white and the black races which will forever forbid the two races living together on social or political equality. There must be a position of superior and inferior, and ***I am in favor of assigning the superior position to the white man."***

In May 1861 the ***Journal of Commerce*** published a list of more than a hundred Northern newspapers that had editorialized against going to war. The Lincoln administration responded by ordering the Postmaster General to deny these papers mail delivery. At that time, nearly all newspaper deliveries were made by mail, so this action put every one of the papers out of circulation.

Lincoln Quote:
"Any people anywhere, being inclined and having the power, have the right to rise up and shake off the existing government, and form a new one that suits them better. This is a most valuable, a most sacred right – a right which we hope and believe is to liberate the world. Nor is this right confined to cases in which the whole people of an existing government may choose to exercise it. Any portion of such people, that can, may revolutionize, and make their own of so much of the territory as they inhabit."

"The Emancipation Proclamation caused a desertion crisis in the United States Army. At least 200,000 Northern soldiers deserted; another 120,000 evaded conscription; and another 90,000 Northern men fled to Canada to evade the draft, while thousands more hid in the mountains of central Pennsylvania 'where' they lay beyond the easy reach of enrolling officers."

Lincoln issued the proclamation was the fear of European intervention. Europe and emancipated slaves were peacefully. and Lincoln feared that if he still supported slavery that the European powers would side with the confederacy and help to end the war with a negotiated settlement. This would have resulted in a split Union. Lincoln time and time again argued that the Civil War was not about slavery. His main concern was forcing the Secessionists to remain within the Union.

On December 10, 1860, The Daily Chicago Times candidly admitted that the tariff was indeed a tool used by Northerners for the purpose of plundering the South. The editor of the newspaper warned that the benefits of this political plunder would be threatened by the existence of free trade in the South:

The South has furnished near three-fourths of the entire exports of the country. Last year she furnished seventy-two percent of the whole...we have a tariff that protects our manufacturers from thirty to fifty percent, and enables us to consume large quantities of Southern cotton, and to complete in whole home marker with the skilled labor of Europe. This operates to compel the South to pay an indirect bounty to our skilled labor, of millions annually.

On March 12, 1861, another Republican Party mouthpiece, the *New York Evening Post,* advocated that the U.S./Navy "abolish all ports of entry" into the Southern states simply because sending hordes of customs inspectors there to enforce the Morrill tariff would be too expensive.

Protectionist tariffs require "a collector, with his army of appraisers, clerks, examiners, inspectors, weighers, gaugers, measurers, and so fourth.

The Newark Daily Advertiser was clearly aware that the free-trade doctrines of Adam Smith had taken a strong hold in England, France, and the Southern states. On April 2, 1861, the paper warned that Southerners had apparently "taken to their bosoms the liberal and popular doctrine of free trade" and that they "might be willing to go...toward free trade with the European powers." Which "must operate to the serious disadvantage of the North. "as "commerce will be largely diverted to the Southern cities." "We apprehend," the New Jersey editorialists wrote, that "the chief instigator of the present troubles—South Carolina—have all along for years been preparing the way for the adoption of free trade," and must be stopped by "the closing of the ports" by military force.

December 17, 1862—**Grant's General Order No. 11.** General Ulysses S. Grant issues his notorious General Order No. 11, which expels all Jews from his department. A Jewish businessman, one Cesar Kaskel, of Paducah, Kentucky was expelled from his home by this order. Furious, he formed a delegation that telegraphed a petition to President Abraham Lincoln. Following Grant's order would, the petition said, "place us...as outlaws before the whole world. We respectfully ask your immediate attention to this enormous outrage on all law and humanity..." There is no record of a direct reply from the President, but five days later, a message from the War Department was sent to Grant, stating, "A paper purporting to be General Orders, No 11, issued by you December 17, has been presented here. By its terms it expels all Jews from your department. If such an order has been issued, it will be immediately revoked."

"After the battle of Gettysburg in July 1863,...reported among the rebel prisoners were seven blacks in Confederate uniforms fully armed as soldiers..."

Within Lincoln's first month in office the U.S. congress with his support passed the Morrill Tariff, which was the highest import tax in U.S. history, more then doubling the import tax rate from 20% to 47%. This tax was why the southern states started to withdraw from the volunteer union.

Abe Lincoln when asked "Why not let the South go in peace?" Lincoln replied: "I can't let them go. Who would pay for the government?"

What other American president, in his first address to the American people, would have threatened a bloody war *on his own citizens* over the issue of tax collections?

Lincoln said, "I intend to make you pay taxes to the government which you say you do not owe, you say you are independent (talking about the southern states-Confederate States of America) I deny it. You are as much a part of the union as you ever were. You are bound to pay the taxes; you must let us occupy the forts we have in your territory: it depends on you whether there shall be bloodshed: If you submit, there will be none at all:" In other words, "If you obey, I will not strike you: If you disobey, my commands, if you decline to give up these forts, if you refuse to pay the *Revenue which I intend to Collect off you:* Your blood will be on your own heads." That is the result to which we are brought. Mr. Lincoln said it is not a treat.

January 14,1861 – **Corwin Amendment.** With the U.S. House Committee of Thirty-three unable to reach agreement on a compromise, Ohio Rep. Thomas Corwin, Chairman of the House Committee of Thirty-three, proposed a constitutional amendment protecting slavery where it exists that could never be further amended without approval of slaveholding states. In a stunning feat of linguistic legerdemain, the Corwin committee delivered to the House floor a draft amendment to protect slavery that never mentioned the words "slave" or "slavery" at all:

"No amendment shall be made to the Constitution which will authorize or give to Congress the power to abolish or interfere, within any State, which the domestic institutions thereof, including that of persons held to labor or service by the laws of said state."

The amendment passed the House as Joint Resolution No. 80 on February 28 by a vote of 133 to 65, which was two-thirds of the members present. In the subsequent parliamentary wrangle over whether that met the Constitution's requirement of two-thirds of the House, opponents of the amendment lost. On March 2, the Senate acted in favor of the proposed amendment by a vote of 24 to 12. Ohio and Maryland passed the Corwin amendment and on January 10, 1862 Illinois lawmakers sitting as a state constitutional convention at the time also approved it. But that action is of questionable validity. The amendment was considered for ratification in several additional states including Connecticut, Kentucky, and New York but was either rejected or died in committee under neglect as other pressing wartime issues came to preoccupy the nation's attention. The Corwin Amendment was never ratified. Abraham Lincoln supported this bill by sending letters to all the governors both north and south asking for their support to pass it.

Ohio Black Codes

In Cincinnati, a three-way fight for jobs, among Black Yankees, Irish, and Germans, led to an attempt to exile Black Yankees from the state. The struggle among Irish, German, and African American laborers for lucrative work on Cincinnati's docks led to demonstrations, then parades, then riots. Previously, Cincinnati's African American community had provided the bulk of construction laborers, porters, vendors, shoeblacks, messengers, and domestic workers—steady work in an expanding economy. The growing political power of Irish and German immigrants struggling to distinguish themselves as White men too, manifested itself in the enforcement of the repressive **Ohio Black Codes,** laws that had long been on the books but ignored. The city expelled Black Yankee children from public schools and forbade the construction of Black private schools.

By the summer of 1829, Cincinnati's African Americans were avoiding going out in public. They stopped going to hotels, restaurants, theaters, or riding public transportation. They found that they were no longer welcome to attend European American church services. Former Virginian John Malvin organized a petition drive calling for a repeal of the Black codes. In angry reaction, the city council gave each Black Cincinnatian thirty days to leave the state or post $500 surety bond (roughly $25,000 apiece, in today's money). Desperate, Malvin negotiated a sixty-day extension from the city in order for the refugees to find new homes in exile. The city's White zealots—led by not-yet-fully-White immigrant German and Irish laborers—responded to the extension on August 19, 1829 with a riot that burned down all of Cincinnati's Black residential areas.

The expulsion order and subsequent arson riot shocked Americans everywhere. It was even reported overseas. Compassion for the victims sparked collection drives for money, food, and clothing even among Southern slave-owners, and brought about the first meeting of the National Convention movement. Zephaniah Kingsley, one of Florida's wealthiest slave- owners, a man who, seven years earlier had been appointed by President Monroe to Florida's Legislative Council wrote that, "(racial tolerance) may be considered as a standard measure by which the comparative state of civilization…may be fairly estimated." He opined that Ohio had stepped outside the limits of civilized society, "in its acts of oppression against its free colored inhabitants, by which their existence seems so far to have been threatened..."

Looked at rationally, immigrant Irish and German resentment of Cincinnati's African—American workers made little sense. From the viewpoint of strict self-interest, the most severe competition that each unskilled Irish worker faced in selling his labor was not from already-employed Black workers, but from the dozen of identically unskilled Irish laborers who had just stepped off the same boat. Membership in an ethnicity in many ways resembled membership in a gang.

"White Slavery"

The Irish Slave Trade – The Forgotten "White Slavery"

They came as slaves; vast human cargo transported on tall British ships bound for the Americas. They were shipped by the hundreds of thousands and included men, women, and even the youngest of children.

Whenever they rebelled or even disobeyed an order, they were punished in the harshest ways. Slave owners would hang their human property by their hands and set their hands or feet on fire as one form of punishment. They were burned alive and had their heads placed on pikes in the marketplace as a warning to other captives.

We don't really need to go through all of the gory details, do we? After all, we know all too well the atrocities of the African slave trade. But, are we talking about African slavery?

King James II and Charles I led a continued effort to enslave the Irish. Britain's famed Oliver Cromwell furthered this practice of dehumanizing one's next door neighbor.

The Irish slave trade began when James II sold 30,000 Irish prisoners as slaves to the New World. His Proclamation of 1625 required Irish political prisoners be sent overseas and sold to English settlers in the West Indies. By the mid 1600s, the Irish were the main slaves sold to Antigua and Montserrat. At that time, 70% of the total population of Montserrat were Irish slaves.

Ireland quickly became the biggest source of human livestock for English merchants. The majority of the early slaves to the New World were actually white.

From 1641 to 1652, over 500,000 Irish were killed by the English and another 300,000 were sold as slaves. Ireland's population fell from about 1,500,000 to 600,000 in one single decade. Families were ripped apart as the British did not allow Irish dads to take their wives and children with them across the Atlantic. This led to a helpless population of homeless women and children. Britain's solution was to auction them off as well.

During the 1650s, over 100,000 Irish children between the ages of 10 and 14 were taken from their parents and sold as slaves in the West Indies, Virginia and New England. In this decade, 52,000 Irish (mostly women and children) were sold to Barbados and Virginia. Another 30,000 Irish men and women were also transported and sold to the highest bidder. In 1656, Cromwell ordered that 2000 Irish children be taken to Jamaica and sold as slaves to English settlers.

As an example, the African slave trade was just beginning during this same period. It is well recorded that African slaves, not tainted with the stain of the hated Catholic theology And more expensive to purchase, were often treated far better then their Irish counterparts.

African slaves were very expensive during the late 1600s, (50 Sterling). Irish slaves came cheap (no more than 5 sterling).If a planter whipped or branded or beat an Irish slave to death, it was never a crime. A death was a monetary setback, but far cheaper than killing a more expensive African.

The English masters quickly began breading the Irish women for both their own personal pleasure and for greater profit. Children of slaves were themselves slaves, which increased the size of the master's free workforce. Even if an Irish woman somehow obtained her freedom, her kids would remain slaves of her master. Thus, Irish moms, even with this new found emancipation, would seldom abandon their kids and would remain in servitude.

England continued to ship tens of thousands of Irish slaves for more than a century. Records state that, after the 1798 Irish Rebellion, thousands of Irish slaves were sold to both American and Australia.

There were horrible abuses of both African and Irish captives. One British ship even dumped 1,302 slaves into the Atlantic Ocean so that the crew would have plenty of food to eat. There is little question that the Irish experienced the horrors of slavery as much (if not more in the 17th Century) as the Africans did. There is, also, very little question that those brown, tanned faces you witness in your travels to the West Indies are very likely a combination of African and Irish ancestry.

In 1839, Britain finally decided on, own to end, participation in Satan's highway to hell and stopped transporting slaves. While their decision did not stop pirates from doing what they desired, the new law slowly concluded THIS chapter of nightmarish Irish misery.

But, if anyone, black or white, believes that slavery was only an African experience, then they've got it completely wrong. Irish slavery is a subject worth remembering, not erasing from our memories. But, where are our public (and PRIVATE) schools ????? Where are the history books? Why is it so seldom discussed?

Do the memories of hundreds of thousands of Irish victims merit more than a mention from an unknown writer? Or is their story to be one that their English pirates intended: to (unlike the African book) have the Irish story utterly and completely disappear as if it never happened.

"White Slavery"

When White servitude is acknowledged as having existed in America, it is almost always termed as temporary "indentured servitude" or part of the convict trade, which, after the Revolution of 1776, centered on Australia instead of America. The "convicts" transported to America under the 1723 Waltham Act, perhaps numbered 100,000.

The indentured servants, who served a tidy little period of 4 to 7 years polishing the master's silver and china and then taking their place in colonial high society, were a minuscule fraction of the great unsung hundreds of thousands of White slaves who were worked to death in this country from the early 17th century onward.

Up to one-half of all the arrivals in the American colonies were White slaves and they were America's first slaves. These Whites were slaves for life, long before Blacks ever were. This slavery was even hereditary. White children born to White slaves were enslaved too.

Whites were auctioned on the block with children sold and separated from their parents and wives sold and separated from their husbands. Free Black property owners strutted the streets of northern and southern American cities while White slaves were worked to death in the sugar mills of Barbados and Jamaica and the plantations of Virginia.

In 1855, Frederic Law Olmsted, the landscape architect who designed New York's Central Park, was in Alabama on a pleasure trip and saw bales of cotton being thrown from a considerable height into a cargo ship's hold. The men tossing the bales somewhat recklessly into the hold were Negroes; the men in the hold were Irish.

Olmsted inquired about this to a ship worker, "Oh," said the worker, "the black are worth too much to be risked here; if the Paddies are knocked overboard or get their backs broke, nobody loses anything."

Before British slavers traveled to Africa's western coast to buy Black slaves from African chieftains, they sold their own White working class kindred ("the surplus poor" as they were known) from the streets and towns of England, into slavery. Tens of Thousands of these White slaves were kidnapped children. In fact the very origin of the word kidnapped is kid-nabbed, the stealing of White children for enslavement.

Ships carrying White slaves to America often lost half their slaves to death. According to historian Sharon V. Salinger, "Scattered date reveals that the mortality for [White] servants at certain times equaled that for [Black] slaves in the 'middle passage.' And during other periods actually exceeded the death rate for [Black] slaves." Salinger reports a death rate of ten to twenty percent over the entire 18th century for Black slaves on board ships en-route to America compared with a death rate of 25% for White slaves en-route to America.

The Hidden History of Slavery in New York

In 1991 excavators for a new federal office building in Manhattan unearthed the remains of more than 400 African stacked in wooden boxes sixteen to twenty-eight feet below street level. The cemetery dated back to the seventeenth and eighteenth centuries, and its discovery ignited an effort by many Northerners to uncover the history of the institutional complicity with slavery.

To all those who think slavery was a "Southern thing," think again. In 1703, 42 percent of New York's households had slaves, much more than Philadelphia and Boston combined. Among the colonies' cities, only Charleston, South Carolina, had more.

The profits from the slave trade and products of slave labor, "fueled the world's first industrial revolution." By 1800 it also fueled moral outrage against slave trading, igniting "the first international human rights movement."

The ship *Sloop of Rhode Island,* which left the Port of New York in 1748 for West Africa under the direction of Capt. Peter James, distributed two New World commodities that had come through the Port of New York: tobacco and rum, connecting the British colonies of Virginia and Caribbean plantation economies into an Atlantic world of inebriation and addiction. In return he loaded up on cloth, guns and other manufactured goods from Europe. Later, as he sailed along the Gold Coast (today's Ghana), he traded those goods for slave, a few at a time.

In James's book that registered the deaths of thirty-eight slaves on the journey home. But even with the loss, the trafficking in slaves was profitable. A table provides a graphic illustration of just how lucrative the business was. In 1675 the average selling price of a slave in dollars in Africa was $354.89. and in New York it was $3,792.66 (that's a 969 percent markup). A hundred years later the trade was still profitable, although with a more modest return of 159 percent.

Slavery in the New England states was big business. There were over a hundred rum factories that made rum for the slave trade. There were hundreds of ships working out of the Ports of New York taking rum and trinkets to Africa to trade with the black African leaders for their people. Most slaves came thru the New England Ports were the Northerners would sell the slaves to both the Northern states and southern states. Most slaves were owned by people in England. There were blacks, Indians, and whites that owned black and white slaves. Most white slaves died because they were treated cruelly and worked to death. The white slavery were hundreds of thousand of English, Irish and Scottish. The English were mostly children taken off the streets of England. The Irish and Scottish were taken from out of their towns and sold into slavery in Jamaica and America.

The First lifetime slavery started in 1654 when Anthony Johnson from North Hampton County, Virginia, a black master convinced the court that he was entitled to lifetime services of his slave.

Johnson's Island Museum / Information Center

The museum has images, artifacts, letters and other material about Johnson's Island prison camp for Confederate soldiers. Hours: 1PM to 4PM on weekends and holidays from Memorial Day to October 1st. Out of state visitors who are unable to visit during the weekend should contact the society by e-mail jipres@johnsonsisland.org to make other arrangements. The museum is located at Ohio Veterans Home I.F. Mack Bldg. 3416 Columbus Ave. Sandusky, Ohio 44870

200 Years of Northern Slavery

The first venture from New England to Africa was undertaken in 1644 by an association of Boston traders, who sent three ships in quest of gold dusts and slaves.

The British took over in 1664, and was known as the Royal African Company..

Between 1709 and 1807, Rhode Island merchants sponsored at least 934 slaving voyages to the coast of Africa and carried an estimated 106,544 slaves to the New World.

New port, was the leading slave port, took an estimated 59,070 slaves to America before the Revolution. In the years after the Revolution, Rhode Island merchants controlled between 60 and 90 percent of the American trade in African slaves.

The colonial governments of Massachusetts, Rhode Island, New York, New Jersey, and Pennsylvania all made money from the slave trade by levying duties on slaves imports. Taxes on slave import in Rhode Island in 1717 and 1729 were used to repair roads and bridges.

The Browns, one of the great mercantile families of colonial America, were Rhode Island slave traders. At least six of them ran one of the biggest slave-trading businesses in New England, and for more than half a century the family reaped huge profits from the slave trade. The Browns played a commanding role in the New England slave trade. Their donations to Rhode Island College were so generous that the name was changed to Brown University.

From 1750 to 1770, African, Irish and Scottish slaves flooded the Northern docks.

Colonial newspapers drew much of their income from advertisements of slaves for sale. New England-made rum, trinkets, and bar iron were exchanged for slaves. When the British in 1763 proposed a tax on sugar and molasses, Massachusetts merchants pointed out that these were staples of the slave trade, and the loss of that would throw 5,000 seamen out of work in the colony and idle almost 700 ships.

The connection between molasses and the slave trade was rum. Millions of gallons of cheap run, manufactured in New England went to Africa and brought black people back. Tiny Rhode Island had more than 30 distilleries, 22 of them in Newport, Massachusetts, 63 distilleries produced 2.7 million gallons of rum in 1774.

Even after slavery was outlawed in the North, ships out of New England continued to carry thousands of slaves to American South. Some 156,000 slaves were brought to the United States in the period 1801-08, almost all of them on ships that sailed from New England ports that had recently outlawed slavery.

Northern slavery was in Vermont, New Hampshire, New Jersey, Rhode Island, Massachusetts, New England, New York, Delaware, Pennsylvania, Connecticut and Ohio.

When slavery in the North was outlawed, Northern slave's masters went South and became plantation owners. Slavery existed right up to the war. In the North General Grant had his slave till the 13th Amendment in 1865. There were more Union Generals that owned slaves then Southern Generals.

Black Slave Owners

The country's leading African American historian is Professor John Hope Franklin from Duke University. Records that in New Orleans in the 1860 census that over 3000 free blacks owned slaves.

In Charleston, South Carolina in 1860, 125 free blacks owned slaves.

Between 1822 and the mid-1840's William Ellison, owning slaves became one of South Carolina's major cotton gin manufacturers.

Ervin L. Jordan Jr. a black author writes that 169 free blacks owned 145,976 acres in Virginia before the war.

1830 census in South Carolina list 464 free blacks owning 2,715 slaves.

In 1860 Black women in Charleston owned 70% of the black owned slaves in the city.

The 1860 U. S. Government census showed more than 10,000 black slave owners. In 1860 there were at least six blacks in Louisiana who owned 65 or more slaves, the largest number 152 slaves were owned by the widow C. Richards and her son P.C. Richards, who owned a large sugar cane plantation. Another black slave owner in Louisiana, with over 100 slaves, was Antoine Dubuclet, a sugar planter whose estate was valued at (in 1860 dollars) $264,000. That year the rich wealth of southern white men was $3,978. In June 1860 there were 261,988 blacks in the south that were not slaves.

John C. Stanly of North Carolina owned 163 slaves in 1820 to work his three turpentine plantations.

Black Americans continued to hold slaves through the civil war. In 1860 black masters owned around 20,000 slaves.

Carter G. Woodson, whose grandparents and father had been slaves. He was one of the first to write about the black slave owners in his book." Free negro owners of slaves in the United States in 1830," "published in 1934"

Slavery in Canada

The first recorded slave was in New France in the region known today as Quebec in 1628.

The slaves were Indians

The citizens of New France received slaves as gifts from their allies among native people.

Many of these slaves were prisoners taken in raids against the villages of the Fox nation.

By the early 1700's Africans began arriving in greater numbers to New Frankce, mainly as slaves of the French.

When the British took over in 1759, Quebec had over 1,000 slaves.

1783 the British brought over 2000 African slaves to British Canada.

Throughout Canadian history there were over 4,092 slaves.

There were 1400 masters.

The British ended slavery in 1833.

August 1, 1834, 781,000 slaves were set free in the British empire.

A hundred million dollars was set aside to compensate the slave owners.

Jefferson Davis
President of the Confederate States of America

Jefferson Davis's Inaugural Address: Montgomery, Alabama, February, 1861

Gentlemen of the Congress of the Confederate States of America:
Called to the difficult and responsible station of Executive Chief of the Provisional Government which you have instituted, FI approach the discharge of the duties assigned me with an humble distrust of my abilities, but with a sustaining confidence in the wisdom of those who are to aid and guide me in the administration of public affairs, and an abiding faith in the patriotism and virtue of the people. Looking forward to the speedy establishment of a provisional government to take the place of the present one, and which, by its great moral and physical powers, will be better able to contend with the difficulties which arise from the conflicting incidents of separate nations, I enter upon the duties of the office for which I have been chosen with the hope that the beginning of our career as a Confederacy may note be obstructed by hostile opposition to the enjoyment of that separate and independent existence which we have asserted, and which, with the Blessing of Providence, we intend to maintain.

Our present position has been achieved in a manner unprecedented in the history of nations. It illustrates the American idea that government rests upon the consent of the governed, and that it is the right of the people to alter or abolish a government whenever it becomes destructive of the ends for which it was established. The declared purposes of the compact of the Union from which we have withdrawn were to establish justice, insure domestic tranquility, to provide for the common defense, to promote the general welfare, and to secure the blessings of liberty for ourselves and our posterity: and when in the judgment of the sovereign States now comprising this Confederacy it had been prevented from the purposes for which it was ordained, and had ceased to answer the ends for which it was established, an appeal to the ballot box declared that so far as they were concerned the government created by that compact should cease to exist. In this they merely asserted a right which the Declaration of Independence of 1776 defined to be inalienable. Of the time and occasion for its exercise, they, as sovereign, were the final judges each for itself. The impartial and enlightened verdict of mankind will vindicate the rectitude of our conduct, and He who knows the hearts of men will judge the sincerity with which we have labored to preserve the government of our fathers, in its spirit and in those rights inherent in it, which were solemnly proclaimed at the birth of the States, and which have been affirmed and reaffirmed in the Bill of Right of the several States. When they entered into the Union of 1789, it was with the undeniable recognition of the power of the people to resume the authority delegated for the purposes of that government whenever, in their opinion, its functions were perverted and its ends defeated. By virtue of this authority, the time and occasion requiring them to exercise it having arrived, the sovereign States here represented have seceded from that Union, and it is as gross abuse of language to denominate the act rebellion or revolution. They have formed a new alliance, but in each State its government has remained as before. The rights of person and property have not been disturbed. The agency through which they have communicated with foreign powers has been changed, but this does not necessarily interrupt their international relations.

Sustained by a consciousness that our transition from the former Union to the present Confederacy has not proceeded from any disregard on our part of our just obligations, or any failure to perform every constitution duty – moved by no intention or design to invade the rights of others – anxious to cultivate peace and commerce with all nations –if we may not hope to avoid war, we may at least expect that posterity will acquit us of having needlessly engaged in it. We are doubly justified by the absence of wrong on our part, and by wanton aggression on the part of others. There can be no cause to doubt that the courage and patriotism of the people of the Confederate States will be found equal to any measure of defense which may be required for their security. Devoted to agricultural pursuits, their chief interest is the export of a commodity required in every manufacturing country. Our policy is peace, and the free trade our necessities will permit. It is alike our interest, and that of all those to whom we would sell and from whom we buy, that there should be the fewest practicable restrictions upon interchanges of commodities.

There can be but little rivalry between us and any manufacturing or navigation community, such as the Northwestern States of the American Union.

It must follow, therefore, that mutual interest would invite good will and kindness between them and us. If, however, passion or lust of dominion should cloud the judgment and inflame the ambition of these States, we must prepare to meet the emergency, and maintain, by the final arbitrament of the sword, the position we have assumed among the nations of the earth. We have now entered upon our career of independence, and it must be inflexibly pursued.

Through many years of controversy with our late associates, the Northern States, we have vainly endeavored to secure tranquility and obtain respect for the rights to which we were entitled. As a necessity, not a choice we have resorted to separation, and henceforth our energies must be devoted to the conducting of our own affairs, and perpetuating the Confederacy we have formed. If a just perception of mutual interest shall permit us peaceably to pursue our separate political career, my most earnest desire will have been fulfilled. But if this be denied us, and the integrity and jurisdiction of our territory be assailed, it will be remain for us with a firm resolve to appeal to arms and invoke the blessings of Providence upon a just cause.

As a consequence of our new constitution, and with a view to meet our anticipated wants, it will be necessary to provide a speedy and efficient organization of the several branches of the Executive departments having special charge of our foreign intercourse, financial and military affairs, and postal service. For purposes of defence, the Confederate States may, under ordinary circumstances rely mainly upon their militia; but it is deemed advisable, in the present condition of affairs, that there should be a well instructed, disciplined army, more numerous than would be usually required for a peace establishment.

I also suggest that for the protection of our harbors and commerce on the high seas, a navy adapted to those objects be built up. These necessities have doubtless engaged the attention of Congress.

With a constitution differing only in form from that of our forefathers, in so far as it is explanatory of their well known intents, freed from sectional conflicts which have so much interfered with the pursuits of the general welfare, it is not unreasonable to expect that the States from which we have parted may seek to unite their fortunes with ours under the government we have instituted. For this your constitution has made adequate provision, but beyond this, if I mistake not the judgment and will of the people, our reunion with the States from which we have separated is neither practicable nor desirable. To increase power, develop the resources, and promote the happiness of this Confederacy, it is necessary that there should be so much homogeneity as that the welfare Of every portion be the aim of the whole. When this homogeneity does not exist, antagonisms are engendered which must and should result in separation.

Actuated solely by a desire to protect and preserve our own rights and promote our own welfare, the secession of the Confederate States has been marked by no aggression upon others, and followed by no domestic convulsion. Our industrial pursuits have received no check; the cultivation of our fields has progressed as heretofore; and even should we be involved in war, there would be no considerable diminution in the production of the great staple which constitutes our exports, and in which the commercial world has an interest scarcely less than our own. This common interest of producer and consumer can only be interrupted by external force, which would obstruct shipments to foreign markets – a course of conduct which would be detrimental to manufacturing and commercial interests abroad. Should reason guide the action of the government from which we have separated, a policy so injurious to the civilized world, the Northern States included, could not be dictated even by the strongest desire to inflict injury upon us; but if otherwise, a terrible responsibility will rest upon it, and the suffering of millions will bear testimony to the folly and wickedness of our aggressors. In the meantime there will remain to us, besides the ordinary remedies before suggested, that well known resources for retaliation upon the commerce of our enemy.

Experience in public stations of subordinate grade to this which your kindness has conferred on me, has taught me that care and toil and disappointments are the price of official elevation. You will have many errors to forgive, many deficiencies to tolerate, but you will not find in me either a want of zeal or fidelity to a cause that has my highest hopes and most enduring affection. Your generosity has bestowed upon me an underserved distinction, one which neither sought nor desired. Upon the continuance of that sentiment, and upon your wisdom and patriotism, I rely to direct and support me in the performance of the duties required at my hands. We have changed the constituent parts, not the system of our government. The constitution formed by our fathers is the constitution of the "Confederate States." In their exposition of it, and in the judicial constructions it has received, it has a light that reveals its true meaning. Thus instructed as to the just interpretations of that instrument, and ever remembering that all public offices are but trusts, held for the benefit of the people, and that delegated powers are to be strictly construed, I will hope that by due diligence in the discharge of my duties, though I may disappoint your expectations, yet to retain, when retiring, something of the good will and confidence which welcome my entrance into office. It is joyous in perilous times to look around upon a people united in heart, who are animated and actuated by one and the same purpose and high resolve, with whom the sacrifices to be made are not weighed in the balance against honor, right, liberty and equality. Obstacles may retard, but cannot prevent their progressive movements. Sanctified by justice and sustained by a virtuous people, let me reverently invoke the God of our fathers to guide and protect us in Our efforts to perpetuate the principles which by His blessing they were able to vindicate, establish and transmit to their posterity, and with the continuance of his favor, ever to be gratefully acknowledge, let us look hopefully forward to success, to peace, and to prosperity.

Source: Confederate Military History

Town Line, New York

In 1861, in the small hamlet of Town Line in upstate New York, 125 voters met and voted 85 to 40 to secede from the Union and join the Confederate States of America. The reasons are unclear, but an article in The Buffalo News from 1945 cites discontent with President Lincoln, treatment of Confederate soldiers at a POW camp in Elmira, the interest of self rule or perhaps an incident by some runaway slaves at a local Underground Railroad stop. It was also reported that Town Line sent five men through the Union lines to fight for the Confederate States under General Robert E. Lee.

During the American Civil War, as casualties on both side increased and the nature of the Civil War changed, the secession was slowly forgotten by members of the community but never revoked.

During World War II, it was discovered that Town Line had not rejoined the Union. The town people voted twice in 1945 and it was rejected and on 26th January 1946, Town Line voted to officially join the Union. Even today, the local volunteer fire company has the words "*Last of the Rebels*" on their shoulder patch. The desk that secession was signed on is located in Town Line, New York at the fire department.

Other parts of Northern States were talking of secession and joining the Confederate States of America. There are no official records of how many Northerners went south to fight for Dixie. It is estimated into the ten's of thousands. It is estimated that 1/3 of the West Point officers joined the Confederate States of America. There was a lot of dissatisfaction of Northerners and Northern newspapers over Lincoln's aggression to the South over taxes. Newspapers were saying, "Why don't you just let the South go in peace?" And Lincoln stated, "I can't let the South go, who is going to pay for the government?"

November 29, 1862
Letter from Confederate Soldier:

My dearest Odessa,

It is with great pain, both physically and emotionally, that I write you this final letter. Though our forces fared well at Shiloh, I became injured during a frenzied fire battle in the pitch black pouring rain night just some 60 hours past. We had secured our post at Corinth and were called by a messenger to meet the forces of a General Shegog in Holly Springs. The march was met with various atrocities and sad sights along the way. Villages and small communities burned, children crying over the crisp corpses of their parents and siblings. Animals slain up and down the road. It looked as if the devil himself had lended the Yanks a hand.

There was fighting outside of Holly Springs. We marched in at dusk, and the air was full of white haze. The ground was black, as was the sky. We couldn't see two feet in front of us. We could only hear the report of the cannon and the pleading cries of men. Our regiment was separated in the fog and night but myself and a handful of men came across the river and followed the bank until we could find a summit to plan our move. We stumbled into a Yankee bunker, caught them by surprise and let them have it good. But our fire and action gave us away and the cannons flared in our direction.

I cannot explain to you the sensation of numbness that accompanied me when my legs were separated from my torso, and the blinding fear that rushed forth as I lay alive yet dying on that bitter field, damp with rain and blood and burned wood.

After their numbers had retreated, I was picked up and bandaged into a mess of tattered sheets, then sent here to Oxford, where the university serves as a hospital for the critically injured. Our numbers are not small, and there are blessed persons here gathering their wits to prepare for the imminent arrival of General Smith and his troops. Yet there is no need for promptness where I'm concerned. My life is spilling away in pools beside my bed. I'm numb with opium and my eyesight is fading.

There is a mad General Shegog here who is quarantining all the men into an underground shelter he has devised. He claims he's going to fight the Yankees from these underground bunkers. He has claimed all our valuable possessions, including, my darling, your ruby heart locket, which you gave me to wear on the battlefield. I had worn it faithfully until the General claimed it at our camp just the night before I reached my last ballet.

If I die, and I know now that I shall, send my brother Maxwell here to Oxford to retrieve your ruby heart from the General. I want you to know that, by the time you read this, I will have died in proud duty to my land and people. In the soggy mist of this Mississippi grove, I feel that all is not lost, nor will be. My sprit will live on and fight through these other scared, scattered men. Do not mourn the loss of my body, it is but weak flesh and form. I send my love and spirit with these words. I will be with you always and will remember you in heaven.

Your loving, dying husband,
John Lucas Beauchamp III

Letter regarding Union Treatment of Slaves:

This is a letter written by Federal Chaplain and Surgeons, dated Dec. 29th 1862, Helena, Arkansas:

General, The undersigned Chaplains and Surgeons of the army of the Eastern District of Arkansas would respectfully call your attention to the Statements and Suggestions following. The Contrabands within our lines are experiencing hardships oppression & neglect the removal of which calls loudly for the intervention of authority. We daily see & deplore the evil and leave it to your wisdom to devise a remedy. In a great degree the contrabands are left entirely to the mercy and rapacity of the unprincipled part of our army (excepting only the limited jurisdiction of Capt. Richmond) with no person clothed with specific authority to look after & protect them. Among the list of grievances we mention these: Some who have been paid by individuals for cotton or for labor have been waylaid by soldiers, robbed, and in several instances fired upon, as well as robbed, and in no case that we can now recall have the plunderers been brought to justice—The wives of some have been molested by soldiers to gratify their licentious lust, and their husbands murdered in endeavoring to defend them, and yet the guilty parties, though known, were not arrested. Some who have wives and families are required to work on the Fortifications, or to unload Government Stores, and receive their meals at the Public table, while their families, whatever provision is intended for the, are, as a mater of fact, left in a helpless & starving condition. Many of the contrabands have been employed, & received in numerous instances, from officers & privates, only counterfeit money or nothing at all for their services. One man was employed as a teamster by the Government and he died in the service (the government indebted to him nearly fifty dollars) leaving an orphan child eight years old, and there is no apparent provision made to draw the money, or to care for the orphaned child. The Negro hospital here has become notorious for filth, neglect, mortality and brutal whipping; so that the contrabands have lost all hope of kind treatment there, and would almost as soon go to their graves as to their hospital. These grievances reported to us by persons in whom we have confidence, and some of which we known to be true, are but a few of the many wrongs of which they complain for the sake of humanity, for the sake of Christianity, for the good name of our army, for the honor of our country, cannot something be done to prevent this oppression and stop its demoralizing influences upon the Soldiers themselves? Some have suggested that the matter be laid before the Department of Washington, in the hope that they will clothe an agent with authority to register all the names of the contrabands, who will have a benevolent regard for their welfare, though whom all details of fatigue and working parties shall be made though whom rations may be drawn and money paid, and who shall be empowered to organize schools, and to make all needful regulations for the comfort and improvement of the condition of the contrabands: whose accounts shall be open at all time for inspection, and who shall make stated reports to the Dept.

All which is respectfully submitted Samuel Sawyer Pearl P. Ingall J.G. Forman

Letter regarding Union Treatment of Slaves:

Another letter by Charles Stevenas to Lt. J.H. Metcalf (Acting Assistant Adjutant General) on Jan. 27, 1863 describes working conditions of contrabands at Kenner, La.

"The reason the Negroes gave for their filthy conditions was that they had no time to clean up in. On inquiry I found they have worked from sunrise till dark, Sundays included, since last Sept—"

"My cattle at home are better cared for then these unfortunate persons." –Col. Frank S. Nickerson, U.S. Army

Elsewhere at Fortress Monroe in the Virginia theatre, Lewis C. Lockwood, U.S. Senator from Massachusetts testifies that this kind of abuse was committed on a widespread extent. In a letter dated Jan. 29, 1862 he writes: "Contrabandism at Fortress Monroe is but another name for one of the worst forms of practical oppression –Government slavery. Old Pharaoh slavery was government slavery and Uncle Sam's slavery is a counterpart..."

"But most of the slaves are compelled to work for government for a miserable pittance. Up to town months ago they had worked for nothing but quarters and rations. Since that time they have been partially supplied with clothing – costing on an average $4 per man. And in many instances they have received one or two dollars a month cash for the past two months.." "Yet, under the direction of Quarter Master Tallmadge, Sergeant Smith has lately reduced the rations, given out, in Camp Hamilton, to the families of these laborers and to disabled, from 500 to 60. And some of the men, not willing to see if their families suffer, have withdrawn from government service. And the Sergeant has been putting them in the Guard-house, whipping and forcing them back into the government gang. In some instances these slaves have been knocked down senseless with shovels and clubs."

"But I have just begun to trace the long catalogue of enormities, committed in the name of the Union, freedom and justice under the Stars and Stripes.

Yours with great respect,
Lewis C. Lockwood

Mrs. Louisa Jane Barker, the wife of the Chaplain of the 1st Mass. Heavy Artillery writes in 1864 regarding a contraband camp near Pt. Albany, in northern Virginia: the camp, referred to as a "village" by Mrs. Barker was ordered to be cleared out by order of General Augur. "This order was executed so literally that even a dying child was ordered out of his house---The grandmother who had taken care of him since his mothers death begged leave to stay until the child died, but she was refused."

"The men who were absent at work, came home at night to find empty houses, and their families gone, they knew not whither! ---Some of them came to Lieutenant Shepard to enquire for their lost wives and children---In tears and indignation they protested against a tyranny worse then their past experiences of slavery---One man said, "I am going back to my old master—I never saw hard time since I called myself a freeman."

In another letter of the same date: "we want to know from the Secretary of War has the Rev. Chaplain James [Capt. James] which is our Superintendent of negroes affairs has any wright to take our boy children from us and from the school and send them to Newbern to work to pay for they ration without they parent consint if he has we thinks it very hard indeed…" "the next is concerning of our White soldiers they come to our Church and we treat them with all the politeness that we can and some of them treats us as though we were beast and we cant help our selves some of them brings Pop Crackers and Christmas devils and throws among the woman and if we say any thing to them they will talk about mobin us, we report them to the Capt he will say you must find out which ones it was and that we cant do but we think very hard it they put the pistols to our ministers breast because he spoke to them about their behavour in the Church…"

Deaths in Union 'Contraband Camps'

Slaves seized under the Confiscation Acts, as well as runaway slaves who turned themselves in to Union forces, were held in so-called "contraband" camps. In his message to the Confederate Congress in the fall of 1863, President Jefferson Davis sharply criticized Union treatment of these blacks. After describing the starvation and suffering in these camps, he said: "There is little hazard in predicting that in all localities where the enemy have a temporary foothold, the Negroes, who under our care increased six-fold...will have been reduced by mortality during the war to no more than one-half their previous number." However exaggerated Davis' words may have been, it remains a grim fact that many blacks lost their lives in these internment camps, and considerably more suffered terribly as victims of hunger, exposure and neglect. In 1864, one Union officer called this death rate in these camps "frightful," and said that "most competent judges place it as no less than twenty-five percent in the last two years. "40"

Sarah Debro, a ninety year-old former slave, gave this account in 1937: "I waz hungry most of de time an 'had to keep fightin' off dem Yankee mens. Dem Yankees was mean folks. "53"

Bisland, Louisiana; During the invasion of Cajun Louisiana, the Yankee targeted slaves as part of the loot to be acquired. "Contraband" was a term used to denote slaves enticed or forced away from their masters' plantations. These poor people very often would end up serving in the Federal army or working on a government plantation. When the Confederate forces recaptured the area around Bisland, Louisiana, they discovered the pathetic condition in which these former slaves were forced to live while enjoying the charity of the United States government. One account states that two thousand of these people perished as a result of following, or being forced to follow, the Federal army in retreat. In view of the shallow graves in which many had been hastily placed, the comment was made, "They have found their freedom." The horror of a local sugar house has been described by at least two separate eyewitnesses who were either Confederate soldiers or masters searching for their former slaves. The small house was filled with dead or dying Negroes. Some were "being eaten by worms before life was extinct." The roads, "were lined with Negroes half starved, almost destitute of clothing, sick and unable to help themselves; the only question of the poor wretches, who had been two months experiencing Federal sympathy and charity, was the inquiry if their master was coming after them." The Federal army, in spite of its abundance, did not provide for these people. When their fellow Southerners discovered short on every necessity. With their fellow Southerners discovering their plight, the Confederate army, short on every necessity, assigned transportation and such food and medicine as it had at its disposal to the salvation of these poor, suffering people. Let it be remembered that it was the compassion of their fellow Southerners and the assistance of the Confederate army that saved the lives of these black Southerners. "74" **Article taken from the book "The South was Right," Authors: Donald and Ronald Kennedy**.

The Confederate Soldiers Terrible Odds that they Fought Against

Honoring the greatest fighting machine to march on the face of the earth, The Confederate Soldier motivated by the profound emotional connection between military service and the protection of home and family.

The Confederate were mostly volunteers, his average age was 21-23, but there were some in their early teens and young as 8 years old and some in their 60's Most of which were illiterate and 60-70% were farmers by trade. They worked their land with their own hands and did this without slaves.

These Southern patriots were raised under the shadow of The War for Independence. They were brought up to honor and respect that struggle by their fathers and grandfathers. They knew from this up bringing. The War for Independence was to insure the people and states the right to rule themselves. It is not too difficult to understand why these Southerners and many Northerners "That's right" Northerners, fought for self rule and state rights.

These Confederate warriors were underfed, under clothed, and almost never paid his $11 a month. They fought until the very end and begged for another to at them when Lee surrendered! They were fighting for the very thing their fathers fought for, Independence.

The following, although written by a Union officer, ought to be in every school history of the South, so that the children of the men who fought the South's battles should know the odds they contended against. In an article which appeared first in the Century Magazine and afterwards in the third volume of "Battles and Leaders of the Civil War," Union General Buell said: "It required a naval fleet and 15,000 troops to advance against a weak fort, manned by less than 100 men, at Fort Henry; 35,000, with navel cooperation, to overcome 12,000 at Donelson; 60,000 to secure a victory over 40,000 at Pittsburg Landing(Shiloh); 120,000 to enforce the retreat of 65,000 entrenched, after a month's fighting and maneuvering at Corinth; 100,000 repelled by 80,000 in the first Peninsula campaign against Richmond; 70,000 with a powerful navel force, to inspire the campaign which lasted nine months, against 40,000 at Vicksburg; 90,000 to barely withstand the assault of 70,000 at Gettysburg; 115,000 sustaining a frightful repulse from 60,000 at Fredericksburg; 1000,000 attacked and defeated by 50,000 at Chancellors Ville; 85,000 held in check two days by 40,000 at Antietam; 43,000 retaining the field uncertainly against 38,000 at Stone River (Murfreesboro); 70,000 defeated at Chickamauga, and beleaguered by 70,000 at Chattanooga; 80,000 merely to break the investing line of 45,000 at Chattanooga, and 100,000 to press back 50,000 increased at last to 70,000 from Chattanooga to Atlanta, a distance of 120 miles, and then let go an operation which is commemorated at festive reunions by the standing toast of "One hundred days under fire," 50,000 to defeat the investing line of 30,000 at Nashville; and, finally, 120,000 to overcome 60,000 with exhaustion after a struggle of a year in Virginia.

The Carpet-Baggers

"His like the world has never seen from the days of Cain or of the forty thieves in the fabled time of Ala Baba. Like the wind, he blows and we hear the sound thereof, but no man knoweth whence it cometh or whither it goeth. National historians will be in doubt how to class him. Ornithologists will claim him, because in may respects he is a bird of prey. He lives only on corruption, and takes his flight as soon as the carcass is picked. He is no product of the war. He is a "canker of a calm world' and of peace, which is despotism enforced by bayonets. His valor is discretion; his industry perpetual strife; and his eloquence' the parcel of a reckoning' of chances as he smell Out a path which may lead from the White House to a custom house, a post office, the internal revenue bureau, or perchance, to either wing of the Federal capitol. His shibboleth is 'The Republican Party.' From that party he sprung as naturally as a maggot from putrefaction. Wherever two or three or four Negroes are gathered together, he, like a leprous spot, is seen, and his cry, like the daughter of the horse leech, is always, Give, give me office. Without office he is nothing; with office, he is a pest and public nuisance. Out of office he is a beggar; in office he grows rich till his eyes stick out with fatness. Out of office he is, hat in hand, the outside ornament of every Negro's cabin, a plantation loafer and the nation's laze-rone; in office he is an adept in 'addition, division and silence.' Out of office he is the orphan ward of the administration and the general sign-post of penury; in office he is the complaining suppliant for social equality with Southern gentlemen." (Norwood.) This is a splendid picture in general of the carpet-bagger during the days of reconstruction.

Alabama had become insolvent, and "Governor Lewis, Republican, said to the legislature that he could not sell for money any of the State bonds." The State debt had grown to the enormous sum of $25,500,000, besides county and city debts of vast sums. "Corruption marked the Republican management as its own. The scoundrel class was in office. Strife between whites and blacks still stirred up by Spencer and his henchmen. Immigration was prevented, emigration from the State by whites going steadily on. Capital shrank from the State into which it had corruptibly rushed a few years ago. For six years the State had been losing at all outlets." Such was Alabama. It was even worse in South Carolina, Louisiana and other States.

In North Carolina, July 4, 1868, "this new State government was organized. Senate, 38 Republicans, 12 Democrats, 12 carpet-baggers. Outside the legislature, in the lobby, a swarm of the same king,...all of them disreputable. The treasury was robbed, the school fund stolen to pay per diems. The educational investments in securities were sold out at nearly one third their par value to the Republican treasurer for himself and his associates...In less than four months, this legislature authorized a State debt of over $25,000,000 in bonds, in addition to $16,000,000 for various minor schemes. The entire debt imposed by reconstruction of North Carolina exceeded $38,000,000, while the taxable wealth of the State at that time was returned at $120,000,000.... Similar Corruption in municipal bonds. Yet not a mile of railroad was built, although $14,000,000 in bonds were actually issued. Not a child, white or black, was educated for two years; not a public building erected, no State improvements anywhere." (Noted Men of the Solid South.)

Alabama's debt, before Republican rule, was $8,336,083; at the end, $25,503,593.

In North Carolina, the assessed property in 1860 was $292,000,000; taxes, $543,000. In 1870, assessed property, $130,000,000; taxes, $1,160,000, showing a difference between local government and enforced military government under carpet-baggers.

In South Carolina, in 1860, the taxable property was $490,000,000; taxes, $400,000. In 1870 (Republican rule), assessed property, $184,000,000; taxes,$2,000,000 a year. In Georgia, in 1860, the taxable property was $672,322,777; in 1870, $226,329,767. When Governor Bullock became governor, the State debt was $5,827,000; at the date of his flight, the debt was reported to be $12,500,000; bond endorsements amounted to $5,733,000, aggregate over $18,000,000.

In Florida, property decreased in value 45 per cent in eight years of Republican rule, from 1867 to 1875.

In Mississippi, 6,400,000 acres of land were forfeited to the State in payment of excessive taxation, and large amounts were collected as taxes and squandered.

In Louisiana, during Republican rule, New Orleans city property decreased in value $58,104,864 in eight years. County property decreased more then one-half, or from $99,266,839 to $47,141,690. One hundred and forty million of dollars were squandered with nothing to show for it; State debt increased more than $40,000,000; city property depreciated 40 per cent, county property 50 percent.

Source: Reconstruction Confederate Military History Vol. 12

"Lieutenant Harry Buford" AKA- Loreta Janeta Velazquez

Estimates there were as many as 250 women in the Ranks of the Confederate Army disguised as men.

The Confederate soldiers appeared to have defeated their Union opponents at the Battle of Shiloh. Confederate Lt. Harry Buford, a handsome, scrappy officer, anticipated a glorious victory for his army. But all that exuberance was to be short-lived.

The next day, April 7, 1862, a retrenched, reinforced Union army miraculously rebounded and crushed the South decisively. Rather than feeling the expected flush of victory, surviving Southern soldiers felt lucky they had escaped the battlefield with their lives.

After the dust of war settled, Buford and some fellow soldiers revisited the Tennessee battlefield. They witnessed the horrible aftermath: dead men and horses, body parts and broken wagons littered the grounds. The aftermath consumed over 23,000 men dead, wounded or missing from both sides. The soldiers knew war was not to end anytime soon.

As Buford rode along the battleground, he was suddenly thrown off his horse and struck the ground forcefully. A soldier helped the shaken lieutenant up. Buford remounted and rode back to camp with an extreme pain in his hand and arm. Enduring the pain until he could no longer avoid medical care, the agonized lieutenant sent for a surgeon. The doctor examined Buford and began to suspect something amiss. Only then did the lieutenant reluctantly disclose the truth. His name wasn't Buford, and he wasn't a man, but a woman who'd been masquerading so well that she'd fooled her commanding officer—her husband!

Loreta J .Velazquez was born June 26, 1842, in Havana, Cuba, of a Spanish father and French-American mother. Her family inherited an estate in Texas, but did have a chance to move in before the Mexican-American War began. Her father served in the Mexican army as an officer. After Mexico's defeat, he abandoned his estate rather than become a Texan and U.S. citizen.

While living in Puerto de Palmas, Cuba, the Velázquez's' hired an English governess to tutor their young daughter. The girl would later live with her aunt in New Orleans and become accomplished in the English language. Throughout her childhood, Loreta was inspired by the story of Joan of Arc. She dreamed of being a war hero and had a growing obsession to be a man. As a child, she would dress as her male role models and heroes, such as Columbus and Capt. James Cook.

Lt. Harry Buford, CSA-AKA-Loreta J. Velazquez at Johnson Island Prison Camp, Sandusky Bay, Ohio

On April 5, 1856, Loreta married a U.S. Army officer whom she referred to only as "William" in her memoirs. Her family disowned her. She was a dutiful wife and mother, but after the deaths of her three children, her grief revived her childhood notions of pursuing battle. William reluctantly resigned his commission from the U.S. Army and hesitantly joined the Confederate army at the wishes of Loreta and his father. Meanwhile, Loreta continued to possess this burning desire for a war to happen and a stronger inclination to dress as a soldier engaging battle. William tried to discourage Loreta by allowing her to disguise herself in one of his Confederate uniforms and accompanying him in a local bar full of men. William assumed that once Loreta saw how vulgar men Acted in the absence of women, she would not be so inclined to pursue her desire. While at the bar, two dear male friends of the couple came up to greet them. They did not recognize Loreta. This boosted her confidence of her new male identity.

On April 8, 1861, William went off to war thinking Loreta had changed her mind about battle. However, the moment he was gone, she pursued her dream of war. With the help of a good tailor, wire body shields and loose undergarments, a handsomely dressed Confederate soldier stood in the mirror ready for a gallant new life. All evidence of a beautiful, slender woman vanished. Now, the aspirations of a child influenced by Joan of Arc were to be realized. Loreta neatly packed a trunkful of Confederate officer uniforms. On the lid of the trunk were the shiny letters of her new name – "Lieutenant H.T. Buford, C.S.A."

She swore a male friend to secrecy and with his help fine-tuned her act –the appearance and mannerisms of a male Confederate officer ready for combat. After that careful preparation, her plan was to recruit a battalion and present it to her unsuspecting husband for his commend. At her own research and expense, Loreta recruited a battalion of men in the name of the state of Virginia. She established a regiment and a chain of command beneath her that included two subordinate officers, a sergeant and a corporal. A friend in Memphis provided transportation for her troops and helped prepare them for war.

Buford and the recruits met up with William in Pensacola. He didn't recognize his disguised wife. In confidence, she revealed herself to her profoundly astonished and aggrieved husband. William knew she would just try somewhere else if he sent her packing. He took command of Buford's troops and started to train them. Loreta, as Lieutenant Buford, went off to New Orleans to get supplies. While there, a terrible message arrived. The commander was dead, killed when a weapon exploded in his hands during training. The unfortunate death of her husband left Loreta alone in the war ahead – and motivated even more by the secret fact she was a widow.

From the skirmish at Blackburn's Ford on July 21, 1861, until the autumn of 1863, Loreta Velazquez pursued war as both a male Army officer and female spy. Few knew the truth about either role. As Lieutenant Buford, Loreta and her fellow soldiers took part in such hard-fought battles as Bull Run, Ball's Bluff, Fort Donelson, and Shiloh. Although her charade was discovered other times, it seems Buford would simply vanish or be "reassigned." Buford would take leaves between battles. Loreta used those times to doff the uniform for dresses and go into enemy territory to spy as a social butterfly. She would later write of the time she met President Lincoln, saying she greatly admired the man, but not his politics. After two and a half years of faithful service, Lieutenant Buford retired from duty. The story about Loreta's disguise had become too well known. She kept up the fight from the autumn of 1863 until the end of the war as Madame Velazquez, full-time Confederate spy. Loreta gathered information in the north and passed it to the South. No union opponent ever saw through her deception.

Loreta Velazquez entering the Federal Lines

While many women on both sides of the war served as spies, Loreta Velazquez is the only one known to have served disguised as a man at the same time and for so long. Soldiers who served beside Buford attested to the lieutenant's valor, integrity, ability and conduct becoming a gentlemanly army officer. Madame Loreta J. Velazquez was not a real man, but a real woman.

The preceding information was the source of information by R. Hull of SCV Camp # 819 in Cooper, Oklahoma

Jim Limber Davis
Rescued by the Confederacy's First Lady

In 1989, magazine article caught my eye which I had to read from beginning to end. This was not an ordinary story but about a black child, a Confederate President's First Lady and the Southern Presidential Family. The story was written by Gulfport, Mississippi freelance writer Mrs. Peggy Robbin's and is entitled, "Jim Limber Davis."

While Black History Month mostly focuses on black adults in history, this story is bout a black child. This a summary, in my own words, of Mrs. Robbin's splendid story.

On the morning of February 15, 1864, Mrs. Varina Davis, wife of Confederate President Jefferson Davis, had concluded her errands and was driving her carriage down the streets of Richmond, Virginia on her way home. She heard screams from a distance and quickly went to the scene to see what was happening.

Varina saw a young black child being abused by an older man. She demanded that he stop striking the child and when this failed she shocked the man by forcibly taking the child away. She took the child to her carriage and with her to the Confederate White House.

Arriving home Mrs. Davis and maid 'Ellen' gave the young boy a bath, attended to his cuts and bruises and feed him. The only thing he would tell them is that his name was Jim Limber. He was happy to be rescued and was given some clothes of the Davis' son Joe who was the same size and age. Joe was tragically killed in an accidental fall later that year.

The Davis family were visited the following evening by a friend of Varina's, noted Southern Diarist-Mary Boykin Chesnut, who saw Jim Limber and wrote later that she had seen the boy and that he was eager to show me his cuts and bruises. She also said, "the child is an orphan rescued yesterday from a brutal Negro Guardian." And "there were things in life that are too sickening, and such cruelty is one of them."

There were some children who addressed Jim as Jim Limber Davis for fun. This was fine with him because he felt he was indeed a member of the family. The Davis letters to friends are indication of his acceptance and they said he was a member of their gang of children.

The Christmas of 1864, would be memorable for the Davis family and probably the best Christmas Jim Limber would ever have. A Christmas tree was set up in Saint Paul's Church, decorated and gifts placed beneath it. On Christmas evening orphans were brought to the church and were delighted with the presents they got. Jim was happy that he helped decorate the tree.

Mrs. Robbin's wrote, in her story, that Mrs. Jefferson Davis was a very good story teller who was able to make sounds of different animals in the stories about the critters. Jim was always eager to help.

The end of the War Between the States was coming and Richmond was being evacuated. Carina and the children left ahead of Jefferson Davis. The president and his staff left just hours before the occupation of Union troops.

Varina and the children were by the side of Jefferson Davis at his capture near Irwinville, Georgia and again the family was separated. Jefferson Davis was taken to Virginia to spend two years in prison.

Mrs. Davis and her children were taken to Macon, Georgia and later to Port Royal outside of Savannah. At Port Royal their Union escort, Captain Charles T. Hudson, made good at his earlier threats to take Jim Limber away.

As the Union soldiers came to forcibly take young Jim, he put up a great struggle and tried to hold onto his family as they took him. Jim and his family cried uncontrollably as the child was taken. His family would never again see him or know what happened to him. The Davis' tried in later years to locate Jim but were unsuccessful. They prayed that he grew to manhood and did well in life.

The Museum of the Confederacy in Richmond, Virginia is home to a portrait of Jim Limber Davis in the Eleanor S. Brookenbrough Library. I thank Mrs. Peggy Robbin's who wrote the Jim Limber Davis story in 1989 and the Southern Partisan Magazine for publishing her story in the second quarter Issue Volume IX of 1989

By: Calvin E. Johnson Jr. Special to Huntingtoonnews.net

CHAPTER XI

ACHIEVEMENTS OF CONFEDERATE VETERANS AFTER THE WAR BETWEEN THE STATES

Achievements Of Confederate Veterans After the War Between The States

Brig. Gen. E. Porter Alexander had a distinguished career after the war as professor of engineering, railroad president, rice planter, and author ("Memoirs").

Brig. Gen. James L. Alcorn became Governor of Mississippi, was elected to the United States Senate, and had Alcorn St. University (predominately black) named for him.

Brig. Gen. Henry W. Allen became Governor of Louisiana.

Pvt. Archer Avary Sr., Co. A, Cavalry, Cobb's Legion. After the War, he attended the Southern Medical College and became a physician. He did post-graduate work at the Universities of Bavaria and Vienna. He was president of the American Cancer Society in 1908.

Brig. Gen. William Brimage Bate- Two terms as Gov. of Tennessee (1883-1887), followed by 3 terms serving 19 years in the United States Senate, of which he was a member at the time of his death in 1905.

Col. R.L.T. Beale (9th Va. Cavalry.) was elected to Congress in 1878.

Gen. P.G.T. Beauregard became president of two railroads, and for many years was adjutant general of Louisiana.

Judah P. Benjamin (Secretary of State-CSA) after the war became a Barrister in England, publishing a classic legal text on the sale of personal property. He was the only Barrister not of English Birth.

John Mercer Brooke (designer of Confederate Ironclads and ordinance), after the war invented an underwater sounding device that became the modern sonar.

Brig. Gen. John C. Brown was twice elected Governor of Tennessee.

Sgt. Philemon N. Bryan 9th Florida Vol. Infantry arrived in what is now Fort Lauderdale, Florida in 1895. He built the first Inn, and the first Ice House. He brought 400 Negro's into the city to work on Flagler's railroad, creating the city's first black community.

Admiral Franklin Buchanan-Former Commandant of the U.S. Naval Academy (before the war), & Commander of the CSS "Virginia", was post-bellum president of Maryland Agricultural College.

Major. Gen. Matthew C. Butler (S.C.) was elected to the U.S. Senate after the war.

Lt. William Burdine (45th Miss. Inf.) moved to Miami & founded Burdine's Department Stores.

Lt. Gen. Simon Bolivar Buckner was Governor of Kentucky, and Democratic Party candidate for Vice-President of the United States in 1896.

John A. Campbell (former Supreme Court Justice-who represented the Southern States in an unsuccessful attempt to mediate the impending conflict with the Lincoln Administration) re-established his law practice and returned to the Supreme Court on several occasions to argue cases.

Dr. Henry Campbell-Became president of the American Medical Association in 1884.

Brig. Gen. Ellison Capers entered the Episcopal Ministry, and was appointed arch-bishop of South Carolina. He was elected Chancellor of the University of the South (Sewanee).

Brig. Gen. Thomas L. Clingman – is for him that "Clingman's Dome" (highest point in the Smoky Mountains) is named.

Maj. Gen. Thomas J. Churchill was elected Governor of Arkansas.

Brig. Gen. Charles Clark was elected Governor of Mississippi.

Maj. Gen. Henry Clayton- retiring as a circuit court judge in 1886, became president of the University of Alabama.

Col. F.M. Cockrell was elected to the United States Senate.

Brig. Gen. Alfred Colaquitt became Governor of Georgia, and was later elected to the United States Senate.

Brig. Gen. Douglas H. Cooper represented Choctaw and Chickasaw tribes in civil claims against the United States government after the war.

Adjutant/Inspector General Samuel Cooper – preserved C.S. records, and assisted in compiling the Official Records of the war.

Brig. Gen. William Ruffin Cox was elected to the United States Congress for three terms.

Lt. Col. Jabez Curry became president of predominantly black Howard University, president of Richmond College, and subsequently United States Minister to Spain.

Major Robert Lewis Dabney (Chaplain, & later Chief of Staff under Stonewall Jackson) authored many books, such as "A Defense of Virginia"', and numerous theological Writings. Became President of Union Theological Seminary, and later chaired the Department of Mental and Moral Philosophy at the University of Texas.

Brig. Gen. Zachary Deas returned to the cotton business, but this time in NYC as a member of the New York Stock Exchange.

Pvt. H.H. Duncan and Major St. Clair Abrams, after the war, established the City of Tavares, Florida and Lake County.

Brig. Gen. Clement A. Evans entered the Methodist Episcopal ministry. He authored the 12 volume "Confederate Military History".

Sir Moses Ezekiel (Fought in War as Sgt. Of Co. C –VMI Cadets) became one of the world's greatest sculptors. Lee counseled Ezekiel , "I hope you will be an artist and do earn a reputation in whatever profession you undertake." He sculpted (among MANY other things) the New South Monument honoring the Confederate Dead in Arlington National Cemetery.

John Robert and Samuel Joseph Fields of Macon, Ga., acquired property in the area now known as Merrit Island, Fl., and raised Oranges. The home still is occupied by the Fields Family and is listed on the Historic Record.

Pvt. William Fletcher returned to Beaumont, Texas and became a thriving lumber man and prominent member of the community. The entire city of Beaumont shut down for his funeral.

Lt. Gen. Nathan Bedford Forrest became president of the Selma, Marion and Memphis Railroad.

Dr. Alexander Y.P. Garnett (physician to Jefferson Davis) became president of the American Medical Association in 1887.

Professors Gildersleeve and Lodge (CSA Officers) while at the University of Virginia after the war wrote one of the finest Latin grammars ever produced, which is still in use today (on the college level). Gildersleeve (at age 18) worked with Edgar Allen Poe, and before he died, recorded the only known version of Poe's "Raven".

Ambrosia Jose Gonzales (Artillery Officer under Gen. P.G.T. Beauregard) after the war helped design the modern versions of the Cuban and Puerto Rican flags.

Brig. Gen. John B. Gordon was three times elected to the United States Senate. He wrote "Reminiscences of the Civil War." He was a prime mover in the organization of the United Confederate Veterans (UCV), and was its first Commander-In-Chief. John B. Gordon became acquainted with Henry Flagler, helping build the Florida East Coast Railroad, in 1901 he bought 62 acres of land in Miami and built a winter home. He also bought Everglades property in what is now Hollywood, Florida and farmed tomatoes. He died in Miami in 1905 and his friend Henry Flagler sent his body home in his personal rail car.

Brig. Gen. George Washington Gordon was thrice elected to the United States Congress. He also served as Commander-In-Chief of the United Confederate Veterans.

Brig. Gen. Josiah Gorgas became Superintendent of Brierfield Iron works, and President of the University of Alabama in 1878.

Lt. Gen. Wade Hampton became Governor of South Carolina, and also a United States Senator.

Pvt. Gardner Sheppard Hardee, 9th Ga. Infantry, became the first white settler in Brevard County, Florida. He established a city Called Rockledge, Florida, outside the Kennedy Space Center, in 1887. He also served as Brevard County Commissioner.

Gov. Isham G. Harris (Confederate Governor of Tennessee, and a member of the staffs of Gen. A. S. Johnson, and J. E. Johnston) after the war served in the United States Senate for 20 years (dying in office).

Brig. Gen. Johnson Haygood – after the war he became Governor of South Carolina.

Lt. Gen. Daniel H. Hill became president of the University of Arkansas in 1877.

Confederate Nurse Juliet Opie Hopkins is the only Confederate female buried with honors in Arlington National Cemetery.

3rd. Sgt. John Houston, Jr., Company A of 3rd. Florida Infantry, served as the first Brevard County, Florida Commissioner in 1871.

Cpl. Julius Franklin Howell held the presidency of Virginia Intermont College, as well as serving as Commander-In-Chief of the United Confederate Veterans.

Brig. Gen. Eppa Hunton served in the United States House of Representatives, as well as the United States Senate. He was the only Southern member of the famed electoral commission of 1877, which decided the disputed Hayes-Tilden Presidential election.

Brig. Gen. William H. ("Red") Jackson founded Belle Meade Stables in Nashville, Tenn.

Major Eli Janney – made railroad history by inventing the automatic coupler in 1868.

Brig. Gen. Adam Johnson, although blinded during the war, surveyed and laid out the streets for the city of Marble Falls, Texas.

Brig. Gen. Bradley Johnson served in the Virginia Senate, and wrote a number of historical and legal works.

General Joseph Johnston served in the United States House of Representatives, and was appointed U.S. Commissioner of Railroads. He also wrote "Narrative of Military Operations".

Maj. Gen. James Kemper (one of Brigade leaders in Pickett's Charge) became Governor of Virginia.

A.N.V. Judge Advocate Lucius Quintus Cincinnatus Lamar (Aide to Gen. Longstreet) was elected to the United States House of Representatives, the United States Senate and appointed to the United States Supreme Court as a Justice.

General Alexander Robert Lawton was appointed U.S. Minister to Austria.

Major Gen. Fitzhugh Lee, led U.S. cavalry unit in the Spanish-American War (as a Maj. General). He also led the founding of the Confederate Soldiers Home in Richmond, giving a sanctuary to 3,000 destitute "Old Soldiers".

Maj. Gen. George Washington Custis Lee succeeded his father, Robert E. Lee, as president of what is now Washington & Lee University.

Brig. Gen. William Henry Fitzhugh Lee served as president of the Virginia Agricultural Society, and in 1887 was elected to the United States Congress.

General Robert E. Lee continued to be a "guiding light" in the lives of young Southerners as president of what is now known as Washington & Lee University.

Brig. Gen. Stephen Dill Lee became the first president of Mississippi State University, and also the first director of the Vicksburg Battlefield Park (in addition to giving the SCV & UDC the famous "Charges").

Major. Gen. George Littlefield made millions in the cattle business, and single handedly saved the University of Texas from closing its doors due to the lack of funds.

Maj. Gen. Lunsford Lomax became president of Virginia Polytechnic Institute (Va. Tech).

Lt. Gen. James Longstreet became U.S. Ambassador to Turkey.

Maj. Gen. Lafayette McLaws became Savannah's Postmaster.

Naval Commander John Newland Maffitt served in the Paraguayan Navy and went on to command the Cuban gun-runner "The Hornet" after his service to the Confederacy.

Maj. Gen. William Mahone founded the Norfolk & Western Railroad. Also served in the United States Senate.

Col. Albert S. Marks served as Chancery Judge, and also as Governor of Tennessee.

Maj. Gen. John S. Marmaduke served as Governor of Missouri.

Major William T. Martin headed the commission which designed the current Mississippi State Flag, which was "re-adopted" last year by a 65% vote of the people of Mississippi.

Brig. Gen. Dabney H. Maury founded the Southern Historical Society, and was appointed U.S. Minister to Colombia.

Commodore Matthew Fontaine Maury's books on Oceanography were considered classics (so much so that he was called "Pathfinder of the Seas"), as well as the book he wrote called "A Vindication of the South"!

Dr. Hunter Holmes McGuire (Stonewall Jackson's surgeon) became president of the American Medical Association in 1892.

Brig. Gen. Evander McIvor Law established the foundation of the Educational System in Florida, and served as Commander of the Florida division of United Confederate Veterans.

Mississippi Men Elected to the US Congress:
J.T. Harrison elected but not seated
Capt. J.C. Morphlis
O.R. Singleton
Co. C.E. Hooker
Col. V.H. Manning
B. Gen. J.H. Chalmers
Col. J.Z. George US Senator
Pvt. H.S. Van Eaton
E. Barksdale
Col. J.B. Morgan
Pvt. J.M. Allen
Major Gen. E.C. Walthall
Pvt. F.G. Barry
Pvt. T.C. Catchings
Col. T.R. Stockdale
Pvt. C.L. Anderson
Pvt. Clark Kewis
Pvt. J. H. Spencer
Pvt. Pat Henry

Capt. John Mizell 7th Florida Vol. Company F became the first Mayor of the City of Pompano Beach, Florida in 1908.

Narciso Monturiol (Spanish inventor who gave designs of his advanced submarine- "Ictineo" – to the Confederacy) inspired Jules Vernes' idea for his "Nautilus" in "20,000 Leagues Under the Sea".

Col. John S. Mosby (the "Gray Ghost") became U.S. Consul to Hong Kong.

Captain John Pleasant Oakes returned to serve as head of Colorado College.

Brig. Gen. William Henry Fitzhugh Payne served in the Virginia House of Delegates, and became general counsel for the Southern Railway.

Lt. Col. John S. Pemberton founded "Coke Cola".

Brig. Gen. William H. Pendleton resumed his rectorship in Lexington, VA. after the war and carried on his struggle against poverty in his desolated parish, and against the hostility of the Federal authorities.

Private George Perry helped found the city of Coral Gables, Florida.

Brig. Gen. Edmund W. Pettus was elected to the United States Senate in 1896.

Brig. Gen. Lucius E. Polk served as a delegate to the Democratic Party's National Convention in 1884, and was later elected to the Tennessee Senate.

Col. James D. Porter served two terms as Governor of Tennessee, and later served as United States Ambassador to Chile.

Confederate Surgeon Horace Porter Founded a Post Office in the 1870s and called it Coconut Grove as a joke, Now one of the upper crust Yuppie sites in South Miami, Fl.

Jose Agustin Quintero (Confederate States Commissioner to Mexico) became a famous Cuban poet and revolutionary.

Col. George W. Rains became Dean of the Medical College of Georgia.

Dr. Tobias G. Richardson (Medical Inspector Under Braxton Bragg) became president of the American Medical Association in 1877.

Brig. Gen. Thomas Rosser became chief engineer of the Northern Pacific and Canadian Pacific Railroads. In 1898 he was appointed Brig. Gen. of U.S. Volunteers (Spanish-American War).

Pvt. Edmund Ruffin –that most STAUNCH of all Confederates (who was given the honor of firing the first shot at Ft. Sumpter), formulated agricultural innovations that are still being used today (although he committed suicide after the War "rather than live in the same Country with damned Yankees").

Gen. Daniel Ruggles became a member of the Board of Visitors at the United States Military Academy in 1884.

Admiral Raphael Semmes (of "Alabama" fame) became teacher, newspaper editor, and a lawyer.

Brig. Gen. Alfred M. Scales was elected to Congress, and also served as Governor of North Carolina.

Brig. Gen. Joseph Orville Shelby ("The Undefeated Rebel") was appointed U.S. Marshall for the Western District by President Cleveland.

Maj. Gen. Edmund Kirby Smith became president of the Pacific & Atlantic Telegraph Company, chancellor of the University of Nashville, and professor of mathematics at the University of the South. His home is located in Saint Augustine, Florida, oldest city in the United States.

2nd Lt. Alexander A. Steward of the 10th Florida Infantry Co. "G" served as the First Brevard County, Florida Court Clerk.

Major Lawrence Sullivan ("Sul") Ross became President of Texas A & M University, and Sul Ross St. College (Texas) bears his name today.

Captain Sally Tomkins (only woman commissioned by Jefferson Davis) of the Confederate Medical Corps. After the war she continued her charity work, and generous hospitality to Confederate Veterans- which exhausted her fortune.

Col. Henry Titus, Blockade Runner, owned the property at Sand Point where the post office opened in 1868, Later the city's name was changed to Titusville, Fla.

Naval Commander John Randolph Tucker became a Vice Admiral in the Peruvian-Chilean Navy, leading the fleet vs. Spanish incursions.

Col. Peter Turney (1st Tenn. Infantry) – Chief Justice of the Tenn. Supreme Court, 2 terms as Governor of Tennessee (1893-1897), and was elected to the United States Senate.

Mark Twain became one of America's finest literary figures. He served with the Marion Rangers for only two weeks before it disbanded, so formal charges of desertion were not levied against him.

Loretta Janetta Velazquez fought for the Confederacy disguised with an alias of "Lt. Harry Buford". After the war, she went on to write of her adventure – "The Woman in Battle"!

Surgeon Wall in 1873 did most of the work in Tampa, Fla. On Yellow Fever that Dr. Walter Reed would receive credit for.

Gen. Joe Wheeler led US Cavalry unit in the Spanish-American War (as a Maj. General).

Brig. Gen. Williams Carter Wickham became president of the Virginia Central Railroad, and later the Chesapeake & Ohio railroad. He served in the Virginia Senate.

Brig. Gen. Cadmus Wilcox was appointed chief of the railroad division of the Land Office, by President Grover Cleveland.

Hiram Smith Williams, 40th Ala. Infantry, he moved in 1873 to the small village of Rockledge and help found it in 1887. He served as Postmaster for the village from 1875 until 1881. He became Brevard County Treasurer and in 1885 was elected to the First State Senator from the area.

Maj. Gen. A.R. Wright was elected to the United States Congress.

Brig. Gen. Marcus Wright also assisted in the compiling of records for the "Official Records" and was rewarded with a military burial plot in Arlington National Cemetery (only 1 other C. S. A .officer, General Joseph Wheeler, is buried in Arlington).

Dr. Davis Yandell became president of the American Medical Association in 1871.

CHAPTER XII

CONFEDERATE SOLDIERS EDUCATED IN THE NORTH CONFEDERATE GENERAL'S NORTHERNERS AND FOREIGN BORN

Confederate Soldiers Educated in the North

Brown University in Rhone Island
Robert Benjamin (Smith) Hilton C.S.A. Captain Virginia Confederate Congress 24 Brown Men entered the service of the Confederacy and six of them died.

Cambridge Mass.
George Wythe Randolph C.S.A. Secretary of War and General

Harvard University
357 Harvard graduates entered the service of the Confederate Army
Albert Gallatin Jenkins C.S.A. General – Virginia
Albert Pike C.S.A. General – Massachusetts
Alexander Robert Lawton C.S.A. General – South Carolina
Ben Hardin Helm C.S.A. General – Kentucky (Abraham Lincoln's Half-Brother-in- Law
John Bullock Clark Jr. C.S.A. General – Missouri
John E. Chols C.S.A. General – Virginia
John R. Cooke C.S.A. General – Missouri
John Sappington Marmaduke C.S. A. General – Missouri
John Smith Preston C.S.A. General – Virginia
Martin Witherspoon Gary C.S.A. General – South Carolina
Richard "Dick" Taylor C.S.A. General- Kentucky (Son of President Zachary Taylor)
Robert Hatton C.S.A. General – Tennessee
William Booth Taliaferro C.S.A. General – Virginia
William Henry Fitzhugh Lee C.S.A. General – Virginia
William Preston C.S.A. General – Kentucky
71 Harvard graduates died wearing the gray.

Miami University Oxford, Ohio
John Stuart Williams C.S.A. General – Kentucky
Joseph Robert Davis C.S.A. General – Mississippi (Jefferson Davis's Nephew)

New Jersey Educated
Thomas Carmichael Hindman C.S.A. General – Tennessee

Pennsylvania Educated
James Hagan C.S.A. General – Ireland

Princeton University, New Jersey

Alfred Holt Colquitt C.S.A. General – Georgia
Allen Thomas C.S.A. General – Maryland
Bradley Tyler Johnson C.,S.A. General – Maryland
James Chesnut Jr. C.S.A. General – South Carolina
James Jay Archer C.S.A. General - Maryland
Lawrence O'Bryan C.S. A. General – North Carolina
William L. Brandon C.S.A. General – Mississippi
The class of 1859 contributed 20 men for the Confederacy. Class of 1861 21 men fought for the South whom 4 were killed.

Yale University
Edward Aylesworth Perry C.S.A. General – Massachusetts
Elisha Franklin Paxton C.S.A. General – Virginia
Henry Rootes Jackson C.S.A. General – Georgia
Isaac Munroe St. John C.S.A. General –Georgia
James Edward Rains C.S.A. General – Tennessee
John Sappington Marmaduke C.S.A. General – Missouri
Joseph Emerson Brown C.S.A. Governor of Georgia – South Carolina
Randall Lee Gibson C.S. A. General – Kentucky
Richard "Dick" Taylor C.S.A. General – Kentucky (Son of President Zachary Taylor)

CONFEDERATE GENERAL'S NORTHERNERS AND FOREIGN BORN

Blanchard, Albert Gallatin C.S.A. General – Massachusetts
Brown, William M. C.S. A. General – England
Clark, Charles C.S.A. General – Ohio - Governor of Mississippi
Cleburne, Patrick Ronayne C.S. A. General – Ireland
Colston, Raleigh Edward C.S. General - France
Debray, Exavier Blanchard C.S.A. General – France
Delagnel, Julius Adolphus C.S.A. General – New Jersey
Duncan, Johnson Kelly C.S.A. General – Pennsylvania
Ewell, Richard Stoddert C.S. A. General – Wash. D.C.
Flanagin, Harris C.S.A. Governor of Arkansas - New Jersey
French, Samuel Gibbs C.S.A. General – New Jersey
Frost, Daniel Marsh C.S. A. General – New York
Gardner, Franklin C.S.A. General – New York
Gorgas, Josiah C.S.A. General and Chief of Ordinance Pennsylvania
Hagan, James C.S.A. General – Ireland
Hatton, Robert Hopkins C.S.A. General – Ohio
Hotchkiss, Jedediah C.S.A. Topographical Engineer – New York
Johnson, Bushrod Rust C.S.A. General – Ohio
Lane, Walter Payne C.S.A. General – Ireland
Leadbetter, Danville C.S.A. General – Maine
Leventhorpe, Collett C.S.A. General – England
Lomax, Lunsford Lindsay C.S.A. General – Rhode Island
Mackall, William Whann C.S.A. General – Wash. D.C.
Maclay, Robert Plunket C.S.A. General – Pennsylvania
Maffitt, John Newland C.S.A. Navy Capt. – Born at Sea
Major, James Patrick C.S.A. General –Missouri
McGlashan, Peter Alexander Selkirk C.S.A. General – Scotland
Memminger, Christopher Gustavus C.S.A. Secretary of the Treasury – Germany
Moore, Patrick C.S.A. General – Ireland
Pemberton, John Clifford C.S.A. General – Pennsylvania
Perry, Edward Aylesworth C.S.A. General - Massachusetts
Reynolds, Daniel H. C.S.A. General – Ohio
Ripley, Roswell Sabine C.S.A. General – Ohio
Ruggles, Daniel C.S.A. General – Massachusetts
Sears, Claudius Wistar C.S.A. General – Massachusetts
Shoup, Francis Asbury C.S.A. General – Indiana
Slidell, John C.S.A. Diplomat - New York

Smith, Martin Luther C.S.A. General – New York
Soule, Pierre C.S.A. General – France
Steele, William C.S.A. General New York
Stevens, Clement Hoffman, C.S.A. General – Connecticut
Strahl, Otho French C.S.A. General – Ohio
Trimble, Isaac Ridgeway C.S.A. General – Pennsylvania
Velaques, Loreta Janeta C.S.A. officer and spy – Cuba

The Rebel Yell

By Monte Akers

None of us have ever heard it,
None of us ever will;
There's no one left who can give it,
Though you may hear its echo still.

You may hear it up near Manassas,
And down around Gaines Mill;
In December it echoes in Fredericksburg,
In May around Chancellorsville.

It's the "pibroch of Southern fealty",
It's a Comanche brave's battle cry;
It's an English huntsman's call to the hounds,
It's a pig farmer's call to the sty.

It's a high-pitched trilling falsetto,
It's the yip of a dog in flight;
It's the scream of a wounded panther,
It's the shriek of the wind in the night.

It was yelled when the boys flushed a rabbit,
It was passed man to man in the ranks;
It was cheered when they saw their leaders,
It was screamed when they whipped the Yanks.

But non of us will ever hear it,
Though some folks mimic it well;
No soul alive can truly describe
The sound of the Rebel Yell.

We wish to thank Carl W. McClung of SCV Camp1934 for posting this stirring poem on the SCV Dispatch.

RECOMMENDED READING:

Stonewall Jackson/The black man's friend
By Richard G. Williams Jr.

Forced into Glory/Abraham Lincoln's white dream
By Lerone Bennett Jr.

Illinois Rebels/A civil war unit history of G company 15th Tennessee Regiment Volunteer infantry
By Ed Gleeson

A south side view of Slavery
By Nehemiah Adams

Why was Lincoln murdered?
By Otto Eisenschiml

Facts the Historians leave out
By John S. Tilley

Slavery and the U.S. Government
By Stanley K. Lott

Black Confederates
By Charles Kelly Barrow, J.H.Segars, & R.B. Rosenberg

The Truth of the War conspiracy of 1861
By H.W. Johnstone

Christian Slaves, Muslim Masters
By Robert C. Davis

How the North Promoted, Prolonged, and Profited from Slavery
By Anne Farrow

The Longest Raid of the Civil War
By Lester V. Horwitz

White Slavery, What the Scots already know
By Kelly D. Whittaker

They were white and they were slaves
By Michael A. Hoffman II

White Cargo
By Don Jordan & Michael Walsh

The Real Lincoln
By Thomas DiLorenzo

The Real Lincoln
By Charley Reese

Lincoln Unmasked
By Thomas DiLorenzo

The Lincoln Legacy Revisited
By Mark M. Alexander

The Known World
By Black author Edward P. Jones

Black Slaves owners: Free Black Slave master in South Carolina 1790-1860
By Larry Koger

The Johnson Family: African-American owners of white and black slaves.
By Robert M. Grooms

Black Masters: A free family of color in the old south
By W.W. Norton

Free Negro owners of slaves in the United States in 1830
By Carter G. Woodson

The Confederate War
By Gary W. Gallagher

A Informational website I recommend is:

Southern Heritage 411 or H.K. Edgerton

General Jubal A. Early Homeplace

The Challenge

The Jubal A. Early Preservation Trust, Inc. has begun a $1,000,000 capital campaign in an effort to preserve and restore the boyhood home of Confederate General Jubal A. Early, in the Red Valley section of Franklin County, Virginia. The home and surrounding area will serve to interpret Early's childhood on a typical old Virginia tobacco plantation, his military experiences, and his immense post war contribution to the printed history of the Southern Cause.

A Virginia foundation has pledged to match contributions up to $250,000 toward this goal, thus making each tax-deductible donation worth twice as much to the preservation effort. The homeplace along with eight acres of land already has been donated to the trust.

Contribute Now

and Double

Your Donation!

$25 = $50
$50 = $100
$100 = $200
$250 = $500

You Can Help Save this Historic Home.
Contributions are tax deductible to the extent allowed by law.

Yes I will help save The Jubal A. Early Homeplace.

Make your check payable to:
Jubal A. Early Preservation Trust, Inc.
P.O. Box 638 Rocky Mount, Virginia 24151 Thank You

The Sons of Confederate Veterans Garland-Rodes Camp # 409 of Lynchburg, Va. proudly announce the latest camp project to—erect permanent monument honoring Confederate General Jubal A Early to Middleton, Virginia on the site of the 1864 Battle of Cedar Creek.

Negotiations are now actively underway with the Town of Middletown to locate it in a proposed park just off Route 11 in Middletown, ground on which Gen. Early most certainly fought upon and where hundreds of young patriots lost their lives. Camp Commander Brian Giles said "Gen Early was in command of the Army of Northern Virginia during the Battle of Cedar Creek and his heroic effort to destroy Union General Philip Sheridan's forces after the "burning" of the Shenandoah Valley has never been forgotten by the Southern people; therefore he needs to make his stand once again only this time in stone and bronze in recognition of our Southern heritage and culture."

Fore more information or to make a donation, contact the Garland-Rodes SCV Camp # 409,Lynchburg, Va. Commander Brian Giles, 167 Ashmont Dr. Madison Heights, Virginia 24572 or scv3rdbrigade@yahoo.com or 434-942-8075

Evergreen Cemetery, Lake County, Ohio picture by Gloria J. Early Page 3
Ray County, Missouri Reflections 4
Centertown Cemetery, Kentucky 5
Robby Beamer 6
Paul McWhorter 7
Randy McNutt "The Cincinnati Enquirer) 8
Mound Cemetery, Marietta, Ohio 10
Sigma Chi-Theta Lota 11
Paul McWhorter – picture by Gloria J. Early 13
Fuller Family Cemetery – Lawrence County, Ohio 14
Picture by Raylene Hlavaty 15
Henry Ebenezer Handerson by Gilbertus Angelicus 16
Henry Ebenezer Handerson by Gilbertus Angelicus 17
Henry Ebenezer Handerson by Gilbertus Angelicus 18
Henry Ebenezer Handerson by Gilbertus Angelicus 19
Paul McWhorter photo by Gloria J. Early 20
National Archives-National Park Service, Civil War soldiers and Sailors System (CWSS) Sept. 2004 http://www.civilwar.nps.gov 21
Randy Chadwick 22
Ohio Historical Society – Ohio History Central www/ohiohistorycentral.org. 23
Ohio Historical Society – Ohio History Central www/ohiohistorycentral.org 24
Randall Howard – Mr. Burnett TSLAC 25
Randall Howard – Mr. Burnett TSLAC 26
Randall Howard photo by Gloria J. Early 27
Willoughby Center Cemetery Lake County, Ohio photo by Curtis A. Early 29
Randy Chadwick 30
Paul McWhorter photo by Historic Spring Grove Cemetery and Arboretum 31
Paul McWhorter 32
West Kirtland Cemetery – Lake County, Ohio photo by Curtis A. Early 33
Paul McWhorter 34
Brakeman Cemetery, Leroy, Lake County, Ohio photo by Curtis A. Early 35

Randolph Harrison McKim photo by Curtis A. Early 38
National Archives –National Park Service- Civil War Soldiers and Sailors
System (CWSS) Sept. 2004 http://www.civilwar.nps.gov 39
Randy Chadwick Confederate Army photo by Curtis A. Early 41
National Archives-National Park Service-Civil War Soldiers and Sailors
System (CWSS) Sept. 2004 http://www.civilwar.nps.gov photo by Curtis A. Early " 39
Cedar Hill Cemetery, Licking County, Ohio 40
Paul McWhorter 41
Claysville Mt. Zion Cemetery, Guernsey County, Ohio Methodist Cemetery
Belmont County, Ohio 42
Illinois Rebels by Ed Gleeson 43
National Archives-National Park Service-Civil War Soldiers and Sailors
System (CWSS) Sept 2004 http://.cicvilwar.nps.gov 44
Paul McWhorter 46
Historic Spring Grove Cemetery and Arboretum 47
National Archives-National Park Service-Civil War Soldiers and Sailors
System (CWSS) Sept. 2004 http://www.civilwar.nps.gov 50
National Archives – National Park Service-Civil War Soldiers and Sailors
System (CWSS) Sept. 2004 http://www.civilwar.nps.gov 49
Historic Spring Grove Cemetery and Arboretum, National Archives-National
Park Service-Civil War Soldiers and Sailors System (CWSS) Sept. 2004
http://www.civilwar.nps.gov 51
Photo by Curtis A. Early 53
Historic Spring Grove Cemetery and Arboretum 54
National Archives – National Park Service – Civil War Soldiers and Sailors
System (CWSS) Sept. 2004 http://www.civilwar.nps.gov 55
National Archives – National Park Service – Civil War Soldiers and Sailors
System (CWSS) Sept. 2004 http://www.civilwar.nps.gov 56
Lebanon Cemetery, Warren County, Ohio 60-61
National Archives –National Park Service- Civil War Soldiers and Sailors
System (CWSS) Sept. 2004 http://www.civilwar.nps.gov 61
Waldschmidt Cemetery Camp Dennison 62
National Archives-National Park Service – Civil War Soldiers and Sailors
System (CWSS) Sept. 2004 http://www.civilwar.nps.gov 63
Sabina Cemetery, Clinton County, Ohio , National Archives-National Park
Service- Civil War Soldiers and Sailors Systems (CWSS) Sept. 2004
http://www.civilwar.nps.gov 65
Historic Spring Grove Cemetery and Arboretum-National Archives-National
Park Service- Civil War Soldiers and Sailors System (CWSS) Sept. 2004
http://www.civilwar.nps.gov 66
Photo by Curtis A. Early 67
New Burlington, Clinton County, Ohio- National Archives- National Park
Service-Civil War Soldiers and Sailors System (CWSS) Sept. 2004
http://www.civilwar.nps.gov 68
Sugar Grove Cemetery, Clinton County, Ohio, National Archives-National Park

Service-Civil War Soldiers and Sailors System (CWSS) Sept 2004 http://www.civilwar.nps.gov 69
Martinsville Cemetery, Clinton County, Ohio, National Archives-National Park Service-Civil War Soldiers and Sailors System (CWSS) Sept 2004 http://www.civilwar.nps.gov 70
Miami Cemetery Corwin, Warren County, Ohio, 71
Miami Cemetery, Corwin, Warren County, Ohio, National Archives-National Park Service-Civil War Soldiers and Sailors System (CWSS) Sept. 2004 http://www.civilwar.nps.gov 72
Historic Spring Grove Cemetery and Arboretum, National Archives-National Park Service-Civil War Soldiers and Sailors System (CWSS) Sept 2004 http://www.civilwar.nps.gov 73
Harry Searles , Ohio History Central 74
National Archives-National Park Service-Civil War Soldiers and Sailors System (CWSS) Sept. 2004 http://www.civilwar.nps.gov 75
Historic Spring Grove Cemetery and Arboretum 76
Historic Spring Gove Cemetery and Arboretum, National Archives-National Park Service-Civil War Soldiers and Sailors System (CWSS) Sept 2004 http://www.civilwar.nps.gov 77
Sugar Grove Cemetery, Clinton County, Ohio, National Archives-National Park Service-Civil War Soldiers and Sailors System (CWSS) Sept. 2004 http://www.civilwar.nps.gov 78
Historic Spring Grove Cemetery and Arboretum 79
Grandview Cemetery, Ross County, Ohio 80
Martinsville I.O.O.F. Cemetery, Clinton County, Ohio, National Archives National Park Service-Civil War Soldiers and Sailors System (CWSS) Sept. 2004 http://www.civilwar.nps.gov 81
Historic Spring Grove Cemetery and Arboretum, National Archives-National Park Service- Civil War Soldiers and Sailors System (CWSS) Sept 2004 http://www.civilwar.nps.gov 82
National Archives-National Park Service-Civil War Soldiers and Sailors System (CWSS) Sept. 2004 http://www.civilwar.nps.gov 83
Historic Spring Grove Cemetery and Arboretum 85
National Archives-National Park Service-Civil War Soldiers and Sailors System (CWSS) Sept. 2004 http://www.civilwar.nps.gov 86
By Scott Morris 89
By Lima Sunday News 90
Ancestry.com 91
National Archives-National Park Service-Civil War Soldiers and Sailors System (CWSS) Sept. 2004 http://www.civilwar.nps.gov 93
New Burlington Cemetery, Clinton County, Ohio, National Archives-National Park Service-Civil War Soldiers and Sailors System (CWSS) Sept. 2004 http://www.civilwar.nps.gov 94
Historic Spring Grove Cemetery and Arboretum 95
National Archives-National Park Service-Civil War Soldiers and Sailors System

(CWSS) Sept. 2004 http://www.civilwar.nps.gov 96
Willoughby Sharp Avenue Cemetery, Lake County, Ohio photo by Gloria J. Early 98
Willoughby Center Cemetery, Lake County, Oh. photo by Gloria J. Early 99
Hanna Cemetery, Crawford County, Ohio 100-101
Historic Spring Grove Cemetery and Arboretum 102
National Archives-National Park Service- Civil War Soldiers and Sailors System (CWSS) Sept. 2004 http://www.civilwar.nps.gov 103
Standing Rock Cemetery, Franklin, Ohio photo by Gloria J. Early 105
Mayfield Jewish Cemetery, Cleveland Hts.,Cuyahoga County, Ohio photo By Gloria J. Early 106
Jack Sullivan Photo by Gloria J. Early 108-109-110-111
Good Hope Cemetery, Fayette County, Ohio 113
Senecaville Cemetery, Guernsey County, Ohio photo by Gloria J. Early 114
National Archives-National Park Service- Civil War Soldiers and Sailors System (CWSS) Sept. 2004 http://www.civilwar.nps.gov 114-115
Oak Street Cemetery, Coshocton County, Ohio, National Archives-National Park Service –Civil War Soldiers and Sailors System (CWSS) Sept. 2004 http://www.civilwar.nps.gov 117
Historic Spring Grove Cemetery and Arboretum 118-119
The Longest Raid of the Civil War by Lester V. Horwitz Pg. 124-125-126
Ohio History Central – Ohio Historical Society 127
Remarkable Ohio-Marking Ohio's History- The Ohio Historical Society 128
Meigs County Historical Society – Meigs County Commissioners Ohio 129
Ohio Travel and Tourist, The Ohio Historical Society 130
Senecaville Cemetery, Senecaville, Ohio photo by Gloria J. Early 131
The Longest Raid of the Civil War by Lester V. Horwitz 132
The Ohio Bicentennial Commission-The Village of Old Washington 133
The Longaberger Company – The Ohio Historical Society-Bottom 133
Old Washington Cemetery, Guernsey County, Ohio 134-135
Heidelberg College Archaeological Project- Buffington@Heidelberg.edu 136-137-138-139-140-141
Erected by Will L. Thompson 142
D.F. Brandon 143
Ohio Bicentennial Commission-The Longaberger Company-The Ohio Historical Society 144-145
Brig. Gen. Roswell S. Ripley Camp 1535 Sons of Confederate Veterans 144
Wikipedia, The Free Encyclopedia 146
Confederate Military History 147
Photo by Gloria J. Early 150
Johnson Island Preservation Society-picture by Bob Ibos- CSN website www.csnavy.org 151-152-153-154-155
Photo by Gloria J. Early 157-158
Atlas Editions – Civil War Cards 159-160
Ohio Historical Society 161

Wikipedia – The Free Encyclopedia 162
Robert W. McComick – About Six Acres of Land Camp Chase Civil War Prison 1994 Timeline Article 163-164
George C. Campbell- George C Campbell on Wikipedia Encyclopedia 165
National Register of Historic Places- National Park Service 167-168
Camp Dennison Civil War Museum/Christian Waldschmidt Homestead 169
Dan A. McCaskill-SCV Camp Benjamin G.Humphreys 1625 172
Scott L. Mingus Sr.-Cannon Ball Civil War Blog York Daily Record www.yorkblog.com/cannonball 173-174
Hatton, Robert Biographical U.S. Congress 1774-present 175-176
Marc Schulman multied@multied.com 177
Robert Patrick Bender – Eastern New Mexico University-Roswell 178-179
Confederate Military History Voc. 5 Pg 418 180-181
Picture John Merrill – Touring Ohio.com 183
Evans, Clement Ed Confederate Military History -vol. VIII-Confederate Publishing Co. Atlanta, Georgia 1899 184-185
2007 David L. Mowery and the Cincinnati Civil War Round Table 188-189-190
Marge Maclean 191-192-193-194
Navy History – Heritage Command-NHHC webmaster nhhcwebmaster@navy.mil 195
Mount View Cemetery- Mount Vernon, Ohio 198
Knox County Convention and Visitors Bureau 199-200
Book- Way Up North in Dixie by Howard L. Sacks and Judith Rose Sacks- Wikipedia The Free Encyclopedia 201-202-203
A Product of the Ohio History Central- Ohio Historical Society 204-205-206-207
FNB Chronicle, Josetta Griffith Editor 210-211-212-213
Mound Hill Cemetery= Seville, Ohio 214
Ohio Historical Society – Mound Hill Cemetery-Seville, Ohio 215
Seville and Medina County Historical Societies 216
Artwork by R.G. Skerrett- Port Lavaca Wave, Port Lavaco, Texas 217-218-219-220-221
Moultrie SCV Camp #27 Mount Pleasant, S. Carolina 222
Charles Kelly Barrow-Commander Army of Tennessee-Calvin Hart 224-234
Photo by Bob Crowell 237-238
Photo by James F. McMurry 239
Confederate Military History 240-241
A.C. Griffith 242
Photo by Waynesville Mountaineer- http://Thomaslegion.net/bodyguard 243
Photo by Confederate Military History 244
S.C.V. Albert Sidney Johnston Camp 67 245
Confederate military History 246-247-248
Lee's Tigers- The Louisiana Infantry in the Terry L. Jones Army of Northern Virginia- Louisiana State University press 1987 249
Calvin E. Johnson Jr. S.C.V. Georgia 252-253-254
Tri S Ranch (sales) Trisranch@gmail.com – Bobby Sherard The Irish Slave Trade 255-256
By Michael A. Hoffman II 257

First 5 columns by Adele Oltman – The Nation 258
By Curtis A. Early 259
Lorenzo Johnston Green – The Negro in Colonial New England from
1620 – 1776 260-261
Philip Burnham Article "Selling Poor Steven" –American Heritage
Feb-March, 1993 261
Wikipedia, The Free Encyclopedia 262
Confederate Military History 263-264-265-266
The Buffalo News 267
Tom Arriola 268
Hank Van Slyke 269-270-271
The South Was Right –Authors Donald and Ronald Kennedy (53-74) 272
David E. Johnston Standard Printing 1906 P.P.285 Volunteer 273
Confederate Military History vol. 12 274-275
Photo-Richmond, Va. Dustin, Gilman and Co. 1876 by Tech.Sgt.
Phillip E. Copeland USAF – R. Hull S.C.V. camp # 819 Cooper, Ok 276-277-278-279
By Calvin E. Johnson Jr. special to huntingtonnews.net 280-281
Robert Niepert 284 thru 292
Special Thanks to – Glenn Venner, Scott Morris, Mark Hankins, Dave Allison
and George Shrader

INDEX

D.

E.

F

G

H.

I

J

T.

U.

W.